INTRODUCTION TO PREHISTORY

McGRAW-HILL BOOK COMPANY

*New York   San Francisco   St. Louis   Düsseldorf   Johannesburg
Kuala Lumpur   London   Mexico   Montreal   New Delhi   Panama
Rio de Janeiro   Singapore   Sydney   Toronto*

IRVING ROUSE

Charles J. MacCurdy Professor of Anthropology, Yale University

INTRODUCTION TO PREHISTORY

A Systematic Approach

This book was set in Granjon by Monotype Composition Company, and printed and bound by Kingsport Press, Inc. The designer was Janet Bollow; the drawings were done by Judith McCarty. The editors were Ronald D. Kissack and Michael A. Ungersma. Charles A. Goehring supervised production.

INTRODUCTION TO PREHISTORY

A Systematic Approach

Printed in the United States of America

Library of Congress catalog card number: 71–173715

234567890   KPKP   798765432

To my wife
Mary Mikami
with gratitude for her
advice, support, and encouragement

CONTENTS

Figures and Tables   *xi*
Preface   *xiii*

1 THE NATURE OF PREHISTORY   1

    1 Prehistory as a historical discipline   1
    2 Prehistory as a scientific discipline   4
    3 Prehistory and archeology   6
    4 Prehistory and ethnography-ethnology   12
    5 Prehistory and anthropology   16

2 THE ARCHEOLOGICAL BASE   26

    1 Importance of archeological evidence   26
    2 Strategy and tactics of archeological research   27
    3 Development of archeology   29

4   *The site, its structure and contents*   *33*
5   *Artifacts*   *40*
6   *Cultural components and assemblages*   *41*
7   *Classes, their formation and identification*   *45*
8   *Classes of cultural remains*   *46*
9   *Classes versus types of artifacts*   *48*
10 *Kinds of types*   *50*
11 *Taxonomic versus typological hierarchies*   *52*
12 *Classes versus modes of features*   *55*
13 *Morphological components, assemblages, and classes*   *57*
14 *Exhibition and publication of the remains*   *58*

3   ETHNIC CLASSIFICATION   *61*

1   *Synthetic versus processual strategy*   *61*
2   *Strategy and tactics of prehistoric research*   *62*
3   *Systematic units: organic versus superorganic*   *65*
4   *Peoples versus societies*   *68*
5   *Development of the study of peoples*   *69*
6   *Cultural classification*   *78*
7   *Cultural complexes*   *84*
8   *Peoples and their cultures*   *87*
9   *Magnitude of peoples*   *89*
10 *Dividing peoples*   *90*
11 *Combining peoples*   *91*
12 *Hierarchies of cultural units*   *92*
13 *Co-peoples and co-cultures*   *94*
14 *Cultural identification*   *96*
15 *Morphological groups*   *98*

4   CHRONOLOGICAL ORDERING   *102*

1   *The chronological approach*   *102*
2   *Relative and absolute dating*   *104*
3   *Development of chronological research*   *107*
4   *Cultural chronologies*   *116*

5 *Other kinds of chronologies*   *118*
6 *Distinguishing local areas*   *121*
7 *Establishing local sequences*   *122*
8 *Synchronizing the sequences*   *129*
9 *Estimating calendrical dates*   *131*
10 *Delimiting ages*   *136*
11 *Converting cultural into ethnic chronologies*   *138*

5 RECONSTRUCTION OF ETHNIC SYSTEMS   140

1   *The conjunctive approach*   *140*
2   *Development of conjunctive research*   *143*
3   *The dimension of form*   *149*
4   *Settlement patterns*   *151*
5   *A model of ethnic relationships*   *153*
6   *The environment*   *158*
7   *Cultures: activities*   *159*
8   *Cultures: norms*   *164*
9   *Cultures: materiel*   *167*
10 *Cultures: reconstruction*   *168*
11 *Morphologies: nature*   *176*
12 *Morphologies: reconstruction*   *177*
13 *Social structures: institutions*   *178*
14 *Social structures: interaction*   *183*
15 *Social structures: norms*   *184*
16 *Social structures: reconstruction*   *184*
17 *Languages*   *189*

6 CHANGES IN ETHNIC SYSTEMS   191

1   *Dynamics and explanation*   *191*
2   *Patterns of change*   *192*
3   *Processes of change*   *194*
4   *Systems versus traits*   *195*
5   *Levels of evolution*   *197*
6   *Role of norms in superorganic change*   *199*

7   Models of macro- and microevolution   202
8   Lines and traditions   207
9   Grades and stages   212
10 Centers and climaxes   216
11 Development of dynamic research   220
12 Processes of change: modification of existing systems 230
13 Processes of change: ethnogenesis   232
14 Processes of change: revolution   233
15 Attitudes toward change   234
16 Reductionism   235

7 CONCLUSION   237

1   Summary of prehistorical methods   237
2   Relevance of prehistorical research   242

Bibliography   246
Glossary and Index   259

FIGURES AND TABLES

FIGURES

1 Potential knowledge about the earth and its inhabitants 2
2 Reliance of the synthetic disciplines upon the analytic disciplines 9
3 Excavation units and components 34
4 Relationship between a class and type of artifacts 49
5 Comparison of the taxonomic and typological procedures for hierarchical classification 53
6 Strategy and tactics of prehistory 63
7 Relationship between a class of cultural assemblages and its characteristics 79

xi

8 *Distribution of typical and transitional assemblages of cultural and morphological remains* *81*

9 *Development of cultural chronologies* *108*

10 *The kind of ethnic chronology recommended in the present volume* *114*

11 *A model of ethnic systems* *154*

12 *Relations among a people's behavior, materiel, and norms* *165*

13 *Models of organic change* *204*

14 *Model of cultural change* *206*

TABLES

1 *Relationships of the anthropological disciplines* *17*

2 *Contents of primary sites* *39*

3 *The midwestern taxonomic system* *75*

4 *Hierarchies of ordinary peoples* *92*

5 *Hierarchies of civilized peoples* *97*

6 *Cultural and social subsystems* *161*

PREFACE

Anthropological theory cannot be covered adequately in a single course. Since anthropologists work empirically from the evidence, they have had to develop a different body of theory for each of their principal kinds of evidence, ethnographic and archeological. The two bodies of theory require separate courses.

The archeological body of theory is treated here, as it is used in the reconstruction of prehistory. This volume presents the concepts of prehistorical research, traces their development, and explains how they enable us to learn about prehistoric life and times. It is the first of three elementary textbooks meant to cover the entire field of prehistory. The other two will present the results of prehistorical research. The second book, also a paperback, will be entitled *African and Western Prehistory*. The third book, in hard cover, will be an expansion of the second book into a synthesis entitled *World Prehistory*.

The three texts are based upon thirty years of teaching prehistory to undergraduates at Yale University. Originally, I covered the entire subject in a single two-semester course, but paid relatively little attention to theory and method. Over the years, I gradually expanded the discussion of these topics until it cut appreciably into the time needed for the synthesis of world prehistory.

In 1963, I began to write a textbook for the course. As I did so, I further increased the course's coverage of theory and method to the point where I had to set up a new single-semester course for the purpose, distinct from the two semesters devoted to the synthesis of world prehistory. At first I taught the new course as an advanced seminar, following after the synthesis, but subsequently I found that better results were obtained by converting it into a regular course, preceding the synthesis. Thus, the original introduction to the synthesis became a separate introductory course; the synthesis itself was divided between two courses, one covering the African and Western worlds and the other, the Eastern, Oceanic, and New Worlds; and I decided to write a separate textbook for each of the three courses.

These changes conform to current trends in American education. Today's teachers prefer a series of smaller textbooks to a single large one, so that they may have greater freedom in selecting and organizing the topics to be covered. Today's students prefer to learn the theoretical structure of a discipline before proceeding to its substantive content, in order to be able to view the facts in theoretical perspective, instead of learning them by rote (Bruner, 1960, pp. 17–32).

My bias is indicated by the subtitle to the present volume: *A Systematic Approach*. This is inspired by the following passage from Petrie (1904, p. 122): "A science can hardly be said to exist until it has a developed system of work, and its possibilities of value for teaching purposes depend entirely upon the organization of its methods. [Historical] geology was in a chaos before the generalization of the successive order of the strata, and the method of the determination of a stratum by its fossils gave the subject a working system...."

I first became aware of the unsystematic nature of prehistory

when I found it necessary in my world prehistory course to reconcile the concepts and terminologies used by the prehistorians work
ing in different parts of the world. Of necessity, prehistorians concentrate on particular regions, and those working in each region
have tended to develop their own approaches. If one attempts, as I
have had to do in my synthesis, to put together the results achieved
in each region, one has to reconcile the differences of approach, in
order not to confuse one's students. For this reason, I gradually
developed, to the best of my ability, a single set of concepts and
terms that incorporates all the regional variations and enables me
to present them to my students in a systematic manner.

When I began to write up this conceptual system in 1963, I discovered to my embarrassment that it was internally inconsistent,
and that I needed to incorporate the latest trends in prehistorical
research. It has taken me seven years to correct these deficiencies.

The internal inconsistencies derive from the fact that words have
multiple meanings, as a glance at any dictionary will reveal. The
more important the words are in our thinking, the more meanings
they have acquired; thus, a whole volume is needed to summarize
the various meanings of the word "culture" (Kroeber and Kluckhohn, 1963). We have a natural tendency to shift back and forth
from one meaning to another, often in successive paragraphs, as a
particular meaning happens to suit our purposes.

Following scientific practice, I have reversed this procedure in
preparing the present volume. First I have attempted to develop a
consistent body of concepts, and then I have applied the best possible term to each concept. I am under no illusion that I have completely succeeded in my attempt to achieve consistency, either in
concepts or in terminology; each time I teach my course, student
reactions bring out new inconsistencies. Nor do I believe that all
inconsistencies ought to be eliminated. (The careful reader will
find, for example, that I use the term "systematic" in several
different senses.) As in other sciences, we need only systematize
our principal concepts and the verbal labels we apply to them.

In my attempt to achieve consistency, I have had to use certain
terms in ways that will be unfamiliar to some readers. I have been
careful not to depart from accepted dictionary definitions. Nevertheless, some of my usages are bound to offend readers' preferences.
Thus, my distinction between "prehistory" and "archeology," while

conceptually sound and in accord with the usage of many specialists, particularly in Europe, is likely to offend other specialists who are accustomed to apply the term "archeology" or the phrase "prehistoric archeology" to the pair of concepts which I am separately calling prehistory and archeology (Sec. 1.3).

Similarly, before starting this volume I had limited my usage of the term "culture" to the norms that mediate human behavior, excluding the behavior itself and the artifacts resulting from the behavior. (This usage was because of my predilection for the dynamic approach, in which norms are the key concept, as opposed to the conjunctive approach, where behavior and artifacts are more important; cf. Secs. 5.5 and 6.6.) I have since been compelled by my desire for consistency and balanced coverage to incorporate both behavior and artifacts into my concept of culture. This change in turn has made it necessary for me to exclude morphological, social, and linguistic norms, which were encompassed in my previous usage (Sec. 5.5). Both of these changes will please some readers and offend others.

The term "evolution" provides a third and final example. A noted biologist whom I consulted advised me to drop the term, since anthropologists use it so differently from biologists and the biological usage has priority. Instead, I have attempted to reconcile the anthropological and biological concepts of evolution, so that I may apply the same term to both (Secs. 6.5 to 6.11).

I do not claim that the usages I have developed for terms such as these are necessarily the best. In fact, I think it a waste of time to argue about terminology—though I have done my share of it. In science, it is one's concepts that are important, not one's terms. As a colleague has suggested, I would avoid much needless antagonism—though at too great a loss of utility—if I were to adopt symbolic logic in order to avoid employing people's favorite terms in ways that offend them.

It is my hope that the reader will find enough of value in the concepts presented in this volume to compensate for my deviations from his terminology. In the case of each concept, I have tried to cite alternative terms, so that each reader may substitute his own favorite if he so desires.

Since the course in world prehistory that I give at Yale was originally conceived and taught by Professor Cornelius Osgood, I owe the inception of the present volume to him. As for the approach used, I wish to acknowledge the influence of my Venezuelan collaborator, José M. Cruxent, who impressed on me the importance of studying people as well as artifacts; my late colleague at Yale, Wendell C. Bennett, whose concept of the Peruvian co-tradition first set me thinking about the use of diagnostic complexes and traditions to distinguish peoples and series of peoples (Bennett, 1948); my present colleague, Kwang-chih Chang, whose insistence upon the study of societies and social structures has made me aware of my own bias toward the study of peoples and cultures; and Sir Julian Huxley, who sensitized me to the fact that cultures are open systems by his criticism of my use of his concept of cultural (superorganic) evolution.

This volume was begun during the course of a sabbatical year in England during 1963–1964. I am indebted to the Guggenheim Foundation for a fellowship that enabled me to go there; to the Institute of Archaeology at the University of London for providing a place where I could write; and to the British prehistorians with whom I came into contact for the many insights I obtained from them. I am particularly grateful to the Guggenheim selection committee for recognizing my parochialism and insisting that I go to Europe to correct it. This slowed me down while I reacted to the "culture shock" of exposure to British anthropology, but has resulted in the production of a much better book.

The manuscript was read in first draft by Peter Ucko, in England, and by Morton H. Levine, in the United States, and I have profited greatly from their criticisms. I have likewise received a number of helpful suggestions from Michael D. Coe and from Ronald D. Kissack, my editor. Whenever the opportunity has arisen, I have sought the advice of other specialists, and I regret that they are too numerous to mention by name. I also would have liked to enumerate the students who have helped me; I have learned much in the process of teaching them. Finally, I wish to thank Mrs. Evelyn Middleton for her patience and skill in typing and retyping so many drafts of this volume.

Irving Rouse

I

THE NATURE OF PREHISTORY

1
Prehistory as
a historical
discipline Though man has been in existence for as much as 2,000,000 years, he did not begin to record his history until the time of the Sumerians, about 3000 B.C., and then he dealt with only a fraction of the earth's surface. The term "prehistory" is applied to the vast periods and areas for which we have no written records. Geologists sometimes extend the term to include events in the history of the earth before the appearance of man, but the discipline of *prehistory,* with which we are here concerned, focuses on mankind (Daniel, 1964).

The scope of prehistory is illustrated in Figure 1. This figure consists of a cube symbolizing the totality of potential knowledge about the earth and its inhabitants. The vertical dimension of the cube indicates time, proceeding from early in time at the bottom to late at the top, and its horizontal dimension indicates space, proceeding from one end of the world at the left to the other end at the right. Geographic space is actually two-dimensional, of course, but the two are here compressed into one so that the third dimension of the cube, running into the page, may be used to symbolize the nature of the human population present at any particular point in time and space on the front face. This third dimension has been termed "form" (Spaulding, 1960a).

The front face of the cube may be termed historical, because it is delimited by the dimensions of time and space. The temporal and spatial positions of human beings may be plotted upon it. Not all of the points of time and space in the front face were occupied by human beings, of course, for parts of the world have been uninhabited from time to time. In addition, the front face includes the very long period between the formation of the earth and the

FIGURE 1 *Potential knowledge about the earth and its inhabitants.*

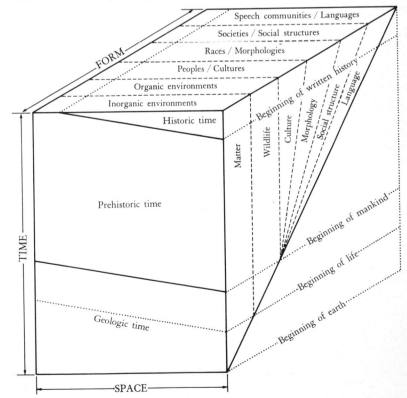

first appearance of mankind, though this representation has been greatly compressed because it is not directly pertinent to the study of prehistory.

The front face is crossed by three inclined lines. The lowest one symbolizes the first appearance of life on the earth; the middle one, the beginning of man; and the top one, the development of written history. These lines are inclined because life, mankind, and written history appeared earlier in some parts of the world than in others. No significance should be attached to the direction of inclination or the distance between the three lines; they are not intended, for instance, to indicate that mankind and written history both appeared earliest in the same part of the world or that each necessarily originated only once, at their lowest points.

The major divisions of the front face may be named and defined as follows:

1.) *Geologic time*—the period from the beginning of the earth through the development of life to the first appearance of mankind.

2.) *Prehistoric time*—the period from the first appearance of mankind to the development of written history.

3.) *Historic time*—the period after man became able to produce adequate historical records.

Prehistorians are by definition specialists in prehistoric time. They take as their field of study the part of the front face of the cube between the middle and upper slanting lines, that is, between the first appearance of mankind and the development of written history. They examine each point in time and space between the two lines, seeking to learn as much as possible about the human beings who lived at that point.

Prehistorians must occasionally go back into geologic time in order to examine the ancestry of the human groups they study. They also find it necessary to follow the development of particular groups from prehistoric into historic time and to investigate the contacts of prehistoric groups with contemporary groups that had already crossed the threshold into history (Daniel, 1967, p. 29). Otherwise, they leave geologic and historic times to the specialists in those divisions of the past.

2
Prehistory as
a scientific
discipline

Geologic time is studied by historical geologists and historic time by human historians. Historical geologists are, of course, natural scientists, whereas historians are humanists (though some prefer to call themselves social scientists). Since prehistory lies between the two, it might be regarded as either a science or a humanity. Actually, Americans classify it as a science and the British classify it as a humanity. (For example, noted American prehistorians are honored by election to the National Academy of Sciences and noted Britishers by membership in the Royal Academy, which is the comparable British organization for the humanities.)

In practice, prehistory is becoming a science in both countries. It is developing regular procedures with which to manipulate its evidence, a specialized body of concepts by means of which to think about the evidence as objectively and as precisely as possible, and a standard terminology with which to refer to the concepts. In other words, it is developing its own peculiar methods and its own technical language.

This development of prehistory as a science is the reason for the present book. Students of prehistory must begin with an introduction, such as this volume, that teaches the methods and language used by prehistorians, before turning to the results of prehistoric research. Students of history, on the contrary, can begin directly with the results of historic research, because that research is carried out in terms of common-sense procedures and everyday language.

The present book discusses the ways in which the methods and language peculiar to prehistory have developed, explains the two, and illustrates their use. The methods are summarized in the last chapter and the language in a Glossary, so as to make it easier to consult this book when reading about the results of prehistoric research. (Some synonyms also have had to be included in the Glossary because prehistorians have not yet been able to reach agreement about their terminology.)

Since man is basically an animal, prehistorians must make use of the methods and language of biology. But they also have had to develop additional methods and a language of their own with which to study man's unique characteristics—those beyond the scope of biology. This dual approach is reflected in the Glossary by the inclusion of biological as well as prehistorical concepts, though the main emphasis is on the latter.

With the scientific nature of prehistoric research in mind, let us return to the cube of knowledge (Fig. 1). The prehistorian must select a point or points on the front face of the cube within the limits of prehistoric time, enter the cube there, and proceed along the dimension of form, studying all of its parts insofar as his data permit. The dimension begins with the inorganic and organic environments present at the points under study and continues with the human beings who inhabited those environments, if any. The human section of the dimension is divided into four parts according to the ways in which individuals are customarily grouped for purposes of scientific study.

When referring to individuals who come from a different background than his own, a layman is likely to say that they belong to a separate ethnic group. This categorization is too gross for scientific study, since ethnic groups usually differ from one another in more than one kind of trait. Scientists have found it necessary to break ethnic groups down into units that differ only in traits of a single kind, as follows:

1. *Cultural groups.* All individuals who engage in similar activities (and who therefore produce similar artifacts) have to be isolated as a group. Such a group is known as a *people* and the activities that characterize its members are termed its *culture* (Childe, 1956, pp. 111ff.). A people and its culture are but sides of the same coin, the term "people" referring to the individuals who compose the group and the term "culture" to the activities that distinguish the group. Hence, "people" and "culture" are juxtaposed on the top face of our cube of knowledge (Fig. 1).

2. *Morphological groups.* Individuals must also be distinguished as a group when their ancestors have interbred, causing them to look alike in their morphological features. We call such a group a *race* and term its distinguishing features the *morphology* of that race (Kroeber, 1948, p. 124). A race and its morphology are, like a people and its culture, but two sides of the same coin (Fig. 1).

3. *Social groups.* Individuals who are organized into similar institutions (and who therefore have the same kinds of social relationships) are said to belong to the same *society* (Firth, 1956, p. 2). The institutions into which the members of a society are organized constitute its *social structure* (Fig. 1).

4. *Linguistic groups.* Individuals who speak the same languages are said to belong to the same speech community (Bloomfield, 1933, pp. 42–56). Each speech community is thus distinguished by its *language,* not by any particular culture, morphology, or social structure (Fig. 1).

In this book, the term *ethnic group* will be used in a general sense to refer collectively to all four of the above kinds of groups. The prehistorian works with all four of them but primarily with cultural groups, for reasons to be given later (Secs. 3.3, 4.5, and 5.2). This is why peoples are placed first in the dimension of form.

3
Prehistory and
archeology

The problems of natural and human history are so complex that a number of academic disciplines have arisen to handle them. In the case of natural history, these include stratigraphy, paleontology, and paleoecology, among others. In the case of human history, a distinction has to be made between (1) *holistic disciplines,* which focus on the ethnic groups of a single period and area; cover their entire range of peoples, races, societies, and speech communities; and study the traits of all these kinds of groups; and (2) *topical disciplines,* which deal with a limited range of traits as they are found among all historic groups. The holistic disciplines include Assyriology, Egyptology, sinology, and others that focus upon "oriental" ethnic groups, as well as classics, medieval studies, and history proper, which are concerned with "western" ethnic groups. The topical disciplines include paleography, which studies inscriptions and writings (e.g., Platt, 1969, p. 20), and history of technology, of art, of religion, of science, and so forth.

In the case of prehistory, too, we must distinguish several disciplines. The first of these, which may be termed *prehistory proper,* is responsible for study of the entire dimension of form during prehistoric time, as explained in the previous section. The second is *archeology,* to which the present section will be devoted.

It is a common practice to group prehistory with archeology and to call the combined subject "prehistoric archeology." In this book, on the contrary, the two will be considered separate disciplines, in order that we may take into account the following differences between them:

1. The term "archeology" means "systematic . . . study of antiquities," that is, of the remains of past peoples (Onions, 1956, p. 92). Archeologists search for remains; excavate, restore, display, and categorize them; and publish reports about them. Hence, archeology has been called "technology in the past tense" (Penniman, 1965, p. 248), though this description is not the whole story; to it should be added "art in the past tense," since some of the remains studied by archeologists are art objects.

Archeology, then, is a topical discipline, like history of technology and history of art. It is limited by definition to the material traits of mankind that have survived in the ground. Prehistory is instead a holistic discipline. It is concerned with the totality of human traits, including social structures and languages, which are not normally represented among archeological remains.

2. The aims of archeology are to recover the remains and learn their nature. To accomplish the latter, it breaks the remains down into categories and studies the relationships among them. Hence, its approach is analytic.

Prehistory takes the results of archeological analysis and combines them with the results obtained in other analytic disciplines, such as linguistics, in order to reconstruct a picture of conditions and events during prehistoric time. Hence, its approach is synthetic rather than analytic.

3. Archeological analysis is not limited to prehistoric remains. Many archeologists study historic remains. The results of these archeologists' research are synthesized by historians rather than prehistorians.

The last point is generally overlooked by the archeologists who excavate in the New World (Hume, 1969, p. 13). Historic time began so late in the United States—not until the arrival of Europeans during the seventeenth century—that the local archeologists are primarily concerned with prehistoric remains, and they tend to equate archeology with prehistory.

The situation in the Old World is quite different. The inhabitants of Mesopotamia entered history at the beginning of the third millennium B.C., and all subsequent remains in that area are historic (e.g., Kramer, 1959). The people of China, Greece, and Rome began to deposit historic remains during the first millennium B.C., and the inhabitants of India, northwestern Africa, and southwestern Europe, during the first millennium A.D. Only in the fringes of the Old World, including northern and eastern Europe and southern Africa, was the advent of history delayed until the present millennium. As a result, the Old World offers major opportunities for research in historic as well as prehistoric archeology. Old World archeologists cannot equate archeology with prehistory, nor shall we do so here.

Even in the Old World, however, archeology is of far greater importance to the student of prehistory than to the student of history. Prehistoric syntheses are based primarily upon the results of archeological analysis, whereas the historian relies upon paleography, that is, the study of inscriptions and other written records. He turns from paleography to archeology only when the former fails him, as when he is studying the dawn of history, before adequate documentation was being produced, and in dealing with mundane matters such as household utensils, which are not likely to be mentioned in the records. It is only historians of art and technology who place great emphasis upon archeology, because they are specialists in particular kinds of objects to be found among the remains.

Archeology may also be compared with a third object-oriented discipline, that of paleontology. Just as archeology, the study of human remains, provides the primary basis for reconstruction of prehistory, so also paleontology, which is the study of nonhuman remains, supplies the primary basis for reconstruction of events and conditions during geologic time.

Paleontologists recover and analyze living organisms, other than man. Hence they cannot go back into early geologic time, before the beginning of life (Fig. 1). Remains dating from that time are practically impossible to identify anyway, because they have been so greatly modified by subsequent events. As a result, no analytic discipline has arisen to study the remains of the period before the development of life. Our best hope of finding out about the nature of the earth during that period is to study the moon and planets, where there is no life.

Only three disciplines, then, are directly concerned with the remains of past life: paleontology, archeology, and paleography. Each of these disciplines may be called analytic, in that it concentrates on the remains themselves, analyzes them, and thereby provides data for the use of other, synthetic disciplines. Paleontological data are utilized primarily by natural historians in studying conditions and events during geologic time; archeological data, by prehistorians in studying the situation during prehistoric time; and paleographic data, by human historians and ethnohistorians in finding out what the world was like during historic time. Each synthetic discipline also uses the others' basic sources of data wherever possible, and each has additional secondary sources of information that need not concern us here.

These relationships are diagrammed in Figure 2. The vertical bars in that figure indicate the degree to which the results of paleontological, archeological, and paleographic analysis are utilized in natural history, prehistory, and the historic disciplines respectively. The paleontological bar is tapered back into early geologic time, the archeological bar into late geologic time, and the paleographic bar into prehistoric time in order to indicate that the syntheses based upon each of these kinds of analysis can be projected back-

FIGURE 2   *Reliance of the synthetic disciplines upon the analytic disciplines.*

TIME		ANALYTIC DISCIPLINES			SYNTHETIC DISCIPLINES
		Paleontology	Archeology	Paleography	
Historic					History, Assyriology, Egyptology, etc.
Prehistoric					Prehistory
Geologic	After beginning of life				Historical geology
	Before beginning of life				

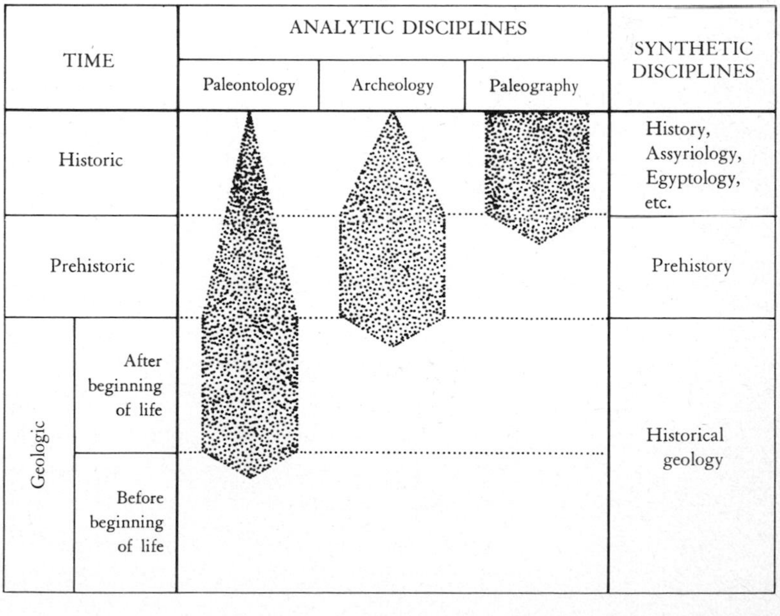

ward to a limited extent. Similarly, the three bars are tapered toward the present in order to indicate that the analyses they symbolize are available for use in studying conditions and events during subsequent time periods.

Some confusion is caused by the fact that a single individual usually finds it necessary to specialize in more than one discipline. He becomes a paleontologist, an archeologist, or a paleographer in order to obtain the evidence he needs, and at the same time he is trained as a natural historian, prehistorian, or historian in order to be able to reconstruct past conditions and events from that evidence. This interdisciplinary approach does not negate the fact that the disciplines are different and must be kept separate in our thinking.

As a teacher of both archeology and prehistory, I am frequently asked by my students about the possibilities of a career in archeology. My reply is that one cannot pursue an academic career in archeology; such a career can only be pursued in a discipline that utilizes the results of archeological research, such as natural history, prehistory, Assyriology, Egyptology, classics, history of art, or history proper. If one wishes to teach or do research of a scholarly nature, one must specialize in one of these synthetic disciplines, using archeology as a means of solving the problems of that discipline (Rowe, 1961a).

In an effort to adjust to this situation, we at Yale University have set up an interdisciplinary undergraduate major in archeology that brings together the courses in archeology taught within each academic department and coordinates them by means of special courses in archeological techniques and in the interpretation of archeological remains. Our aim is to give the student a broad background in all kinds of archeological research before he goes to graduate school and must specialize in the use of archeological remains to resolve the problems of a particular academic discipline, such as prehistory or art history. (For another, more traditional way of handling this problem, see Ascher, 1968.)

For the student who is interested in applied science, on the other hand, there are increasing opportunities to pursue a professional career in archeology. Like other countries, America has become more and more aware of the need to preserve its national heritage of archeological remains, prehistoric as well as historic, and this awareness has produced an increasing demand for salvage archeologists to recover the heritage and for technicians and curators to preserve and display it in monuments and museums. The methods of archeology have become increasingly complex, as more and more recourse is made to the techniques of the exact sciences (e.g., Aitken, 1961; Biek, 1963; Brothwell and Higgs, 1969; Pyddoke, 1963). Prehistorians, historians, and art historians can no longer master all of these techniques, and there is a growing need to train archeologists who are willing to specialize in them and to forsake the status of academicians in favor of applied science.

Unfortunately, the American system of education has not yet adjusted to this development. We continue to train only scholars to teach and do research in prehistory, and often the castoffs from this training end up doing the archeological analysis. Europeans have been more sensitive to the problem and have developed programs for training students in the profession of archeology, for example, at the Institute of Archaeology in the University of London. We in America need to organize similar programs, emphasizing the application of scientific techniques to the analysis of archeological remains rather than stressing the reconstruction of prehistory.

Students trained in such programs may be expected to specialize in one kind of remains and thus to work in prehistoric, industrial, medieval, or underwater archeology, all of which are now recognized in Europe as separate specialties within the discipline of archeology (e.g., Harden, 1957–; Hudson, 1963, 1964–; Dumas, 1962). The prehistoric archeologists trained in this way will have received a different education than the prehistorian, who is trained to teach and do research along the lines of the present volume. He will have become a professional archeologist rather than a specialist in prehistory. But the difference between the two will be merely one of emphasis. The prehistoric archeologist must know some prehistory in order properly to categorize remains, and conversely, the prehistorian must use the categories produced by the archeologist. To a greater or lesser extent, each tries to become proficient in the other's discipline in order to obtain knowledge he needs in his own research, but he finds proficiency increasingly difficult to achieve as the two disciplines become more and more complex.

Having placed prehistory with respect to the other disciplines that are concerned with the past, let us now look at its relation to the disciplines that study the present. For this purpose, we must turn to the top face of the cube (Fig. 1), which is bounded by the dimensions of space and form, the dimension of time being zero.

The dimension of space runs along the front edge of the top face. Each point on that edge represents a particular spot on the earth's surface. The investigator selects one of these local areas for study and moves perpendicularly across the top face from that point, along the dimension of form. First he encounters the physical and organic environments of the area, with which he must familiarize himself in order to understand the ethnic groups that live there. Next comes the first kind of ethnic group, peoples. Each people occupies a part of the area, which the investigator must delimit before proceeding to study cultures. There will also be one or more races, societies, and speech communities, which are depicted in the back three parts of the top face. These groups must similarly be delimited and then studied in terms of their morphologies, social structures, and languages respectively.

The top face is crossed by a dotted line, which is a projection of the line on the front face separating prehistoric from historic time. The ethnic groups to the left of this line are nonliterate, in the sense that they do not write about themselves and therefore can only be studied by observation and questioning. The ethnic groups on the right side of the line are literate and furnish documentary evidence about themselves.

A variety of disciplines have been developed to deal with the subject matter represented on the top face of the cube. We may leave aside the various professional disciplines, such as architecture, engineering, and law, because, like applied archeology, they are nonacademic. Physical geology, biology, and the other natural sciences are of peripheral interest only, since they deal with environments per se. Our primary concern is with the social sciences and humanities, which focus on man.

Contemporary ethnic groups, like those of the past, can be studied analytically or synthetically. The analytic study is known as *ethnography* (Onions, 1956, p. 637). Ethnographers select a particular part of the earth's surface, that is, a specific point on the front edge of the top face of our cube of knowledge, along the dimension of space, and study the inhabitants by moving back along the dimension of form from the local environments to the different kinds of ethnic groups that live there. They obtain samples of the tools, clothing, and other artifacts made by each people; where possible, they also collect human skeletal material to exemplify each race. They install these objects in museums alongside the comparable remains of past peoples and races recovered by archeologists. As a result, there has developed a series of museums of archeology and ethnography—often misnamed ethnology—which display specimens characteristic of the ethnic groups of the world, past and present, with an emphasis upon nonliterate groups. The artifacts of literate groups are more commonly displayed separately in museums of folklore or art.

Ethnographers are not forced by the limitations of their data to restrict themselves to the collection and analysis of artifacts and human bones, as archeologists must do. They can also observe or inquire about all kinds of cultural, morphological, social, and linguistic traits. Hence, they produce incomparably richer analyses than archeologists can. In effect, their analyses are holistic rather than topical.

In organizing these analyses, ethnographers utilize the ethnic groups into which local populations divide themselves (e.g., Moerman, 1965; Barth, 1969). As among ourselves, these ethnic groups are normally based upon a mixture of cultural, morphological, social, and linguistic criteria. The ethnographer must disentangle the criteria, distinguishing separate peoples, races, societies, and speech communities and, when necessary, coining names for each of them, in order to fill out the dimension of form as it is given on the top face of our cube of knowledge (Fig. 1).

Turning from the analytic to the synthetic study of contemporary nonliterate populations, we encounter a discipline known as *ethnology*. This discipline is "the science which treats of ... [living groups], their relations, [and the development of] their distinctive characteristics" (Onions, 1956, p. 637). Ethnologists approach these groups in the same holistic and synthetic manner in which prehistorians and historians approach past groups. They observe the changes that are taking place in the culture of each people, the morphology of each race, the structure of each society, and the language of each speech community; work out the relationships among these changes; and attempt to determine the reasons for them. In so doing they utilize the categories of culture, morphology, social structure, and language that have resulted from ethnographic analysis.

Since the holistic approach is practicable only in dealing with the simpler, nonliterate groups, both ethnographers and ethnologists leave the study of more complex, literate groups to the members of other, topical disciplines, including art and architecture, comparative literature, economics, folklore, geography, linguistics, political science, religion, and sociology. Thus we have the same duality of interpretative approaches to the top of the cube as to the front. Ethnographers and ethnologists, like prehistorians and most historians, use the holistic approach, whereas the remaining social scientists and humanists, like archeologists and the historians of art, science, and technology, limit themselves to particular topics.

We have seen that prehistorians sometimes cross the boundary between prehistoric and historic time in order to investigate the relationships among groups living in the two. In like manner, ethnographers and ethnologists frequently study the relationships between nonliterate and literate groups on the contemporary scene. They also have begun to study among literate peoples individual communities or other kinds of subgroups that are simple enough to be viewed holistically, even though the people in their entirety cannot be. This kind of approach is often called "community study," though the phrase is a poor one, since it fails to distinguish the ethnographer's and ethnologist's holistic approaches to communities from the topical approaches used by sociologists and other social scientists (Steward, 1950, pp. 20–43).

So far, we have been considering the traditional way of studying contemporary literate populations, by dividing them up among the various social sciences and humanities along the dimension of form. In recent years, there has been some tendency to use the alternative dimension, that of space. This approach has produced a series of area studies, in which social scientists and (to a lesser extent) humanists of all disciplines pool their knowledge and experience regarding a particular part of the world. In the case of each area, ethnographers and ethnologists contribute their knowledge of the nonliterate peoples, races, societies, and speech communities; and geographers, economists, political scientists, linguists, and the like, their knowledge about the literate groups. This trend is, of course, linked with our growing awareness of the underdeveloped parts of the world, as a result of World War II and the founding of the United Nations. The trend therefore has a practical cast, and the area student is likely to be an applied rather than a pure scientist.

It is generally recognized that area students need to have some knowledge of history, for they cannot understand the population of an area without knowing something about its background. If all or part of the population is nonliterate, prehistory also must be studied. In this respect both history and prehistory cooperate with the disciplines that approach the top face of the cube, even though their main task is to approach the cube from the front.

Summarizing the discussion to this point, we may say that archeologists and ethnographers complement each other, the former studying the remains of past ethnic groups and the latter the lives of contemporary groups (cf. Mead, 1964, p. 506). They use different field methods, adapted to the differences in their data, but have similar motives. Much archeological field work, as we have seen, is designed to salvage remains that are threatened with destruction. Similarly, ethnographers are frequently motivated to study living groups before these become extinct. In so doing, both function as applied scientists, but they also make important contributions to scholarship by carrying out ever more complex analyses of their data.

By contrast, prehistorians and ethnologists are synthesizers. Just as prehistorians use the results of archeological analyses to reconstruct the nature and development of prehistoric groups, so ethnologists rely upon ethnographic analyses in studying changes in contemporary ethnic groups.

Of the individual disciplines that approach the cube through its top face, prehistory is most closely related to ethnography and ethnology. It shares with these two disciplines a common interest in nonliterate ethnic groups and a common use of the holistic approach. Ethnographers and ethnologists often have occasion to refer to the time perspective that prehistory has worked out for the nonliterate groups of the past. Conversely, prehistorians use the knowledge that ethnographers and ethnologists have accumulated about contemporary nonliterate groups in order to reconstruct the nature and development of past groups.

5
Prehistory and
anthropology

Anthropology has not yet been mentioned. How does it relate to prehistory, ethnology, and the other disciplines that study our cube of knowledge? Most importantly, it is not a single science, like the previously mentioned disciplines; rather, it is a profession, consisting of a number of sciences that are united by possession of a common set of goals, common methods and theories, and a common professional organization (Rouse, 1969).

Anthropology has been defined as "the science[s] of man or of mankind in the widest sense" (Onions, 1956, p. 74). From this definition, one might assume that anthropology includes all of the scientific disciplines that study the human part of our cube of knowledge. Actually, it is less comprehensive. At its core, it is limited to the disciplines that focus on nonliterate man (Table 1): archeology and prehistory, which study the nonliterate groups of the past; and ethnography and ethnology, which study contemporary nonliterate groups (e.g., Kluckhohn, 1965, pp. 15–23).

As we have seen, both prehistorians and ethnologists make excursions from this core into the realm of literate man, past and present. By applying their conceptual approach to historic peoples, they have developed a new discipline, which is known as *ethnohistory* (Wheeler-Voegelin, 1954–). The application of this approach to contemporary literate peoples has not received the status of a separate discipline but is simply considered an extension of ethnography and ethnology (Table 1).

The profession of anthropology also includes a number of disciplines that have not yet been discussed. Some, such as educational and medical anthropology, are applied sciences and hence do not fall within the scope of the present study. Four others are pertinent: *cultural, physical, social,* and *linguistic anthropology* (or, more simply, linguistics). Each of these four disciplines generalizes the pertinent results of the disciplines already mentioned and hence cuts across them (Table 1). Each compares the peoples, races, societies, or speech communities of the past, as studied by archeologists, prehistorians, and ethnohistorians, and the comparable ethnic groups of the present, as studied by ethnographers and ethnologists, in order to draw general conclusions.

Anthropology, then, may be said to consist of three sets of disciplines (Table 1). In the first set are archeology, which processes the remains of past populations, and prehistory and ethnohistory, which study the cultural, morphological, social, and linguistic groups present in each population and attempt to work out the nature and development of each group. In the second set are ethnography, which analyzes the nature of the corresponding groups of the present, and ethnology, which synthesizes the changes in these groups. The third set consists of cultural, physical, social, and linguistic anthropology, each of which focuses on groups of a single kind and proceeds comparatively from one group to another. The first two sets of disciplines operate holistically, but the third is topical, as the names for the different kinds of anthropology imply.

In dealing with the first two sets earlier in this chapter, we noted that archeologists and prehistorians approach our cube of knowledge through its front face, whereas ethnographers and ethnologists approach it through the front edge of the top face (Fig. 1). At first

TABLE 1   *Relationships of the anthropological disciplines*

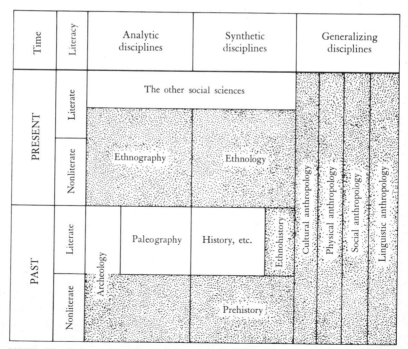

NOTE: The shading indicates the disciplines included in the profession of anthropology.

glance, cultural, physical, social, and linguistic anthropologists might also seem to approach the cube through the front edge of its top face, though from a topical rather than a holistic point of view. This, however, is not the case. Before entering the cube through the front edge, one must choose a particular locality, and this choice requires one to work holistically and therefore to assume the role of an ethnographer or ethnologist or both. One may decide to concentrate upon the peoples of the locality, in order to learn about their cultures; upon the races, to get at their morphologies; upon societies, in order to analyze their social structures; or upon speech communities, in order to study their languages, but it is hardly likely that one will be able to limit oneself to a single kind of ethnic group. For example, one must know the local language in order properly to study culture and social structure. Hence, despite the emphasis upon a single kind of group, one will still be operating in a holistic manner; that is, one will be making a partial rather than a complete study of the local ethnography-ethnology.

The same is true when one enters the cube lower down in the front face, for example, with the aim of studying the physical qualities of early man. One will have to select a particular point in time and space for one's field work, and this will put one in the roles of archeologist and prehistorian. One will dig for human bones, but the chances are that, in so doing, one will also encounter cultural remains. Hence, one can hardly limit oneself to physical anthropology; and even if one does, one will simply be making a partial study of the local archeology and prehistory.

Cultural, physical, social, and linguistic anthropologists do not approach the cube as persons in other disciplines do. They are not field workers and analysts, except insofar as they may have assumed the role of ethnographer or archeologist in order to obtain and analyze missing facts; nor are they synthesizers, except insofar as they may also have had to assume the role of ethnologist or prehistorian in order to fill gaps in their own subject matter. They study the results of both analysis and synthesis, either in terms of the dimensions of form alone, that is, along the top edge of the side face of the cube, or else in terms of the dimensions of form and time, that is, lower down on the side face. Let us consider each of these approaches in turn.

1. The dimension of form is laid out from left to right along the top edge of the side face of the cube. Each anthropologist focuses upon the division of the edge in which he specializes, whether it be culture, morphology, social structure, or language. (It is also possible to specialize in ecology, within the environmental sections; in material culture or art, within the cultural section; in psychology or medicine, in connection within the morphological section; or in economics, within the section on social structure; but these are not generally recognized as anthropological specialties.) Proceeding across the top face within, for example, the cultural division, the anthropologist encounters all the peoples in existence today and is able to select a representative sample of these peoples for comparative study. He then examines the cultural forms present among the peoples in his sample, determines the range of forms, and makes correlations among the forms. The specialist in physical, social, or linguistic anthropology is similarly able to make comparative studies of morphological, social, and linguistic forms respectively.

2. If, instead of limiting himself to the present time, the anthropological specialist proceeds through time, from the bottom of the side face of the cube to the top, he will be studying the succession of forms, which is indicated by the expanding divisions of the side face. The first division starts at the bottom of the face with a point that symbolizes the beginning of matter, that is, of the earth itself. The division expands rapidly upward from that point in order to indicate an increase in the variety and organization of matter, culminating in the beginning of life. Thereafter, little change in width is shown, on the assumption that fewer new kinds of matter came into existence.

Similarly, the second division begins with a point symbolizing the appearance of life. The expansion of this division expresses the subsequent increase in the variety and complexity of life that climaxed in the beginning of mankind. Thereafter, the number of new forms of wildlife was presumably more or less balanced by the number of forms that became extinct, and so the division is shown with little further change in width (Huxley, 1955, p. 6).

The first human beings had only rudimentary cultural, morphological, social, and linguistic forms, but these human attributes became increasingly diverse and intricate with the passage of time, as is indicated by the expansion of the wedges that refer to these forms. The actual widths of all the wedges are, of course, purely arbitrary, and no significance should be attached to them.

The task of the anthropological specialist is to investigate the wedge in which he specializes, whether it be culture, morphology, social structure, or language. He seeks to determine the manner in which the relatively small range of forms present among the earliest human groups expanded, as increasingly complex forms evolved during the course of man's existence. In so doing, he must go beyond the beginning of written history, as symbolized by the horizontal line at the top of the side face, and back before the appearance of man, to study the sources of human forms among the lesser animals (e.g., White, 1959).

Comparing the approaches to the three faces of the cube, we may say that archeologists and prehistorians, on the one hand, and ethnographers and ethnologists, on the other, approach the front and top faces respectively in a particularistic and historical manner, for they are interested in particular points in time and space and want to find out about the remains or inhabitants of those points. By contrast, cultural, physical, social, and linguistic anthropologists approach the side and top faces in a general and scientific way, since they are interested in determining the range of forms and in framing and testing hypotheses about how they evolved (cf. Driver, 1965, p. 325).

Both groups of specialists start with the knowledge acquired by archeologists and ethnographers. Prehistorians and ethnologists treat this knowledge as their data, synthesize it, and explain it by use of the method of multiple working hypotheses; that is, they consider all alternative hypotheses that might account for a particular set of data and select the hypothesis that best fits the data (Chamberlin, 1965). Cultural, physical, social, and linguistic anthropologists eschew this explanatory approach in favor of experimentation. They start with a particular set of hypotheses, for example, as to the evolution of social forms, and proceed to test the validity of these hypotheses by means of cross-cultural study (e.g., Murdock,

1949). Hence, they proceed deductively from one or more hypotheses to the data, whereas prehistorians and ethnologists proceed inductively from the data to consideration of all possible hypotheses that might account for the data.

This distinction does not mean that prehistorians and ethnologists avoid experimentation. They have actually done much experimental research, for example, by working out how different kinds of flint artifacts were made (Ascher, 1961b). But when they do this kind of research, they are shifting from the role of prehistorian or ethnologist to that of cultural anthropologist, in the terminology being used here.

Neither prehistorians nor ethnologists are unfamiliar with the testing of hypotheses. Their work on particular cultural, morphological, social, or linguistic groups often suggests a new hypothesis; and, shifting to the role of a cultural, physical, social, or linguistic anthropologist, they proceed to test the hypothesis by comparative study. This is as it should be; if prehistorians and ethnologists did not constantly shift to the role of an anthropological specialist, and vice versa, there would be no point of including all of them under the label of "anthropology."

Prehistorians and ethnologists, then, use hypotheses to explain data about particular ethnic groups, whereas cultural, physical, social, and linguistic anthropologists test the hypotheses, either in a laboratory situation or by comparative study of archeological and ethnographical data. The cube (Fig. 1) is intended to diagram these relationships. Basically, it is composed of the knowledge about past and present populations that is being accumulated and analyzed by archeologists and ethnographers respectively. Other specialists use this basic information to produce additional knowledge. Prehistorians and ethnologists, approaching the cube through its front and top faces respectively, synthesize it inductively. Cultural, physical, social, and linguistic anthropologists, approaching the cube through its side face, employ the results of analysis and synthesis deductively as a means of testing hypotheses.

The foregoing, developed for use in this book, is a logical way to organize the subject matter of anthropology. In actual practice, anthropologists are not so logical. Indeed, there is considerable variation from country to country. The English-speaking world alone has two different ways of dividing up the field of anthropology, neither of which corresponds to Table 1. In the United States, the divisions are as follows:

1. *Archeology* includes archeology and prehistory, as listed in Table 1.

2. *Cultural anthropology* comprises the subjects of ethnography, ethnology, ethnohistory, cultural anthropology, and social anthropology, much as these are listed in Table 1, though with the exceptions noted below. (This division is alternatively called ethnology or social anthropology. Recently, there has been a tendency to subdivide it into ecological anthropology, economic anthropology, political anthropology, psychological anthropology, religious anthropology, and so forth.)

3. *Physical anthropology* includes both archeological and ethnographic field work on the human organism, as well as the discipline of physical anthropology as listed in Table 1.

4. *Linguistics* covers the linguistic aspects of ethnographic field work and ethnological interpretation, as well as the discipline of linguistic anthropology listed in Table 1.

These four divisions are grouped together in a single department of anthropology at each major American university. In theory, they form coordinate parts of the department, but in practice some are more equal than others. Since cultural anthropology includes five of the units listed in Table 1 and the term itself indicates the highest level of integration, it has come to be regarded as the core of anthropology. Physical anthropology and linguistics also enjoy a certain prestige because they are on the highest level of integration and, in the case of linguistics, because it has developed more systematic methods than the other three divisions. Archeology derives a certain advantage from the fact that it includes prehistory, but it has the disadvantage that the term "archeology" refers to a relatively low level of research.

The British organize anthropology in a somewhat different manner. They exclude linguistics and divide the rest of the subject into three parts:

1. *Prehistory* (alternatively called prehistoric archeology) includes both archeology and prehistory, as listed in Table 1.

2. *Social anthropology* covers the subjects of ethnography, ethnology, cultural anthropology, and social anthropology, as listed in Table 1.

3. *Physical anthropology* is the same as in Table 1.

Unlike their American colleagues, the British have come to view these as separate, though related, academic departments, so the problem of equality among them does not arise. Prehistorians, social anthropologists, and physical anthropologists are each trained as specialists and acquire only a superficial background in the other two specialties, relative to American practice (Forde, 1951).

The differences between American and British practice are rooted in the subject matter and the academic environment of anthropology in the two countries. Americans have traditionally emphasized the study of the local Indians, in which archeology, ethnology, physical anthropology, and linguistics complement one another. Students of the prehistoric Indians need to know about the present-day Indians in order to interpret the remains they find, and students of the contemporary Indians cannot fully understand them without knowing something of their prehistoric past. By contrast, students of the prehistoric British populations have little in common with students of contemporary nonliterate populations because the two are situated in different parts of the world and are separated by long periods of history. British prehistorians, therefore, do not have the incentive of their American colleagues to join forces with social and physical anthropologists and to associate with linguists.

A second reason for the difference is that American students are not accustomed to specialize so early in their academic careers as British students do. When Americans first take work in anthropology during the freshman or sophomore year of college, they are still in the process of acquiring a general education and hence are offered broad courses, including a combination of archeology, cultural and physical anthropology, and linguistics. The comparable British student will have begun to specialize several years earlier, while still in secondary school, and so is prepared when he begins his undergraduate education to concentrate almost exclusively on either prehistory, social anthropology, or physical anthropology. For this reason, British universities recognize separate undergraduate majors in prehistory, social anthropology, and physical anthropology. They do not insist, as American universities do, that a major in prehistory be at the same time a major in social and physical anthropology and vice versa; instead, they argue that the three disciplines have become so complex that students cannot be expected to acquire a thorough knowledge of all three and had better be allowed to concentrate on only one of them.

This difference in undergraduate education intensifies the difference in graduate schools. American universities expose their graduate students to all branches of anthropology so that they will be prepared to teach introductory courses that encompass all of them, whereas British graduate students are trained to teach only prehistory, social anthropology, or physical anthropology, as the case may be. The result is a single profession of anthropology in the United States and multiple professions in Great Britain.

This is not the place to attempt to reconcile the differences between British and American practices ... if, indeed, they are capable of reconciliation. The differences have been discussed here only in order to warn the reader that the logical definitions of terms developed for use in this book do not correspond to the actual practices. Our definitions may be summarized as follows:

Cultural, physical, social, and *linguistic anthropology* are the disciplines that frame and test hypotheses about the variability and development of culture, human morphology, social structure, and language respectively. The hypotheses are tested against the evidence provided by ethnographic, archeological, ethnological, and prehistoric research.

Ethnography is the study of the nature of contemporary ethnic groups. It is largely restricted to nonliterate groups that can be treated holistically. It distinguishes peoples, races, societies, and speech communities and then proceeds to determine what each group was like by making complex analyses of its characteristics.

Ethnology is the study of changes in contemporary nonliterate groups. It focuses on the changes that are taking place in the cultures, morphologies, social structures, or languages of the groups; notes interrelationships among these changes; and theorizes about the reasons for the changes.

Archeology is the study of human remains, historic as well as prehistoric. It seeks to determine their nature, and has developed highly technical methods for discovering, recovering, and analyzing them. It also makes the remains known by preparing monuments, museum exhibits, study collections, monographs, and other analytic publications.

Prehistory is one of several disciplines that synthesize the data provided by archeologists. Its field is the time between the first appearance of man and the development of written history, and it seeks to reconstruct both the ethnography and the ethnology of this period. It does so by applying the accumulated knowledge of cultural, physical, social, and linguistic anthropology to the archeology of the period.

This is a book about prehistory, and so the reader should not expect it to give him an adequate introduction to archeology or to cultural, physical, social, or linguistic anthropology, as these terms are defined here. The book is intended to introduce the reader to the methods prehistorians have developed for bringing together archeological evidence and anthropological knowledge for the purpose of reconstructing the ethnography and ethnology of prehistoric time.

SUPPLEMENTAL READING

CLARK, GRAHAME, _Archaeology and Society_ (1960), pp. 17–37.

DANIEL, GLYN, _The Idea of Prehistory_ (1964).

DANIEL, GLYN, _The Origins and Growth of Archaeology_ (1967), pp. 13–32.

HOLE, FRANK, AND ROBERT F. HEIZER, _An Introduction to Prehistoric Archeology_ (1969), pt. I.

KLUCKHOHN, CLYDE, _Mirror for Man_ (1965).

MEAD, MARGARET, _Anthropology: A Human Science_ (1964).

OLIVER, DOUGLAS, _Invitation to Anthropology_ (1964).

2

THE ARCHEOLOGICAL BASE

1
Importance of
archeological
evidence We have seen that specialists in prehistory work primarily with archeological evidence (Fig. 2)—so much so that the words "archeology" and "prehistory" are often used as synonyms. Not all reconstruction of prehistory is based upon archeological evidence, however, nor is all archeology done in order to reconstruct prehistory. Hence, it is necessary for the sake of clear thinking to distinguish separate disciplines of archeology and prehistory.

Among the non-archeologists who contribute to the study of prehistory are geologists, who follow changes in the earth, its flora, and its fauna up from geologic into prehistoric time (Figs. 1 and 2), and historians, who move back from historic into prehistoric time, for example, when they encounter oral traditions written down after a group passed from prehistory into history or when they are able to study historic groups' writings about the prehistoric groups with whom they come into contact (Vansina, 1965). Ethnologists contribute even more to our knowledge of man's prehistoric past by studying the traces of the past that survive among contemporary groups (e.g., Sapir, 1951).

Why do prehistorians concentrate upon archeological evidence and themselves become specialists in archeology more often than in paleontology, paleography, and ethnography, the disciplines from which geologists, historians, and ethnologists draw their evidence when they assume the role of prehistorian? Why, in particular, do prehistorians place so little emphasis upon the linguistic aspects of ethnographic data when present-day languages contain so many survivals from the past (e.g., Swadesh, 1960)? The reasons are that paleontological evidence tells us only about organisms, not about cultures, social structures, and languages, while paleographic and ethnographic evidence can only be used in reconstructing the latter part of prehistory. Archeological remains are the sole kind of evidence that applies to all of prehistory, throughout the dimensions of space and time, and that also provides information about all aspects of human life, throughout the dimension of form (Fig. 1).

Prehistorians must therefore base the main outlines of their syntheses upon archeological evidence, and should use paleontological, paleographic, and ethnographic evidence, as well as the interpretations of these kinds of evidence by geologists, historians, and ethnologists respectively, only in order to check and embellish the outlines already reconstructed from archeological remains (Trigger, 1968a, pp. 1–6). It follows that we must begin our survey of prehistorical theory and method with a discussion of archeological research, in order to become familiar with the basic data of prehistory.

2
Strategy and
tactics of
archeological
research

Any person planning to study archeological remains is faced with a choice among three goals: (1) he may seek to learn the nature of the remains under study, (2) he may wish to obtain the evidence needed for a synthesis of prehistory or history, or (3) he may be after the evidence with which to make a comparative study of particular kinds of human traits and of the processes of change in those traits. Each of the three goals requires a different strategy, and these strategies may be termed *analytic, synthetic,* and *processual* respectively (Rouse, 1970).

The analytic strategy, with its interest in remains for their own sake, characterizes the discipline of archeology and will therefore be the subject of the present chapter. The synthetic and processual strategies are instead characteristic of prehistory and history, and of cultural, physical, social, and linguistic anthropology (Sec. 3.1).

The analytic strategy requires a three-step procedure, as follows:

1. *Recovery of the remains.* This is accomplished by means of field work, designed to discover all possible kinds of remains and to obtain an adequate sample of each kind.

2. *Processing of the remains.* The archeologist does this in his laboratory, except in the case of buildings and other structures that cannot be removed from their sites. He preserves and records the remains and categorizes them in order to determine their nature.

3. *Exhibition and publication.* Both activities usually take place in a museum or other institution where the archeologist deposits the remains, but again, nonportable objects must be exhibited in situ, by converting them into monuments or open-air museums. From an analytical point of view, both exhibits and publications should be designed to give interested people an opportunity to learn the nature of the remains.

At this point, it is necessary to make a distinction between strategy and tactics. *Strategy* is the logical order of procedure, whereas *tactics* are the order that is followed in any particular instance. Tactics may or may not correspond to the strategy. When, for example, an archeologist first goes into the field to collect remains, his tactics conform to the strategy. If he subsequently finds upon analysis of the material obtained that it contains an obvious gap, he will have to go back into the field in order to fill that gap. He will then be using tactics that are contrary to the strategy; that is, he will be reversing the logical order of the steps by proceeding from step 2 to step 1.

In the remainder of this chapter, we shall consider archeological research in the logical order of the analytical strategy and shall ignore the tactical alternatives, since they are not pertinent to the study of prehistory. Before beginning, let us consider the manner in which archeological research developed.

3
*Development of
archeology*
Mankind has probably always had an interest in human remains, for many prehistoric sites have yielded objects that can only have been picked up from previous sites and kept as curiosities, eventually to be redeposited with the inhabitant's own artifacts (e.g., Rowe, 1961b, p. 326). This process of collection and subsequent deposition is still going on, as exemplified by the finding within the last century of medieval Norse objects redeposited on the North American continent (Brøndsted, 1954, pp. 399–400).

The Sumerians, who were the first historic peoples, were also the first to leave records of an interest in archeological remains. According to these records, the Sumerian kings were instructed by their gods, appearing to them in dreams, to excavate and restore or enlarge the temples built by previous kings. This work involved not only archeology itself, in the sense in which that term has been defined in Chapter 1, but also historic interpretation, for it was the practice of each king, when he built a new temple, to have its bricks stamped with the name of the god for whom it was built and of himself as builder, in order to help his successors to identify the temple or its ruins in the event of reconstruction. To make doubly sure, clay nails bearing the same information on their heads were inserted into the walls of the temple at regular intervals (Chiera, 1938, pp. 91–96). The practice of excavating and restoring temples continued into the subsequent Babylonian period; and in the sixth century B.C. Bel-Shalti-Nannar, daughter of Nabonidus, the last king of Babylon, established a museum of local antiquities in the city of Ur (Woolley, 1965, pp. 202–204).

Both the Greeks and the Romans also had an interest in remains. A number of them traveled around the classical world, as we still do, and recorded their observations. The most famous of these was Pausanius, who in the second century A.D. wrote a description of Greece containing many references to archeological monuments. Unlike the Sumerians and the Babylonians, the Greeks and the Romans made no effort to restore the monuments; they seem to have regarded them only as curiosities (Wace, 1962).

The classical peoples also collected artifacts. Many were kept in temples and public buildings; for instance, the spear of Achilles was preserved in the temple of Athena at Pharsalus. There were also private collectors in Rome, supplied by dealers in antiquities and works of art. For example, when the Roman colonists settled by Julius Caesar at Corinth accidentally discovered ancient cemeteries containing pottery vessels and bronzes, they were able to sell these works at high prices to Roman dealers.

The Chinese, too, became interested in artifacts about this time, though as much for their use in historical research as for their own sake. The earliest Chinese historians, of the Han dynasty, used artifacts to piece out their documentary evidence; for example, Ssu-ma Ch'ien visited many ruins and studied many relics in compiling the data for his *Shih Chi (Book of History)*. The post-Han scholars preferred to base their histories entirely on documents, but artifacts were still collected, especially bronze vessels and stone tablets; they were regarded either as curios or as heirlooms, as in Greece and Rome (Chang, 1968, pp. 1–3).

In Europe, the tradition of collecting, displaying, and describing artifacts disappeared with the decline and fall of the Roman empire. Europeans of the Middle Ages viewed the past in terms of the Bible, and any remains that did not fit the Biblical accounts were explained away by means of superstitions. For example, ax blades ground from stone, to which the technical term "celt" is now applied, were thought to be "thunderstones" that had fallen out of the sky in the company of lightning—a belief that is still current among the country people in Europe and the Americas (MacCurdy, 1926, vol. 1, pp. 11–12).

The collection of artifacts was revived during the Renaissance, along with the rest of classical learning (Daniel, 1950, pp. 16–28). Popes, cardinals, and other prominent citizens of sixteenth-century Italy took the lead in this revival, even to the point of sponsoring archeological excavations. They were primarily interested in classical antiquities and especially in those which could be considered art objects. They decorated their homes with such objects, and they developed the subject of art history, which need not concern us here.

North of the Alps, classical antiquities were neither so much in evidence nor so artistic, and therefore the collectors were more catholic in their tastes. They turned their attention to prehistoric as well as classical artifacts and gradually dispelled the superstitions about them that had existed during the Middle Ages.

The collection of artifacts like these continued sporadically but with increasing momentum during the sixteenth, seventeenth, and eighteenth centuries. At the same time, more systematic attention was paid to monuments, especially in England. The pioneer in this area was William Camden (1551–1623), who traveled around the country collecting information about prehistoric mounds and earth-works, Roman inscriptions and ruins, and medieval structures. He brought this material together in a book, *Britannia* (first edition 1586), that laid the groundwork for field archeology in Britain (Crawford, 1953, pp. 22–23).

It was not until the nineteenth century that the collection of portable artifacts reached a comparable stage of systematization. In 1806, the Danish government appointed a scientific commission to direct studies of the local archeology and natural history. The artifacts excavated under the sponsorship of this commission formed the nucleus of a Royal Danish Museum of Antiquities, established in Copenhagen in 1816, and this institution eventually developed into the Danish National Museum (Daniel, 1950, pp. 38–53).

The British Museum established a Department of Antiquities of Art in the early 1800s, but it was not until the 1860s that the museum divided this department into Departments of Oriental Antiquities, Greek and Roman Antiquities, Coins and Medals, and British and Medieval Antiquities and Ethnography, the last of which handled the museum's prehistoric artifacts from Britain and the rest of the world. Similar developments took place on the continent of Europe, in North America, and, to a lesser extent, in Argentina. For example, one of the first projects undertaken by the Smithsonian Institution, after its formation in Washington, D.C., in the 1840s, was a systematic survey of the mounds and earthworks of the eastern United States. The first systematic collections in the New World were those of the U.S. National Museum and the Harvard Peabody Museum in the 1870s (Shetrone, 1941, pp. 1–26).

The nineteenth century also saw the beginning of synthetic interpretation of archeological remains, including use of the remains in studies of prehistory, Assyriology, Egyptology, sinology, and the like. These studies, however, do not concern us in the present stage of our discussion. From an analytic point of view, the greatest

achievement of the century was the discovery of hitherto unrecog-
nized kinds of remains, such as the shell heaps (middens) of Denmark, the pile dwellings of Switzerland, and the Paleolithic stone
tools and cave paintings of western Europe. Many of these finds
were accepted as archeological remains only after prolonged opposition by people who still believed in a literal interpretation of the
Bible or who refused to go beyond the bounds of their own experience to identify new and exotic kinds of remains.

Analytically, the twentieth century has been marked by expansion of archeological research from Europe and American to the rest
of the world and, in Europe and America, by recognition of the
need to recover remains before they are destroyed by the construction of buildings, dams, and highways. The Soviet Union has
pioneered in this activity, which is known as salvage archeology
(Chard, 1969a). In America, salvage archeology is supported not
only by the federal and state governments, but also by private industry, all of which now appropriate money to excavate remains
that are in danger of being destroyed by construction crews (e.g.,
Petsche, 1968).

At the same time, archeologists have begun to pay attention to
the conceptual side of their analyses. They have devised systematic
methods of classification and identification, which enable them to
think about the specimens instead of simply viewing them as objects. They have also realized the need to record the context of the
specimens as they are found, in order to be able to reconstruct the
order and manner of deposition. They are even studying the
changes that take place after deposition, in an effort better to understand contexts and to reconstruct the original nature of the remains
(e.g., Dimbleby, 1965). As a result, analytic archeology can no
longer be regarded as merely the collection of curios. It has become the science of human remains, investigating the nature of the
remains, the manner of their deposition, and the processes whereby
they have been preserved or modified while in the ground (e.g.,
Piggott, 1965a, pp. 24–50).

Important technical innovations also have occurred. Complex
chemical and physical techniques are now being applied to the
problems of discovery and restoration (e.g., Aitken, 1961). Sampling procedures, classification, and description have been improved
by the adoption of statistical methods and by the use of computers

(e.g., Gardin, 1965). These techniques are beyond the scope of the present volume; here, we need only consider the concepts used in analytic research.

The basic concept used by archeologists in recovering remains is that of *site,* by which is meant any place in which archeological remains have been found (e.g., Webster, s.v. "site"). Sites may be either *primary,* if a people has deposited its own remains there, or *secondary,* if the remains have been redeposited by another people or by a natural agency. If, for example, a primary deposit of refuse on a river terrace has been bulldozed into another part of the terrace, the place of redeposition is a secondary site. Secondary sites are of relatively little use to the archeologist, because the structures of the original sites and much of the contents will have been destroyed, but if the sites have been redeposited by natural agencies, the geologist may find them extremely valuable places in which to obtain evidence of the natural processes involved.

A primary site may be either *disturbed* or *undisturbed.* Actually, the difference is one of degree rather than kind, for any site will have undergone some modification since its formation, if only through the action of roots and burrowing animals. An experiment is now under way in England to determine the degree of modification in an earthwork constructed especially for the purpose (Jewell and Dimbleby, 1966). When, therefore, an archeologist says that a site has been "disturbed," he means that it has been subjected to more than the usual degree of modification, as when later occupants dug into the refuse left by earlier occupants in order to bury their own refuse. Archeologists try to avoid disturbances like these, because they will have destroyed part of the structure of the site, if not some of its contents.

What is meant by the *structure* of a site? The structure is the position of the remains relative to one another, or as it is often put, the "context" in which the specimens are found (e.g., Clarke, 1968, p. 114). Thus, it is an extension of the concept of site itself. Just as a site is a place that contains remains, so its structure consists of the distribution of the remains within that place. Site and structure are both concepts of locality rather than content.

Untrained archeologists, especially amateurs, overlook the structure of sites because they are interested only in content, that is, in collecting specimens. But trained archeologists recognize that the structure of any undisturbed site is as important as the content and that they have an obligation to investigate and record both. If they fail to record the structure, they will be destroying evidence that is essential for proper characterization of the remains (see Sec. 2.6).

The archeologist's problem is that by the very act of excavating a site to recover its contents, he destroys its structure. He must, therefore, record the structure while he digs it, so that it will not be lost. As is often stated, he must provide a basis for reconstructing the site in the laboratory, which means that in the laboratory he must be able to put his finds back into the positions in which they occurred at the site.

To achieve this aim, archeologists divide each site into *excavation units* and record the positions of their finds with reference to the excavation units (e.g., Heizer and Graham, 1967, pp. 81–87). The units are often produced by laying out a rectangular grid, the parts of which are called sections, and digging each section in terms of arbitrary levels, measured from the surface downward (Fig. 3). If

FIGURE 3 *Excavation units and components: The outline of a circular shell heap is shown on top of the figure. This shell heap and the adjacent ground are divided into four 2-m square sections, A1, A2, B1, and B2. Each section is dug through four arbitrary 25-cm levels, numbered from 1 to 4. As a result, there are sixteen excavation units: Section A1, Levels 1 to 4; Section A2, Levels 1 to 4; Section B1, Levels 1 to 4; and Section B2, Levels 1 to 4. If the remains from all these units are alike, they may be said to constitute a single component, but if, for example, the units above the heavy line are marked by one kind of pottery and those below the heavy line by another kind, we may say that the site consists of two components, divided by the heavy line.*

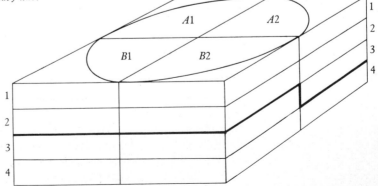

the site consists of a series of small refuse heaps, or if there are clearly marked layers of deposition, these may be used as excavation units in place of, or in addition to, a system of sections and levels. Rooms, burials, or other features constructed by the occupants of the site may also be used as excavation units. The nature of the units has to be adapted to conditions in the site, and it is a test of a good archeologist whether he is able to design his units in such a way as to achieve the goal of reconstructing the site in the laboratory.

Finally, there are the *contents* of the site, by which is meant the materials deposited in it. Following Cornwall (1958, pp. 20–21), we may distinguish between natural and human deposits. Natural deposits are those which would have been laid down even if the site had not been occupied by man, such as waterborne silt, windblown sand, and the remains of wild plants and animals that happened to die at the site. They may occur as separate layers, or they may be mixed in the human deposits.

Human deposits are those which have resulted from occupancy of the site by man. Two kinds are found: (1) remnants of the substances used by the occupants, and (2) the remains of the occupants themselves. The first may be termed *cultural remains* and the second, *morphological remains*. Let us consider them in turn.

In studying cultural remains, we must distinguish between the materials that a people brought to the site to consume as food or fuel or in the course of some other activity, such as manufacture, and the equipment that the people used in their various activities. The *materials* will include some that are still raw, perhaps having been stored at the site for eventual use, and others that show signs of having been processed for consumption, such as the flint "blanks" that certain peoples were accustomed to rough out at a quarry and bring back to their homes for manufacture into arrowheads, knives, and the like. Still other materials can be identified as the by-products of consumption, for example, chips discarded during the manufacture of arrowheads and animal bones split for the extraction of marrow.

The equipment may be divided into two categories, objects used in their natural state, with little or no modification, and objects that were manufactured in order to improve their utility. The unworked objects are often overlooked, particularly by beginners in archeology, but they present a major problem for the experienced archeologist. He must learn to recognize and preserve them, along with the cultural materials he encounters, instead of discarding them as parts of the natural deposits in his site. Recognizing such objects is not easy. It is difficult, for example, to identify a stone flake that has been very slightly chipped along one edge for use as a knife, since the chipping may have been produced by stream action rather than by man. It is equally difficult to identify objects that have been modified only through use. For example, a pebble with traces of battering on the end may have been a hammerstone or it may have resulted from buffeting of stones in a stream. More difficult still is identification of an object that the occupants of the site preserved in its natural condition, for example, a pebble kept as a charm. The only evidence for distinguishing such a pebble from one deposited by natural action may be the fact that it is not likely to have been transported to the site by natural means.

Objects such as these, which were picked up by man and used in their natural state, with little or no modification, may be termed *unworked equipment*. Contrasting with them are objects that were modified by a process of manufacture before being used. These may be called *worked equipment*. Unworked equipment includes all the objects in a site that were utilized, rather than consumed, with little or no preparation. Presumably, the occupants selected these objects because they already had the qualities necessary for use, and hence they show few, if any, traces of manufacture. Traces of use may be present but are likely to be slight, for unworked equipment, being relatively easily replaced, does not tend to be reused so much.

By contrast, worked equipment is the result of manufacture. Its makers designed it to serve particular functions and then proceeded to work it more or less thoroughly in order to enable it more efficiently to perform those functions. Having invested so much effort in it, the makers had an incentive to use it over and over again until it broke or wore out, and so worked equipment is likely to show more traces of use than does unworked equipment.

Both unworked and worked equipment can include structures as well as portable objects. For example, we may say that when early man lived in rock shelters, these constituted part of his natural equipment, and that when he learned to construct pit dwellings, these were part of his worked equipment, for both rock shelters and pit dwellings served the same need of obtaining shelter from the elements. The stick that man picked up and used to dig for roots we may consider part of his unworked equipment, but the stick he sharpened to make digging easier we may call an item of worked equipment.

It is not always easy to draw a line between unworked and worked equipment. Objects without any modification are obviously unworked. So also are objects that bear only evidences of use, not of manufacture. Specimens that are slightly worked present a more difficult problem. So long as the working is only sufficient to accentuate a natural feature, the specimen may still be considered unworked, but if it has been modified enough to produce an entirely new, artificial feature, it must be called worked. If, for example, the digging stick mentioned above has been cut only enough to scar its end, it is natural, but if it has been cut or ground to a point, it becomes worked equipment.

Thus far, we have assumed that all the materials and equipment to be found in a site are human, but this assumption is not necessarily correct. Wild animals can also bring materials into human sites for their own use, as when a pack rat builds up a midden in an area of human activity (e.g., Heizer and Brooks, 1965). Wild animals may also utilize unworked equipment, as when bears and man compete for the use of rock shelters. It is even possible for wild animals to produce worked equipment, as when beavers construct dams, birds make nests, and apes make and use tools (e.g., White, n.d., Eimerl, DeVore, and others, 1965, pp. 153–154). If such worked equipment, or part thereof, was brought to a human site by man, it must be regarded as part of his unworked equipment, but if it was brought there by the wild animals who made it, it must be considered part of their worked equipment.

How are we to distinguish objects destined for consumption or use by wild animals from the materials and equipment of man? In theory, the two should be quite different. Wild animals consume their materials and make and use their equipment without the benefit of either language or culture. They act purely by instinct and in response to specific stimuli, building up habit patterns that are activated by the stimuli.

By contrast, man possesses language, which enables him to think conceptually about what he does and to plan his procedures in advance. He is not limited to the few steps that lead directly to the satisfaction of a particular stimulus but can include steps that are related only conceptually to the desired result. Consequently, he has developed procedures that are much more complex than those possible for wild animals, which are not capable of conceptual thought (Lorenz, 1966, p. 238).

Man also has the advantage of culture. As we shall see in Section 5.8, his actions are mediated by the standards and customs, as well as the beliefs, of the ethnic group to which he belongs, that is, by its cultural norms. This means that, in working with materials and equipment, he follows the traditional procedures of his group. Older procedures tend to persist alongside new ones, for example, hunting alongside agriculture; hence a much greater range of possible procedures are available to man than to wild animals. Moreover, man is enabled by his possession of culture to organize his work far more efficiently than wild animals can, and this ability has also facilitated the production of more elaborate materials and equipment, such as steel and automobiles.

We see these differences under modern conditions, when language and culture are so advanced that it is easy to distinguish most cultural remains from the materials and equipment of the wild animals. When, however, we turn our attention to the time when man began to differentiate from other animals, that is, to domesticate himself, we experience great difficulty in distinguishing cultural from noncultural remains. At that time, language and culture were so rudimentary that man's materials and equipment differed little from those of other animals (R. and M. Ascher, 1965).

Fortunately, culture tends to be cumulative, as already noted, and therefore even the least advanced procedures for producing materials and equipment are still to be found in use among contemporary peoples, especially the so-called primitive peoples. These procedures and the resulting products are studied by specialists in cultural anthropology (Sec. 1.5), and we may use the findings of this discipline to help identify the earliest cultural remains. Also, it is possible to project back from the time when cultural materials and equipment were complex enough to be clearly identified into the transitional period when there was very little difference between cultural and noncultural remains (e.g., Hockett and Ascher, 1964).

From cultural remains, we turn now to morphological remains, consisting of human skeletal material and other remnants of man himself. The chances of finding such remains vary greatly from site to site. The occupants of the site may have deposited their dead elsewhere; for example, they may have put them in separate cemeteries or have thrown them into the sea. Even if they did bury them at the site, these remains usually constitute only a small part of its contents and will be less likely than many of the cultural remains to survive the ravages of time, since flesh and bones disintegrate rapidly, except under unusual conditions of preservation. Hence, man's morphological remains comprise only a small portion of the specimens recovered by archeologists, except when they are dealing with burial sites.

The contents of a primary site are summarized in Table 2. They comprise both natural and human deposits. The natural deposits consist of materials laid down by water, wind, or other geologic agency, and those brought to the site by wild animals, including the materials the animals brought to the site for their own consumption, the materials they processed for consumption, the natural objects they used as equipment, and even structures or tools manufactured by them. There may also be remains of the animal and plant occupants themselves. The human deposits cover the same range as the animal deposits. There are first of all man's materials and equipment, which can collectively be called his cul-

TABLE 2   *Contents of primary sites*

Kinds of deposition			Natural deposits	Human deposits	
Deposits made by geologic agencies			Water-and wind-laid materials	— — — —	
Deposits made by the occupants of the site	Products of the occupants' activities	Raw materials	Materials brought by animals for their own consumption	Materials brought by man for his consumption	Cultural remains
		Processed materials	Materials prepared by animals for their consumption, including by-products	Materials prepared by man for his consumption, including by-products	
		Unworked equipment	Structures, tools, etc., used by animals in their natural state	Structures, tools, etc., used by man in their natural state	
		Worked equipment	Structures, tools, etc., manufactured by animals	Structures, tools, etc., manufactured by man	
	The occupants themselves		Remains of the animals and of plant occupants	Morphological remains (of the human occupants)	

tural remains, since they are selected or produced in accordance with the dictates of culture. The materials may be either raw or processed and the equipment either natural or worked, as in the case of the remains produced by wild animals. Finally, there are the remains of man himself, which may be called morphological.

5
Artifacts

The archeologist is, of course, primarily interested in the human rather than the natural deposits at a site, and especially in the items of worked equipment. There are several names in the archeological literature for these worked objects. Archeologists specializing in historic remains tend to call them "antiquities," which is a shorthand way of saying "objects made in antiquity." They include monuments and other, portable objects (Webster, s.v. "antiquity").

Archeologists specializing in the remains of nonliterate peoples prefer to use the term "artifact" instead of "antiquity," presumably because "artifact" has scientific rather than historic connotations. (It is equivalent to "ventifact," an artifact being an object fashioned by man and a ventifact an object fashioned by the wind.) "Artifact" is more limited in scope than "antiquity," in that it normally refers only to portable objects and not to monuments and other structures. It is "a usu. simple object (as a tool or ornament) showing human workmanship or modification as distinguished from a natural object" (Webster, s.v. "artifact").

The word "artifact" has one advantage over "antiquity" for our purposes. It is applicable to objects being made and utilized at the present time as well as to those of the past. This applicability is important. If we are to correlate our archeologically based interpretations with those of the ethnologist, as explained at the beginning of the chapter, we need to use a term that is equally applicable to both, that is, to the front and top faces of the cube of knowledge discussed in Chapter 1. Hence, "artifact" will be used here in preference to "antiquity."

However, the scope of the word "artifact" will be enlarged to that of "antiquity" by including all manufactured objects, structures as well as portable devices. This enlargement is justified by the fact that structures are the same kind of phenomenon as portable objects, the only difference between them being that structures are difficult, if not impossible, for the archeologist to remove from sites, whereas portable objects are usually brought back to museums or archeological laboratories. Since the two are alike, they must be studied in the same way, and it will be convenient for us to be able to apply the same term, "artifact," to both in dealing with the conceptualization of archeological remains.

An *artifact* may be defined as any natural object to which a people have added at least one artificial feature in accordance with their customary manufacturing procedures, so as to make the object more suitable for use in their activities. Since this definition will be used throughout the book, it is important to note how it differs from common usage of the term "artifact." We have seen that it includes structures as well as tools and other portable equipment, but that not all structures and not all tools are artifacts. They qualify as artifacts *only if they are the result of manufacture by a people in accordance with its culture.* This distinction eliminates the tools made and used by wild animals, as well as those human tools that bear traces of use but not of manufacture. Thus, plain pebbles used as hammerstones are a part of unworked equipment, but hammerstones that have been pitted so that they may be more easily held qualify as artifacts, because an artificial feature, the pits, has been added.

6
*Cultural
components and
assemblages*

The archeologist need not preserve any of the natural deposits he has excavated, unless they present a special problem of deposition about which he must consult a specialist. Ideally, he brings all the human deposits he has been able to excavate back to his laboratory to be processed, but if the site is rich, he may have to adopt a sampling procedure, especially in dealing with materials. He will also, of course, have to leave behind the larger, nonportable artifacts, such as buildings and graves. Structures like these are studied in the laboratory by means of photographs and notes.

The specimens available for study in the laboratory normally include both of the kinds of human deposits listed in Table 2: cultural remains, consisting of raw materials, processed materials, unworked equipment, and artifacts (worked equipment); and morphological remains, mainly human skeletal material. The two must be studied separately, and so we shall consider them in turn, beginning with the cultural remains, since they are much more numerous, and taking up the morphological remains at the end of the chapter.

In the laboratory, the investigator lays out his cultural remains according to excavation units and compares them unit by unit, looking for differences in the content of the units. If there are no significant differences, he proceeds to study the collection as a whole, on the assumption that it has been deposited by a single group of people. If, on the other hand, he finds that some excavation units have yielded markedly different cultural remains, he will be obliged to divide the site into two parts and make a separate study of the remains obtained from each part. For example, in the case of the excavation shown in Figure 3, he may find that all of the units above the heavy black line have yielded similar potsherds, whereas all the units below the heavy line have yielded potsherds with a different set of traits, in which case he will have to deal separately with the remains obtained from above and below the heavy line.

Similarly, an excavator may have encountered two superimposed layers of refuse, with the remains of sea food, fish hooks, and net sinkers in the first layer and the remains of domesticated animals and of agricultural implements and utensils in the second layer. He will then conclude that the site was successively occupied by fishing and agricultural peoples and will proceed to deal separately with the remains from each layer.

Divisions of a site such as these are known as *cultural components,* and the remains obtained from each component are termed a *cultural assemblage* (e.g., Willey and Phillips, 1962, pp. 21–22; Goodwin, 1953, p. 21). Alternatively, components or assemblages or both are sometimes called "occupations" or "settlements" by those who prefer to emphasize the groups of people who produced the assemblages (e.g., Chang, 1967a, pp. 38–56).

A component may be defined as the part or parts of a site that have yielded similar cultural remains, indicating occupation by a single group of people. An assemblage comprises all the cultural remains recovered from a component. Any site may consist of a single component, in which case the specimens retrieved from it will constitute a single assemblage, or of several components, in which case there will be several assemblages, each deposited by a different people.

The archeologist does not attempt to determine who the peoples were. He leaves this problem to the prehistorian, unless he himself is also trained to do prehistoric research (Sec. 3.8). On the other hand, if the prehistorian has already distinguished peoples in the area under study, the archeologist will proceed to identify the people who were responsible for each component and assemblage (Sec. 3.14).

It can now be explained why archeologists avoid disturbed deposits. If, for example, the second people to occupy a site have disturbed the refuse of the first occupants and mixed it with their own, it will be difficult to distinguish the components and assemblages of the two groups of people. It may be necessary to divide the site into three components, two undisturbed and the third disturbed, and consequently to separate the collection into three assemblages, two "pure" and the third mixed. In such a case, laboratory study will be concentrated on the pure assemblages, with the mixed assemblages being used only as supplementary data. Even so, the results will always be open to question, for their reliability will depend upon the archeologist's success in recognizing the disturbed portions of the deposit.

It can now be explained, too, why the archeologist needs to record the structure of his site while removing its contents. If he has failed to do so, or if he has designed his excavation units poorly, so that they do not provide an adequate record of the structure of the site, he will be unable to determine empirically whether the site was single- or multi-component. To return to the example given above, that of a two-layer refuse deposit, the excavator can readily demonstrate that each layer constitutes a separate component if he has dug the site by section and layer, for he will then be able to lay out the remains in the laboratory and establish that (1) they differ from layer to layer within each section and (2) they are uniform from section to section within each layer. He would not be able to make this demonstration, however, if he had dug the site by artificial levels, cutting across the layers. He might then suspect that the two layers constitute separate components, but he would be unable to prove it.

As is illustrated by this example, there are two main criteria for distinguishing between components: contrast between the excavation units assigned to one component and those assigned to other components, and uniformity within the units assigned to one component. There may also be physical breaks between sets of units, as in our example of the two-layer site, but the archeologist is rarely that lucky; if he were, he would have a much easier job distinguishing components.

Application of the criteria of contrast and uniformity is, of course, a matter of judgment. How much difference must there be among parts of a site and how much uniformity within each part before they can be identified as separate components? These questions are beyond the scope of the present book, and in any case they cannot be answered by rules. One's division of a site into components must be a matter of intuitive judgment, and the division can be considered valid if it works—if it produces assemblages that are manageable for purposes of laboratory analysis and meaningful for prehistoric or historic interpretation.

One complicating factor is the tendency for a people to lay down different kinds of remains in the parts of the site in which they carried on different activities. Such differences in the remains may be very marked, as when a people were accustomed to manufacture grave goods unlike their normal cultural equipment, so that different artifacts occur with their burials than in their refuse, yet these differences must be disregarded when formulating components and assemblages. Fortunately, they are not hard to recognize, especially if they are associated with different kinds of structures, such as graves and houses.

If the differences are sharp enough, the archeologist will find it convenient to study them separately in his laboratory. For example, he will deal first with grave goods and then with the materials encountered in residential areas. We may refer to the remains segregated in this fashion as *activity assemblages*. Such an assemblage may be defined as a number of specimens that occur together within a component as the result of one or more linked activities carried out by the people who occupied the component.

Each component of a dwelling site normally contains several activity assemblages, though these are often difficult, if not impossible, to distinguish, even by carefully plotting the distribution of individual specimens. On the contrary, components of nonresidential sites may yield remnants of only a single activity, as when a people visited a place only for the purpose of butchering game. In such a case, the cultural and activity assemblages will coincide. The relationships among different kinds of assemblages do not concern

us here, however, for we are focusing on the remains themsel,
and not on the people that produced them. The problem of articulating the activity assemblages deposited in different sites will be
considered in connection with the procedures of prehistoric research (Sec. 5.10). To be certain, once the articulation has been
completed, an archeologist may apply it to the remains he is studying, but when he does so he is not carrying out original research;
instead, he is applying the results of research in prehistory to his
own discipline.

7
Classes, their formation and identification

Assemblages are concepts of structure, referring to the coexistence
of specimens in particular sections of sites. Now we must turn to
the concepts of content, expressing the nature of the specimens in
the assemblages. The most important of these is *class,* which may
be defined as "a group [of specimens] marked by common attributes" (Webster, s.v. "class").

The archeologist assigns the specimens of each assemblage to
classes, using one of two alternative procedures.

If the specimens are unlike any previously known, he will have
to form new classes in order to accommodate the specimens, in
which case he is said to "classify" them. If suitable classes are already in existence, he will instead "identify" the classes to which
specimens belong.

The procedure of *classification,* then, is one of forming new
classes or, if it seems advisable, of revising previously established
classes. The archeologist sorts his specimens into trial classes, examines the members of each class to see how many attributes they
have in common, and then sorts the specimens into revised classes
in an effort to achieve greater homogeneity within each class. This
procedure may have to be repeated over and over again until the
classes become reasonably homogeneous and share all possible
attributes.

Once this homogeneity has been attained the archeologist names
each class and defines it. He may either set up one or more type
specimens to serve as standards for the class, or else he may specify
a set of attributes that characterizes the class. In other words, a
class may be defined in terms of either type specimens or a set of
diagnostic attributes.

The procedure of *identification* is one of using the type specimens or sets of diagnostic attributes to assign specimens to classes. The archeologist matches the specimens to be identified with those typical of each class or else determines which set of diagnostic attributes is present on each specimen. Thus he learns the class of each specimen and is able to apply the name of that class to it.

The essential difference between the procedures of classification and identification is that only the former involves originality. Only the classifier forms new classes and establishes criteria for them. These are matters of judgment, like the differentiation of components and assemblages (Sec. 2.6), and cannot be determined by rule. A good archeologist is distinguished from a bad one by his ability to make valid classificatory judgments. The test of his classification is whether it works—whether it produces classes that so accurately reflect the nature of the specimens that those classes and the criteria that define them can be used to identify additional specimens of the same kinds.

In recent years, some scientists have turned to statistics in an attempt to rationalize the intuitive basis of classification (e.g., Sokal and Sneath, 1963). This effort is based upon a vain hope, because statistical procedures are no better than the attributes to which they are applied and the attributes must be intuitively formulated. Nevertheless, statistics do enable the archeologist to use a greater number of attributes in his classifications, to manipulate them more efficiently, and to discover similarities and differences that might otherwise be missed.

8
Classes of
cultural remains

In dealing with raw materials, the archeologist normally uses the procedure of identification, since these materials are so little modified from their natural state that they can be identified in terms of the classes established by geologists, biologists, and other natural scientists (e.g., Rosenfeld, 1965). Archeologists acquire as much training as possible in the natural sciences in order to be able to identify materials, but obviously they cannot become equally expert in all branches of science and so they must enlist the aid of specialists in "the identification of nonartifactual . . . materials" (Taylor, 1957). Obtaining this aid is often difficult, because the specialists are loath to take time off from their own research in order to accommodate archeologists. As a result, certain archeologists are developing specialties in identifying materials, not only in order to satisfy the demands of their own research, but also for the benefit of other archeologists. The Institute of Archaeology at the University of London has been a leader in this development through its Department of Environmental Archaeology, which has produced a series of works on the identification of materials (Cornwall, 1956, 1958; Dimbleby, 1967; Rosenfeld, 1965; see also, e.g., Olsen, 1961; Wells, 1964).

A different situation is created by the discovery of raw materials that are so new that natural scientists have not yet set up classes for them. Unless the archeologist has been exceptionally well trained in a natural science, he will be incapable of using the procedure of classification to set up classes of this kind and will find it necessary to enlist the aid of a specialist. In this case, however, aid is relatively easy to obtain, because the specialist will be making a contribution to his own discipline when he forms new classes.

It is not sufficient to assign processed materials to natural-science classes; instead, specially designed classes must be used. For example, iron slag cannot simply be identified as iron of a certain kind. Instead, it must be assigned to the class "iron slag," which is based upon the changes made in the material by man. The natural scientist is not normally qualified for such nonnatural identification or classification; he leaves it to the archeologist, who is a specialist in the modification of natural objects by human agency.

Cultural equipment, too, must be handled by the archeologist. Classifying this equipment is his specialty and the heart of his laboratory research. Much of his training is spent in learning how to classify and identify this material, and a large body of literature has grown up around the procedures, including treatises on classification, which explain how to formulate new classes (e.g., Clarke, 1968; Gardin, 1965; Rouse, 1960, 1970; Spaulding, 1953, 1960b), and handbooks, dictionaries, and encyclopedias, which are in effect definitions of established classes (e.g., Colton and Hargrave, 1937; Cottrell, 1971; Hodges, 1964; Réau, 1953; Shepard, 1957; Sprague, 1968; Stewart, 1958; Trent, 1959).

Unworked equipment is relatively easy to classify. By definition, it consists of specimens that have been used in their natural condition. These specimens, therefore, lack attributes of manufacture and must be classified solely in terms of attributes of use. The names of classes of natural equipment reflect this fact, for example, rock shelters, hammerstones, charm stones, and the like.

Worked equipment or artifacts must be classified in terms of attributes of manufacture as well as use. If the attributes produced by manufacture serve mainly to improve the utility of the original objects, then the artifacts also are given names that reflect uses, for example, houses, axes, vessels, and the like. Such a noun is usually accompanied by an adjective referring to material or shape, for example, shell midden or pit house. If, on the other hand, many of the attributes built into the artifacts are designed to express qualities of style, then it is necessary to employ names based upon what may be called stylistic attributes. In such a case, the archeologist often combines a descriptive name with that of a region or typical site, which symbolizes the stylistic attributes of the class, for example, Micoquean hand axes or Mogollon Red-on-brown pottery (Bordes, 1961, pp. 57, 75; Colton and Hargrave, 1937, pp. 47–48).

We may, then, distinguish between *stylistic* and *functional attributes*. Both result from manufacture, but the stylistic attributes are designed to enhance the appearance of the artifacts, whereas the functional attributes improve their utility. There are also *technological attributes*, which reflect the manufacturing process without contributing to either the appearance or the utility of the artifacts.

9
Classes versus
types of artifacts

As we have seen, the term "class" refers to the artifacts or other specimens that have been grouped together because they share certain diagnostic attributes. These attributes, taken together, are known as a type. Following Spaulding (1960a, p. 443), we may define a *type* of artifacts as the cluster or pattern of attributes that distinguishes a group of specimens and that defines them as a class.

To illustrate the difference between a class and a type, let us consider the nature of celts, the "thunderstones" of the Middle Ages (Sec. 2.3). These artifacts have (1) an ovoid shape, (2) a pointed butt, tapering so that it could be fitted in a wooden shaft, and (3) a semicircular bit, used, for example, in chopping wood. Taken together, all the artifacts that have these three attributes constitute a single class, that of celts. But we also speak of the type "celt," in the singular, and by this usage we mean the three attributes that distinguish all celts and cause them to be grouped together as a class.

Such a class and type are but two sides of the same coin (Fig. 4). The class is indicative of the type and is constantly being expanded as new artifacts of the same type are found. Conversely, the type is a definition of the class and can be fully understood only by examining examples from the class. The class is an objective entity, which the archeologist can lay out on a table in his laboratory (to the extent that he has recovered it), whereas the type is an abstraction from the objects in the class.

To this point, we have concentrated on classes because they are the archeologist's primary concern. He is a specialist in artifacts, seeking to determine their nature and to express it. The class helps him by bringing together all like artifacts and enabling him to describe them as a group instead of treating them individually. Description of artifact classes is a major part of his research.

The prehistorian, on the contrary, is more interested in types than in classes. As we have seen, he focuses on the people that made the artifacts. Types consist of qualities that a people built into its artifacts. These qualities are, in effect, cultural norms, that is, cus-

FIGURE 4 *Relationship between a class (a) and type (b) of artifacts: A class of artifacts and its type are two sides of the same coin, the class being composed of all the artifacts (A_n) that have a particular set of attributes (a_n). The archeological classifier uses all the attributes; the prehistoric classifier instead selects those dimensions of attributes that are most significant for his purposes, as indicated by the hatched area in (b). Hence, the types produced by an archeologist are based upon the entire circle of attributes (b), whereas the types produced by a prehistorian are based only upon the hatched part of the circle.*

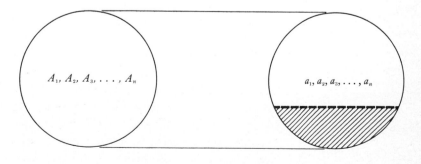

$$A_1, A_2, A_3, \ldots, A_n \qquad\qquad a_1, a_2, a_3, \ldots, a_n$$

(a)   (b)

toms to which the artisans conformed in making their artifacts. Since cultural norms are a major concern of the prehistorian, he focuses on types, describing each one in terms of its constituent attributes instead of describing each class in terms of its constituent artifacts, as an archeologist would do (cf. Figs. 4*a* and 4*b*).

The class, then, is the basic unit of archeological research, and the type is subsidiary to that unit. The archeologist classifies in order to form classes and regards the type as a device for identifying additional members of the class—if, instead, he does not use type artifacts for the purpose (Sec. 2.7). By contrast, the type is the basic unit of prehistoric research. The prehistorian classifies in order to obtain types and regards the class as a means of studying types. Type artifacts do not interest him, since they are members of classes, not components of types.

10
Kinds of types

Given these differences in viewpoint between the archeologist and the prehistorian, we should not be surprised to find that the two produce different kinds of types. For the archeologist, there is only a single kind, that which he uses to define classes for use during the second and final steps in the strategy of his discipline (Sec. 2.1). Having recovered artifacts, he proceeds to sort them into classes, comparing them attribute by attribute. Then he defines each class by listing the "cluster" of attributes that is shared by all those artifacts in the class or by a specified proportion of the artifacts (Spaulding, 1960a, p. 443). Such an attribute cluster comprises a kind of type that has variously been called "morphological" (Steward, 1954, p. 54), "descriptive" (Rouse, 1960, p. 317), "phenetic" (Clarke, 1968, p. 229), "natural" (Thomas, MS), and *intrinsic* (Rouse, MS), in order to indicate that it is designed to bring out the nature of the artifacts under study.

The prehistorian works with other kinds of types, which are designed to resolve problems of prehistory rather than to reveal the intrinsic nature of the artifacts (see Sec. 3.2). If, for example, he wishes to learn the nature of the people that produced an assemblage of artifacts, he will focus upon the features of the artifacts that are most likely to be indicative of peoples, such as rim profiles and designs, and will ignore all other features, such as material and shape (Sec. 3.7). If, instead, he aims to find out when the people made the artifacts, he will concentrate on the features that are likely to furnish good time-markers (Sec. 4.7). In either case, the features used will be primarily stylistic (Sec. 2.8), since stylistic attributes are the best indicators of peoples and periods.

When, on the other hand, the prehistorian wishes to know the manner in which the people made and used the artifacts, he will work primarily with technological and functional features, since these enable him to reconstruct the activities of manufacture and use (Sec. 5.10). He also focuses on these features in investigating a people's development, since the efficiency of a people's artifacts is a measure of its development (Sec. 6.4).

Whatever his choice of features, the prehistorian proceeds by trial and error. He sets up tentative types, each consisting of a "pattern" of attributes to be found on the set of features he has chosen to study, and sorts the artifacts into classes in terms of these types. If the types prove to be satisfactory for their purpose—if each pattern of attributes proves to be an efficient indicator of a people, period, activity, or degree of development—he concludes that the trial types are valid. If not, he has to revise them by selecting another set of features and formulating new patterns of attributes from them. He then tests the revised patterns by using them to reclassify the artifacts. He repeats this procedure until he achieves patterns of attributes that produce the desired results (Krieger, 1944, fig. 25).

Steward (1954, p. 5) has coined names for the types produced in this manner. He calls them "historical-index types" if their purpose is to distinguish peoples or periods, and "functional" if instead they are intended to furnish knowledge about the uses of the artifacts. Both these kinds of types are distinguished from his descriptive—our intrinsic—types by the fact that their constituent patterns of attributes are based upon features selected for specified purposes, whereas all features are utilized in the formulation of intrinsic types (Fig. 4b). Historical-index and functional types are, therefore, *extrinsic* rather than intrinsic. They are designed to abstract various qualities from the artifacts for purposes of prehistoric research, not to express the qualities inherent in the artifacts, as in the case of intrinsic types.

It is important to note that both intrinsic and extrinsic types are created by the investigator. They consist of clusters or patterns of attributes that he has discovered in the artifacts by means of classification and that he conceptualizes as types in order to be able to communicate them to other investigators and to facilitate their use in archeological or prehistorical research. They exist, therefore, in the minds of the investigator and of the people with whom he communicates.

Contrasting with these two kinds of types is a third, consisting of the categories that were in the minds of the artisans as they made their artifacts. These are the categories obtained by ethnographers when they study the manufacture of artifacts. They have variously been called "emic" (as opposed to etic or intrinsic types) and *cognitive* (Arnold, 1971).

Authorities differ as to the relationship between cognitive types, obtained from the artisans, and types based upon archeological evidence. Some authors (e.g., Chang, 1967a, p. 78) assume that the two are identical or nearly so, while others (e.g., Harris in Binford and Binford, 1968, pp. 359–361) deny this. The mere fact that we have found it necessary to distinguish different kinds of archeologically based types—intrinsic and several varieties of extrinsic types—indicates that there cannot be a one-to-one relationship between cognitive types and those based upon archeological evidence. We must distinguish between the two.

We must also be careful to distinguish the cognitive types that were in the minds of the makers and users of the artifacts from cognitive types that are in our minds because they are parts of our own culture, that is, from our own ways of categorizing artifacts. We are concerned with other peoples' cultures, not our own.

Actually, intrinsic types are the only ones directly pertinent to archeological (i.e., analytic) research, which is our present interest. We shall discuss the use of extrinsic and cognitive types in later chapters, in connection with the problems of prehistoric (i.e., synthetic) research.

11
Taxonomic versus
typological
hierarchies

Thus far, we have assumed that both the archeologist and the prehistorian are interested only in setting up single series of classes and types. Both, however, often work with hierarchies, the archeologist because hierarchies provide him with a means of organizing his classes systematically and the prehistorian in the hope that they will serve to express the manner in which the types developed and thus provide an answer to the question "How and why?" (Sec. 3.2).

The obvious way to form a hierarchy is to use the procedure known as *taxonomy*. In its simplest form, taxonomy is accomplished by breaking the collection under study down into classes on the basis of an arbitrarily chosen series of alternate attributes, for example, by sorting the specimens in terms of their material—stone, bone, shell, and so forth. The classes are then divided into subclasses on the basis of another series of alternate attributes, for example, the presence or absence of various kinds of decoration. This process of subdivision is continued until the classes are small enough and are characterized by large enough clusters of attributes to serve the needs of archeological or prehistoric research (Fig. 5*a*). (For a more sophisticated taxonomic procedure, see Clarke, 1968, fig. 158.)

Taxonomic classification has the advantage that it enables the classifier to construct a key for purposes of identification. He ar-

FIGURE 5 *Comparison of the taxonomic (a) and typological (b) procedures for hierarchical classification: In both taxonomic and typological classification, artifacts are sorted into classes (C_1, C_2). In the taxonomic approach, the classes are then divided into subclasses (SC_{1-5}). In the typological approach, however, the artifacts are re-sorted into subclasses. The types (t_{1-2}) or subtypes (st_{1-5}) diagnostic of each class or subclass are shown as the other side of its coin (see Fig. 4). It will be seen that taxonomic classification permits the formulation of only two classes and four subclasses, whereas typological classification permits the formation of an additional subclass (SC_5/st_5), transitional between the two classes.*

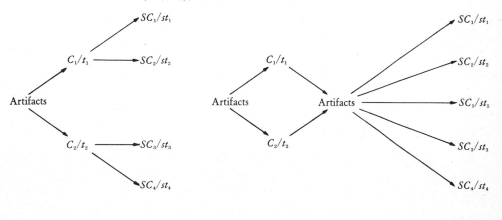

(*a*)   (*b*)

ranges the diagnostic attributes within this key in the order in which he used them to set up the classes, subclasses, sub-subclasses, and so forth, thereby producing a hierarchy of attributes. A person who wants to identify artifacts may then proceed down through the hierarchy, differentiating the artifacts first by means of the attributes at its top, then by the attributes on successively lower levels, and ending up with classes based upon all the attributes in the key (e.g., Colton and Hargrave, 1937, pp. 36–41).

Taxonomic classification has the further advantage for the biologist who is studying species that its successive divisions into classes, subclasses, sub-subclasses, and so forth, can be used not only to express the degree of similarity among units—the species within one genus being more alike than the species within another genus—but also to show the evolutionary relationships of the units (Sec. 4.1). Ethnographers who study kinship systems similarly use genealogies, which are a form of taxonomy, to express both the degree of similarity among relatives and the manner in which the members of kin groups gave birth to one another (Conklin, 1964, pp. 39–40).

Taxonomies can serve both of these functions because on each level they are composed of mutually exclusive alternates. The procedure of dividing and subdividing an assemblage into classes and subclasses in terms of these alternates is the same as the manner in which one species divides into several new ones or a mother gives birth to several children. In both cases, new units are produced by splitting, and these units are self-contained, without the possibility of exchanging any of their genes.

Unfortunately, the same is not true of artifacts. They are a product of cultural norms, that is, of ideas in the minds of their makers, and when an artisan makes a new artifact, he need not limit himself to the ideas he employed in the last artifact he made. He can draw ideas or cultural norms from many previously made artifacts, including not only his own products, but also those of other artisans. As a result, taxonomic hierarchies are inappropriate for the study of artifacts (Brew, 1946).

This fact does not mean that the archeologist or prehistorian should avoid hierarchies of classes or types, but only that the hierarchies should not be taxonomic. It is entirely appropriate for the classifier of artifacts to formulate two or more levels of classes/ types so long as he operates independently on each level, working with discrete clusters or patterns of attributes that bear no necessary relationship to the patterns or clusters on any other level. This procedure has become known as *typological classification* (Krieger, 1944; Conklin, 1964, pp. 40–41). It produces a separate classification for each hierarchical level, contrary to taxonomic classification, and as a result incorporates all possible combinations of attributes on each level, instead of being limited to mutually exclusive combinations as in the case of taxonomy (cf. Figs. 5*a* and 5*b*). Moreover, it permits the formation of superclasses and supertypes, which are precluded by the taxonomic procedure of division and subdivision. (See, e.g., the concepts of ceramic series in Colton and Hargrave, 1937, pp. 1–5, and type group in Clarke, 1968, p. 228.)

12
Classes versus
modes of features

Classification of artifacts is normally followed by description, in which the archeologist proceeds feature by feature. He starts by describing the materials of which the artifacts are made, next their elements of shape, then their surface finish, and finally their decoration, if any.

If he is dealing with only a single artifact, such as a monument, he will proceed to describe each of its features in turn. Otherwise, he will jointly describe all the artifacts that belong to the same class, treating the comparable features of the artifacts in turn, so long as these features are alike. For example, if all the handles on the pottery vessels of a certain class are alike, he will describe them as a unit. If, on the other hand, the features under study differ considerably from artifact to artifact, he will first have to group the features into classes and then will describe each class of features separately. For example, he may have to distinguish between D-shaped and loop handles and describe the two separately.

Features, like the artifacts of which they are a part, can be assigned to classes either by the process of identification or by means of classification. The terms *partitive identification* and *partitive classification* are applied to these procedures in order to distinguish them from the identification and classification of whole artifacts (Thomas, MS).

If the features are still in their natural state, they may be identified by assigning them to the pertinent classes of the natural sciences. For example, to determine the materials of which stone artifacts are made, the archeologist identifies these materials as basalt, flint, and so forth, often with the assistance of specialists in identifying rocks. But if the features have been produced by man, he has to assign them to purely archeological classes. For example, he cannot use natural-science classes to identify the rims of pot-sherds, since the rims are culturally determined; he must assign them to classes of rim profiles, defined in terms of attributes that were significant to the potters. The same will be true of any other features of material, shape, finish, or decoration that have been culturally produced. But once the archeologist has set up new, purely archeological classes, he can use them to identify additional features of the same kinds.

Over the years, archeologists have developed many sets of classes for use in identifying the culturally significant features of artifacts. Part of the training of an archeologist is learning these classes, and they are treated in detail in the works on identification that have been mentioned above. When, therefore, an archeologist is faced with the problem of assigning artificial features to classes, he will first try to fit them into established classes by means of the process of identification. If that proves to be impossible, he will proceed to partitive classification. For instance, he may sort incised designs in terms of their appearance in an attempt to discover new classes, which he will then define by noting which attributes are diagnostic of each class. One class, for example, may consist of nested triangles and another of herringbone lines.

When one engages in partitive identification and classification, one finds that each class of features extends across several classes of artifacts. For example, a class of materials, such as *Strombus gigas,* may be common to shell celts, shell hammers, and shell vessels. Similarly, a class of designs, such as feline heads, may occur on pottery vessels, stone celts, shell pendants, and textiles. Classes of features, therefore, will have very different distributions than classes of artifacts.

The diagnostic attributes that serve to define a class of features and to identify the members of the class are often called "types." Thus, one can speak of types of materials, types of rim profiles, types of handles, and so forth. Since types of artifacts are likely to be confused with types of features such as these, we shall restrict the term "type" to types of artifacts and shall apply a different term, *mode,* to types of features (Rouse, 1960, pp. 313–314). "Type," then, refers to the attributes diagnostic of a class of artifacts and "mode" to the attributes diagnostic of a class of features.

Like types, modes can be either intrinsic, extrinsic, or cognitive (Sec. 2.10). An *intrinsic mode* is one that expresses the inherent nature of a class of features; it tells us what the features in the class are like. An *extrinsic mode* instead expresses a way in which the features were made or used; it is either a technique of manufacture or a function that can be inferred from the features. In the presence of closely related ethnographic or ethnohistorical evidence, the prehistorian also can reconstruct *cognitive modes,* consisting of the sets of attributes that the artisans themselves used to distinguish classes of features (Arnold, 1971).

Classes of features and modes need be formulated only for artifacts that are relatively complex and that vary appreciably in their features. If one were to form classes of features and modes for simpler artifacts, they would coincide with the classes of artifacts and types, and it would be pointless to work with both of them.

The class and mode of feature are again but two sides of the same coin, like the class and type of artifact. The class of feature is an objective entity, composed of the like features of actual specimens, whereas the mode is an abstraction from those features, consisting of the qualities that distinguish them from the features assigned to other classes. Presumably, the artisan built these qualities into the features in accordance with his customs, and hence each mode is indicative of a custom, standard, or belief to which artisans conformed in making features. Like the type, it expresses a cultural norm and therefore is of primary interest to the prehistorian or historian.

The archeologist, on the contrary, shows little interest in the concept of mode, and there is less reason why he should. For him, a mode can only serve to define a class of features. That it is, in addition, an expression of a cultural norm is immaterial, so far as he is concerned.

13
Morphological
components
and assemblages

We turn now from cultural to morphological remains, that is, to the remains of man himself. These are normally limited to human skeletal material, for only under exceptionally favorable conditions of preservation are the flesh, skin, and hair preserved (e.g., Glob, 1969).

The procedure of studying morphological remains parallels that of studying cultural remains. One must first distinguish components, next segregate the assemblage of morphological remains obtained from each component, then assign the specimens within each assemblage to classes, and finally describe the classes. Having already discussed this procedure in detail as it is applied to cultural remains, we need concern ourselves only with two special problems that arise in applying it to morphological remains.

First, cultural components should not be used to distinguish morphological assemblages. To use them for this purpose would be to assume a one-to-one relationship between cultural and morphological groups, which is not likely to exist (Secs. 1.1 and 5.5). The archeologist should treat his sites as single components unless he finds significant differences in the nature and distribution of their morphological remains.

Second, the archeologist normally confines himself to the identification of morphological remains, since he is not enough of an expert to undertake classification. Two kinds of identification are necessary, identification of the bones themselves and identification of the races or species to which the bones belong. For the former, the archeologist utilizes classes formed by the biologist, but for the latter, he uses classes formed by the prehistorian in a manner to be described in the next chapter (Sec. 3.15).

14
Exhibition and publication of the remains

The amateur often assumes that an archeologist's research has been completed when he has excavated and restored his finds. We have seen, however, that excavation and restoration is only the beginning. It must be followed by identification and, where necessary, classification of the remains and by preparation of exhibits, catalogs, and monographs in order to make the remains known.

Technical monographs are the most important aspects of archeological research for our purposes, since they provide the primary basis for prehistoric research. In the monographs, remains are normally discussed in order of sites and, within sites, in order of cultural, morphological, and activity assemblages. Within each assemblage the archeologist deals with the classes of cultural materials and equipment or else the morphological remains that he has found. He ordinarily does not bother to describe the classes of cultural materials or the morphological remains in any detail, except to note certain unusual features, such as evidences of disease, but he is expected to present a thorough analysis and description of the unworked equipment and artifacts. If the artifacts are complex and variable, he will also identify or discover classes of features, that is, of material, shape, finish, and decoration, and describe the features in each class.

A by-product of the foregoing procedure is the establishment of types of artifacts and modes of features, consisting of the attributes diagnostic respectively of each class of artifacts and of features. These are important units of prehistoric research and will be discussed as such in the following chapters.

For the archeologist, on the contrary, it is the remains themselves that are important. His goal is to know them and to impart his knowledge to others. He develops an appreciation of the remains, which he attempts to communicate to others. It is a measure of his success that so many archeological monuments and museums have been set up and that each year they are visited by increasing numbers of people.

This is not to say that the archeologist never goes beyond the nature of the remains. On the contrary, he frequently discusses their historic, prehistoric, or ethnological significance in his publications and in the labels for his monuments and museum exhibits. But when he does so, he will be utilizing the results of research by the historian, prehistorian, or ethnologist, unless he has himself become an expert in one of those disciplines and is able to do original research in it. Here, he is faced with the same option as when identifying and classifying natural objects: that of enlisting the aid of a specialist, whether it be in paleontology, mineralogy, history, or prehistory, or of himself learning to do research in one of those disciplines.

The historian is not interested in remains for their own sake but for what he can learn from them about history (e.g., Wainwright, 1962, pp. 1–11). Remains are meaningful to him only if they can be used to identify events or conditions mentioned in the documents or if, by studying them, he can fill gaps in the documents. Hence, he does not normally include references to archeology in his writings, unless the written records are incomplete or unless he thinks it would be interesting to illustrate some point with archeological materials.

The prehistorian likewise views the remains as a means rather than an end, using them to reconstruct past events and conditions. However, the remains are far more important to him than to the historian because, in the absence of written records, they must serve him as the main basis for reconstruction. We shall see how he makes use of archeological remains in the following chapters.

SUPPLEMENTAL READING

CARPENTER, RHYS, *Archaeology* (1963).

CLARK, GRAHAME, *Archaeology and Society* (1960), pp. 38–131.

CLARKE, DAVID L., *Analytical Archaeology* (1968).

HEIZER, ROBERT F., ed., *Man's Discovery of His Past: Literary Landmarks in Archaeology* (1962).

HOLE, FRANK, AND ROBERT F. HEIZER, *An Introduction to Prehistoric Archaeology* (1969), pts. II and III.

KENYON, KATHLEEN M., *Beginning in Archaeology* (1961).

RAPPORT, SAMUEL, AND HELEN WRIGHT, eds., *Archaeology* (1964), pp. 3–59.

WHEELER, SIR MORTIMER, *Archaeology from the Earth* (1956).

WHITE, LESLIE A., *On the Use of Tools by the Primates* (n.d.).

3

ETHNIC CLASSIFICATION

We turn now from archeology, which focuses on human remains, to prehistory, which concentrates on the human beings who produced the remains. From now on, we shall be studying the remains, not for their own sake, but as a means of learning about man's past.

Man's past can be approached in two alternative ways. Prehistorians and ethnohistorians are concerned with ethnic groups, including those which are cultural, morphological, social, and linguistic. Specialists in the four kinds of anthropology focus instead upon the nature and evolution of cultural, morphological, social, and linguistic forms respectively (Table 1).

This difference results from the fact that prehistorians and ethnohistorians approach the study of man by way of the dimensions of space and time (the front face of our cube of knowledge, Fig. 1), while anthropological specialists approach it by way of the dimensions of form and time (the side face of the cube). Like ethnohistorians and ethnologists, prehistorians choose to focus upon a particular section of space and time and to study the groups of people who occupied that section. Anthropological specialists prefer to focus upon particular kinds of forms, selected without regard for when and where they occurred.

It follows that prehistorians and anthropological specialists must use different strategies of research. Prehistorians start with the archeological facts and from them synthesize a picture of ethnic groups and their distribution, nature, and development, using an inductive strategy (Rouse, 1965b). Anthropological specialists, on the other hand, develop hypotheses to explain the nature of particular forms and then test the hypotheses by making "case studies" of selected ethnic groups (Binford, 1962; Flannery, 1967). Their strategy is experimental rather than synthetic. They call it "processual" in order to distinguish it from the strategies of archeology and prehistory (Wilmsen, 1970, pp. 689–691).

Prehistorians and anthropological specialists complement each other (Sec. 1.5). Anthropological specialists build upon the work done by prehistorians, and the validity of their results depends to a great extent upon how well prehistorians have done their research (Table 1). Conversely, prehistorians employ anthropologists' processual conclusions in their own research, as we shall see in the following section.

2
Strategy and tactics of prehistoric research

In reconstructing prehistory, it is necessary first to select an objective and then to bring together the archeological evidence and anthropological knowledge required to achieve that objective. Figure 6 illustrates how this is done. The principal objectives of prehistoric research are shown as circles, extending across the middle of the figure. The archeological evidence is symbolized by the rectangle at the bottom of the figure and the pertinent anthropological knowledge by the rectangle at the top.

The objectives are expressed in the figure as four questions that the prehistorian attempts to answer by means of his research: (1) Who produced the archeological remains under study, that is, to which ethnic groups did the producers belong? (2) Where and when did each group live? (3) What was each group like in its culture, morphology, social structure, or language, as the case may be? (4) How and why did each group become that way? (Rouse, 1965b.)

These four questions form a logical sequence that constitutes the strategy of prehistoric research. The strategy need not always be followed, however. A prehistorian who is primarily interested in a question toward the end of the strategy may decide to start his research with it and leave the previous questions to be answered by other investigators. He will then be adopting a tactic contrary to the strategy (Sec. 2.2). The heavy curved lines in Figure 6 indicate the strategic order and the light curved lines, the tactical alternatives.

FIGURE 6. *Strategy and tactics of prehistory: The thick lines indicate the logical order of procedure, that is, the strategy. The thin lines indicate tactics that may be more practical under certain circumstances.*

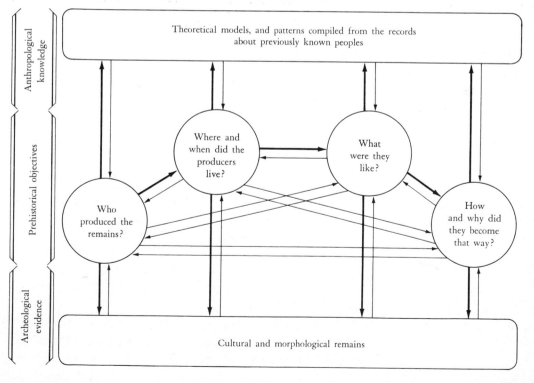

Once the investigator has selected a question, he should seek the evidence needed to answer that question, that is, he should proceed in accordance with the heavy line in Figure 6 that extends from the circle he has chosen to the bottom rectangle. The evidence he seeks may be available among the results of previous archeological research. If not, he himself will have to practice archeology in order to obtain the necessary evidence. When he does, circumstances may cause him to alter his tactics. For example, he may search for homogeneous assemblages with which to answer the first question (Sec. 3.6) and instead find a stratigraphic sequence that provides an answer to the second question (Sec. 4.7). He will then find it advisable to shift from the first to the second question and answer "Where and when?" before obtaining an answer to "Who?" Thus he will follow the alternative tactic indicated by the light line connecting the bottom rectangle with the second circle.

The investigator is aided in obtaining the evidence and in interpreting it by his knowledge of anthropology, which is symbolized by the rectangle at the top of Figure 6. This knowledge includes models developed by theoretical reasoning and also patterns that have been recorded for previously studied peoples. The heavy black lines extending from the circles to the rectangle indicate that the prehistorian chooses different models and patterns in order to answer each question. Sometimes a pattern or model will suggest another line of evidence not yet taken into consideration, in which case the investigator will adopt a tactic contrary to the strategy by proceeding in the order of the light lines extending from the rectangle to the circles.

There is a fundamental difference between the first two and the last two questions with respect to the relative emphasis placed upon archeological evidence and anthropological knowledge. The first two questions establish the systematic framework of prehistory; that is, they result in formulation and ordering of the primary units of prehistoric research. The third and fourth questions are substantive; by answering them prehistorians learn the nature of each systematic unit, the manner of its development, and the factors that produced it.

In the systematic part of his strategy, the prehistorian works primarily with archeological evidence rather than with anthropological knowledge, for he seeks consensus with his colleagues in the organization of his subject, and consensus may best be obtained by concentrating upon the empirical evidence of archeology and avoiding differences of interpretation. Hence, when we come to discuss the first two questions in the remainder of this chapter and in the following one, we shall be dealing primarily with the manipulation of archeological evidence and shall cite anthropological knowledge only insofar as it helps in manipulating the evidence.

When we turn to the two substantive questions in Chapters 5 and 6, however, we shall focus upon anthropological knowledge rather than archeological evidence, for the prehistorian's aim in answering these questions is to find remnants of particular models and patterns and to reconstruct the models and patterns from the remnants (Rouse, 1971). For this reason, some authors refer to the substantive part of prehistoric research as "anthropological archeology" (e.g., Anthropological Society of Washington, 1968).

Here we have the reason why the prehistorian has to be trained in anthropology and must become a professional anthropologist (Sec. 1.5). If he were to concentrate on historic, classic, or some other kind of remains, then historic, classic, or some other kind of knowledge would have to be substituted for anthropological knowledge in the top part of Figure 6, and the investigator would have to become a professional historian, classicist, or some other kind of academician rather than a professional anthropologist.

3 Systematic units: organic versus superorganic

We are now concerned with the formulation of systematic units in answer to the question "Who?" The obvious way to formulate such units is by use of the biological taxonomy. We all know that man is a member of the human species, *Homo sapiens,* but our answer would be incomplete if it stopped there. When possible, prehistorians also distinguish races within the human species and determine which races produced the remains under study. If studying the dawn of prehistory, before men had evolved into the human species, they also have to work with the species that preceded *sapiens* within the genus *Homo* and with the genera ancestral to the genus *Homo* itself.

Prehistorians are able to distinguish races, species, and genera by studying morphological remains (Table 2). They classify and identify such remains and thereby supply one kind of answer to the question "Who?" This answer may be called *organic* because it is based upon the kinds of traits that man shares with other organisms.

The organic answer would suffice if man were just another animal, but he is not. He possesses traits of culture, social structure, and language that differentiate him from all other organisms. These traits may be termed *superorganic,* because they are superimposed on the morphological traits that man possesses as an organism (Kroeber, 1948, pp. 253–255).

We need to answer the question "Who?" in terms of man's superorganic traits as well as his organic traits. To do so, we must develop a second, superorganic set of systematic units to complement the races, species, and genera that comprise the organic set of units. To put this another way, we need to work not only with races, species, and genera, which are organic, but also with peoples, societies, and speech communities, which are superorganic.

Ideally, the superorganic answer to the question "Who?" should include peoples, societies, and speech communities. In practice, it is only possible to work with peoples, for the archeological remains upon which the answer must be based are cultural, not social or linguistic (Table 2). The institutions that distinguish a society can only be inferred from remains and then only under favorable circumstances (Sec. 5.13). Written records, which would make it possible to distinguish historic speech communities, are not ordinarily found among prehistoric remains.

By contrast, the cultural objects called artifacts are a principal constituent of human remains. As we have seen (Secs. 2.7 and 2.8), archeologists customarily classify them, thereby forming types and modes, which are cultural norms (Secs. 2.9 and 2.12). These norms provide a solid basis for distinguishing cultural groups, that is, peoples. Indeed, it is much easier to distinguish peoples than races, species, and genera, since the overwhelming majority of the remains are cultural rather than morphological.

The prehistorian, then, must limit his superorganic answer of the question "Who?" to cultural groups and must forego the study of socially and linguistically defined groups. He need not, however, forego the study of social and linguistic traits. After he has completed his systematic study of cultural and morphological groups by answering the questions "Who?" and "Where and

When?" and in answer to the question "What?" has reconstructed the traits of these groups, he may likewise attempt to reconstruct social and linguistic traits in order to complete his answer to the third question (Secs. 5.13 to 5.17).

The dimension of form in our cube of knowledge (Fig. 1) has been laid out with these considerations in mind. Peoples are placed first, immediately after the organic environment, because cultural norms, the criteria by which peoples are distinguished, are best represented in the remains. Races are placed next, because the morphological traits upon which they are based are likewise empirically observable, so that races, too, can be used in systematic research. Social groups come next, because they are defined by institutions, which cannot adequately be inferred from the remains, and linguistic groups are placed last, because in the absence of written records it is only possible to project languages back from historic time and then only under exceptionally favorable circumstances.

Historians and ethnologists do not suffer from these limitations. Their paleographic and ethnographic sources normally provide them with adequate information about all four kinds of groups, cultural, morphological, social, and linguistic. They have the further advantage that their sources provide them with the peoples' own ways of dividing themselves into groups, together with the peoples' names for, and definitions of, their groups (e.g., Barth, 1969).

In the absence of records and of the people themselves, prehistorians are obliged to create their own cultural and morphological groups by classifying the remains. They also have to coin their own names for the groups and produce their own definitions. This is a much more lengthy process than the historians' and ethnographers' simple identification of groups, as the following pages will illustrate.

Summarizing the argument to this point, we may say that the prehistorian gives two answers, one superorganic and the other organic, to the question "Who?" The superorganic answer is expressed in terms of peoples, and it is much the fuller of the two, since most of the archeological evidence upon which it is based is cultural. The organic answer is expressed in terms of races, species, and genera, that is, the units of biological taxonomy. The greater part of the present chapter will be devoted to the superorganic answer, in terms of peoples, because we can do so much more with it. At the close of the chapter, we shall consider the organic answer, in terms of morphological groups.

4
Peoples versus
societies

The term "people" is not easily confused with "race" or "speech community," since the cultural traits used to define peoples are distinct from the morphological and linguistic traits used respectively to define races and speech communities. However, the words "people" and "society" are sometimes regarded as synonymous (e.g., Childe, 1958a, pp. 9–10), and hence it will be well to clarify the differences between them before proceeding.

A *people* consists of all persons who engage in similar activities, including the production of similar artifacts. The activities are alike because the people's behavior is mediated by similar standards, customs, and beliefs, that is, by the same cultural norms. Hence, we may say that a people is distinguished by its cultural norms (Linton, 1936, pp. 397–400).

By contrast, a *society* consists of all persons who have similar institutions. The institutions are alike because the members of each one interact according to a common set of standards, customs, and beliefs, which we may call social norms. These mediate the behavior of interaction and thereby determine the nature of the institutions. Since a society is characterized by its institutions and the nature of an institution is determined by its norms, it follows that each society, too, is distinguished by a common set of social norms (Beattie, 1964, pp. 34–41).

Taken together, a people's cultural norms cover its entire way of life. They include, for example, its food customs, manufacturing techniques, methods of burial, styles of behavior, esthetic forms, moral values, and religious beliefs. Only a part of these norms, however, are diagnostic of a people. Thus, the recent immigrants to the United States belong to distinct cultural groups that differ from the rest of the American population in some, but not all, of their food customs, moral values, and so forth.

A society's norms similarly cover its entire array of institutions, ranging from families to nations and from factories to international religious bodies, such as the Roman Catholic church. Examples of norms include kinship relationships, laws, ownership of property, and social statuses. As in the case of a people, only part of a society's norms are diagnostic; others, such as the office of prime minister, may be shared by several different societies.

Since peoples are distinguished by cultural norms and societies by social norms, the two cannot be expected to coincide. A people often consists of several different societies (e.g., Narroll, 1964). Conversely, a single society is sometimes composed of several different peoples, each having its own distinctive cultural norms. (It may or may not also have its own morphological traits or language; these are irrelevant to the present comparison.) The so-called plural societies of the West Indies are an example; each is actually a single society composed of plural peoples (M. G. Smith, 1965, p. 14).

The contrast between a people, which is culturally distinct, and a society, which is socially distinct, lies behind the separation in Chapter 1 of cultural from social anthropology (Table 1). Anthropologists interested in comparative research are accustomed to specialize either in cultural norms, as they exist among peoples, or in social norms, as they occur among societies. In the former case, they call themselves cultural anthropologists and in the latter case, social anthropologists (e.g., Lévi-Strauss, 1963, p. 370).

This separation of cultural from social research is necessary only when dealing with the comparative (side) face of our cube of knowledge (Fig. 1). When approaching the cube from the top, as a student of contemporary peoples, or through the front, as a student of past peoples, one normally combines the two kinds of study. One first distinguishes peoples, explicitly or implicitly, and then proceeds to study each people's culture. When possible, one must also study races and their morphologies, societies and their social structures, and speech communities and their languages, in order to obtain a rounded picture of the peoples' lives and of their development—hence the terms "ethnography" and "ethnology" (Sec. 1.4).

5
Development of the study of peoples

In Section 2.3 we saw that prehistoric man has probably always had an interest in archeological remains. It is reasonable to assume that he attributed some of these remains to previous peoples, since many contemporary nonliterate peoples have traditions about their predecessors. For example, the Eskimo tell of the Tunit, a people who preceded them in the central and eastern Arctic (Bandi, 1969, pp. 147–148).

Neither the Sumerians nor the Chinese, among early historic peoples, had reason to be concerned with the problem of previous peoples. They belonged to cultural groups that had been in existence since late prehistoric time, and hence they saw only Sumerians or Chinese as they looked into the past (Kramer, 1959, p. 35; Chang, 1968, pp. 1–3). They were completely ethnocentric in their view of history and prehistory—as, indeed, the Chinese still tend to be.

The Greeks and Romans had more reason to be concerned with the question "Who?" because they had been immediately preceded by peoples who were culturally different from themselves (Phillips, 1964). The Greeks possessed legends about the previous peoples and occasionally attributed archeological remains to them. For example, Pausanius claimed that the great walls of Mycenae and Tiryns in Greece had been built by the cyclopes, a people mentioned in the Homeric legends (Wace, 1962, p. 153).

Speculation about previous peoples disappeared from the Western World with the decline and fall of the Roman empire, along with the archeological knowledge upon which it was based. As we have seen (Sec. 2.3), medieval men viewed the past strictly in terms of the Bible, which does not refer to the prehistoric peoples of Europe.

When Italians revived the activities of collecting and interpreting artifacts during the Renaissance, along with other aspects of classical learning, they had a ready answer to the question "Who?" Their finds were classical and hence must have been produced by the Greeks or the Romans, as the case might be. North of the Alps, where prehistoric artifacts attracted more attention, it was customary to attribute all such artifacts to the Gauls, who were known to have preceded the Romans in the area. Even stone celts were attributed to the Gauls, although it has since been learned that celts antedated their appearance upon the scene by a considerable length of time (MacCurdy, 1926, vol. 1, p. 10).

The Renaissance scholars were not alone in naïvely attributing all prehistoric remains to the people who inhabited an area at the dawn of history. Some contemporary prehistorians have fallen into the same trap, for example, by calling the distinctive ground-stone artifacts of the Lesser Antilles "Carib stones," when in fact they were made before the arrival of the Carib in the Lesser Antilles (Rouse, 1964b). Unsophisticated students of prehistory often fail to realize that all areas have been occupied by previous peoples—even Mesopotamia and China, when one goes back far enough in time—and to recognize that one must distinguish the previous peoples archeologically before making correlations with historic or ethnographic groups, in accordance with the principle that the main outlines of prehistory have to be based upon archeological evidence (Sec. 2.1).

Until the nineteenth century, scholars were too preoccupied with tasks of identifying, excavating, and describing artifacts to develop more systematic methods of prehistoric interpretation; they limited themselves almost entirely to the role of archeologist and did not assume that of prehistorian. Soon after the turn of the nineteenth century, however, artifacts began to be used to establish prehistoric chronology, a development that will be discussed in the next chapter. Use of the remains to distinguish prehistoric peoples, which is the subject of the present chapter, did not arise until toward the close of the nineteenth century. The Germans pioneered in this approach, being led to it by the rise of nationalism in their own country (Childe, 1956, pp. 28–29). As they became conscious of themselves as a people, they began to look for the remains of the ancestral German people. For some time, they had been obtaining similar assemblages of artifacts from some sites and different assemblages from others; and now they attempted to show which assemblages had been produced by their own ancestors and which by other peoples. They applied the term *"Kulturgruppe"* to each people thus identified, frequently shortening this to *Kultur* (Kossinna, 1920). The longer phrase was more accurate, since it means "a group of people distinguished by its culture," that is, by the presence of similar assemblages of artifacts in all its sites.

Kossinna (1920) termed this approach *"Siedlungsarchäologie,"* that is, "settlement archaeology," because it aimed to determine the extent of German settlement of Europe during prehistoric time. Menghin (1931, p. 7) labeled it *"chorologische,"* which is to say that it focused upon the geographic distribution of peoples, German and non-German. It thus contributed to the German national policy of the time by indicating which areas had previously been occupied by Germans and by providing a pretext for conquest of those areas.

The interest in peoples spread from Germany to the rest of

western Europe during the first part of the twentieth century, but with a significant change of attitude. The Germans had aimed to identify their own ancestors and had used cultural assemblages as a device for so doing. In effect, they had ignored the principle of establishing purely prehistoric peoples, based solely upon archeological evidence, before proceeding to make correlations with a historic people (themselves). Prehistorians in the rest of western Europe did not make this mistake. Instead, they used the assemblages they excavated as the basis for discovering hitherto unknown peoples. They were led to this approach by two factors. First, they were culturally too diverse to be able to trace themselves back into prehistory. The British, for example, could not have carried their ancestry back into prehistory because they are the result of fusion of many different prehistoric peoples. Second, the West Europeans recognized that the process of fusion makes it impossible to trace any ethnological or historic people back as far as the early part of prehistory. Hence, the specialists in early prehistory, which was coming into prominence at the time, had to look for a different way in which to interpret their remains.

Cultural assemblages were being obtained from both early and late prehistoric sites. The assemblages that were alike were grouped together and given the name of a typical site or region, to which the suffix "-ian" was added, for example, Danubian. Units like this could have been regarded as cultural groups of people—*Kulturgruppen* in the German terminology—but the West Europeans preferred to concentrate upon the assemblages rather than the people who produced them—upon *Kulturen* in the German terminology. As a result, they called each unit a "culture" or else an "industry" (Childe, 1956, p. 23).

Seeking a name for this approach, Childe (1956, pp. 15 and 173) termed it "chorological classification." He used the term "classification" because the procedure is to group together similar assemblages of artifacts, and he adopted "chorological" from Menghin, though deploring its ugliness. It is not very appropriate either. "Chorology" means the study of geographical distributions. As we have seen, Menghin used it because the Germans were primarily interested in the geographic distribution of their ancestors. Childe, however, stressed instead the recurrence of similar cultural traits from assemblage to assemblage. It is therefore more appropriate to call his procedure "cultural classification" (cf. Rouse, 1965b; there, I used the term "ethnic" in place of "cultural").

By the 1950s cultural classification had become standard practice throughout western Europe, except in dealing with the very latest prehistoric remains—"protohistoric," as they are sometimes called— where the names of historic groups are substituted, contrary to the principle of correlation advocated here. For example, it is still the practice to interpret Iron Age remains by applying to them the names of Celtic tribes mentioned in the Roman sources, instead of first establishing prehistoric peoples by the study of assemblages and then correlating the prehistoric units with the historic tribes (Hodson, 1962). With this exception, west European prehistorians classify assemblages to distinguish cultures. They pay less attention to the other side of the coin, that is, to the peoples that produced the cultures. Childe (1956, pp. 111–134) did pose the question "Who?" but failed to follow through by distinguishing peoples as well as cultures.

The study of peoples developed differently in eastern Europe. Soviet prehistorians originally rejected cultural classification in favor of a strictly Marxian interpretation of prehistory that, as we shall see in Section 4.3, causes them to focus on the question "Where and when?" rather than "Who?" With the resurgence of Russian nationalism during the 1930s, they began to apply the concept of peoples to the late prehistoric remains in order to work out the origins of the Russian people, but they continued to apply only the Marxian approach to their early prehistoric remains, where it was obviously impossible to distinguish Russians from non-Russians (M. W. Thompson, 1965). Thus, they adopted the outmoded German tactics of using cultural classification as a device for projecting historic peoples back into prehistory, and they failed to recognize the need to apply cultural classification to all of prehistory for purely prehistoric purposes.

American prehistorians were likewise slow to develop an interest in cultural classification. They finally took it up in the 1930s in several different forms, two of which will be discussed here:

1. Prehistorians working in the midwestern part of the United States became interested in peoples because of the existence in their area of large mounds and the prevalence of a belief that these

mounds had been built by an earlier and more advanced people than the American Indians. This people was popularly called the "Mound Builders" and was thought to have descended from the Phoenicians, the Israelites, or some other migrants from the Old World. During the nineteenth century, American prehistorians had to spend much time in refuting these beliefs, which they finally did by excavating the mounds and showing that they contained artifacts comparable to those of the American Indians (Shetrone, 1941, pp. 5–26).

Eventually, it became apparent that several groups of American Indians have been involved in construction of the mounds. These sites are so variable in structure and content that they cannot all have been produced by the same people; for example, many have intrusive burials in the tops of them. So the problem arose of distinguishing between various groups of mound-building and mound-using Indians.

Midwestern prehistorians first attempted to solve this problem by means of chorological classification, in the Kossinna-Menghin sense of the term. They studied the distribution of traits from mound to mound in the hope of being able to distinguish geographic groupings of people. This study, however, failed to reveal any consistent patterning of traits. The reason was soon recognized: the peoples that produced the mounds had lived at different times and had had overlapping geographic distributions. These overlaps were obscuring the boundaries between peoples.

One way out of this difficulty would have been to set up a chronology in order to study the distribution of peoples at different times. Unfortunately, the midwesterners had not yet been able to do anything with the question "Where and when?" because they had spent so much time on the problem of defining peoples, that is, in answering the question "Who?" Therefore, they decided to disregard both temporal and spatial distributions and to define their peoples purely in terms of cultural traits. They reasoned that they might better forget about the question "Where and when?" until they had answered the question "Who?" in a more satisfactory manner.

The procedure they developed for concentrating solely on cultural traits became known as the "midwestern taxonomic system" (McKern, 1939). Recognizing that a site might have been successively occupied by several peoples, the midwesterners first separated such sites into components, each containing the remains of a single people. Then they classified the components, grouping into a single class all those which were alike in their cultural norms. Like Childe they did not distinguish between a people and its culture. They simply applied the name of a typical site or area to each class of components and to its distinctive culture, often adding the suffix "-ian" as in western Europe, for example, Hopewellian. They referred to this unit as a "focus." Unlike Childe, they recognized that they had not based their definition of a focus upon all of its cultural norms; they referred to the norms diagnostic of each focus as its "determinants."

Differentiation of components and classification of the components in order to form foci were the basic parts of the midwestern taxonomic system and the only parts that were intended to be permanent (McKern, 1940). In the absence of chronology, however, the midwesterners felt it necessary temporarily to erect a taxonomic superstructure, in which they successively grouped the various foci into aspects, phases, and patterns (Table 3). As in all taxonomies

TABLE 3 *The midwestern taxonomic system*

Cultural classification		Taxonomic ordering of the classes		
Assemblages	Classes	First level	Second level	Third level
Component 1 Component 2	Focus 1	Aspect 1	Phase 1	Pattern 1
Component 3 Component 4	Focus 2			
Component 5 Component 6	Focus 3	Aspect 2		
Component 7 Component 8	Focus 4			
Component 9 Component 10	Focus 5	Aspect 3		
Component 11 Component 12	Focus 6		Phase 2	
	etc.	etc.	etc.	etc.

(Fig. 5), these were hierarchical units. Like the foci, they were supposed to be based solely upon similarities and differences in cultural norms, not upon geographic distributions or chronological positions. Those foci that shared most of their determinants were grouped into a single aspect; the aspects that shared most of their diagnostic norms were grouped into the same phase; and the phases that shared most of their diagnostics were placed in the same pattern. There were three main patterns, Archaic, Woodland, and Mississippi.

This superstructure of aspects, phases, and patterns was intended to serve as a sort of filing system within which to organize the various foci until such time as it should become possible to arrange them in chronological order. It was not until after World War II that chronological control was developed to the point that the hierarchical superstructure could be abandoned. The foci were then arranged in their proper order in time and space by fitting them into a chronology (e.g., Griffin, 1952, fig. 205).

The aspects and phases of the former midwestern taxonomy have largely gone out of use, but the three major patterns—Archaic, Woodland, and Mississippi—are still employed in modified form. Some authorities have redefined them to serve as major divisions of the chronology, in effect converting them from answers to the question "Who?" into answers to the question "When and where?" Other authors prefer to treat them as "traditions," or groupings of similar foci, which in effect means that they continue to serve as answers to "Who?" (cf. Griffin, 1952, and Willey, 1966, fig. 8–1).

2. A different approach has been developed in the southeastern United States. There, much more is known about the early historic Indians than in the Midwest, thanks to the writings of Spanish explorers, and so the prehistorians decided to start with the historic period that they knew and to work back into the unknown of pre-history. They call this approach the "direct historic" method (Steward, 1942). Each prehistorian focuses upon a small, local area and works out the succession of cultural "periods" within that area, proceeding from the historic periods back into prehistory (e.g., Ford, 1962). This approach is chronological and therefore more properly discussed in connection with the question "Where and when?" (Sec. 4.7). Here we need only note that peoples and cultures can be derived from such a local sequence by assuming that

all the people of a given period belonged to a single cultural group or, if it is obvious that they did not, by separating them into two or more groups through the process of cultural classification. Some southeastern prehistorians simply refer to these peoples or cultures or both as "periods" (e.g., Ford, 1962, fig. 7), but other prehistorians who are culturally more sophisticated prefer to use the term *phase* (Willey and Phillips, 1962, pp. 22–24).

The direct historic method is a good example of the difference between strategy and tactics, that is, between the logical way of doing prehistoric research and the most practical way, given the nature of the available evidence (Sec. 3.2). The logical approach is to distinguish peoples before determining the areas and periods in which they lived, that is, to answer the question "Who?" before proceeding to the question "When and where?" Nevertheless, in regions like the Southeast, where so much chronological evidence is available, it is better tactics to begin by delimiting local periods and assigning one's assemblages to them. Then one may proceed to determine by means of cultural classification whether all of the assemblages assigned to a given period have been produced by a single people.

We have now examined the methods developed to answer the question "Who?" in two parts of Europe and two parts of the United States, and we have encountered a number of different approaches. If we were to continue into other parts of the world, we would find still more variety; for example, cultural units are called "facies" in California and "styles" in Peru and the Caribbean region (Heizer and Graham, 1967, pp. 158–161).

Until recently, the prehistorians of each region have been working more or less in isolation and therefore have not been concerned by the differences in procedure and terminology from one region to another. Now, however, research has progressed to the point where it is possible to make interregional syntheses, and as a result it is becoming necessary to reconcile the differences in the regional approaches. Prehistorians are beginning to hold conferences for the purpose but so far have failed to reach agreement (cf. J. D. Clark et al., 1966, 1968, and Clarke, 1968, pp. 24–32). Indeed, some argue that argeement is impossible, since one's units should vary depending upon the objectives of one's study (e.g., Brew, 1946).

The present survey is intended to cover all possible objectives.

However, in the absence of a consensus about the best way to attain each objective, the author has had to make a personal selection of the procedures and terminologies that seem to him to be the most logical and practicable. These will be discussed in the following sections.

6
Cultural
classification

The basic procedure is *cultural classification,* by which is meant the formulation of new classes of cultural assemblages. The classes are formed by grouping the assemblages solely in terms of their types and modes. The spatial and temporal positions of the assemblages are not involved, for they answer the question "Where and when?" rather than "Who?" However, any cultural classification should subsequently be checked by studying the distribution of the resultant units in space and time, for, if they show no consistency of distribution, the classification is obviously wrong and will have to be redone. Conversely, if one has established cultural units by delimiting their position in space and time, one should subsequently check their validity by means of cultural classification, since consistency in the answers to the questions "Where and When?" and "Who?" is the ultimate test of the validity of both.

The procedure of cultural classification should not be confused with that of classifying cultural remains, as described in Section 2.7. In that procedure, the aim was to set up new classes of artifacts, cultural equipment, or materials, viewed as individual specimens. In cultural classification, on the contrary, the aim is to establish new classes of assemblages of the specimens. Classes of specimens and classes of assemblages are established for different purposes. As we saw in Section 2.9, classes of specimens are important to the archeologist in their own right and to a prehistorian because they are indicative of types of artifacts. Classes of assemblages are significant only to the prehistorian, not per se but because each is indicative of a cultural group or people.

This difference may be seen by comparing Figures 4 and 7. In the former, only two circles are needed to portray the results achieved by classifying individual specimens, one circle for the class of specimens and the other circle for its characteristics, that is, for the other side of its coin. In Figure 7, four circles are required, one pair for the class of assemblages and its characteristics and the other pair for the people that produced the assemblages and its characteristics.

To understand why this difference exists, let us return to Section 2.6. There we saw that archeologists customarily divide sites into components (a term adopted from the midwestern taxonomic method), each of which is characterized by a different assemblage of artifacts and other cultural remains (a term overlooked in the midwestern method, presumably because of the local prehistorians' emphasis upon mounds, where structure is more important than content). So far as the archeologist is concerned, assemblages are purely objective units, to be distinguished by the techniques discussed in Chapter 2, but with the implication that each assemblage was produced by a single group of people. It is the prehistorian's task to make this implication explicit. He does so by grouping the

FIGURE 7. *Relationship between a class of cultural assemblages (a, bottom) and its characteristics (b, bottom): A class of assemblages and its characteristics are two sides of the same coin, the class being composed of all the assemblages (As) that share a particular set of types (t) and modes (m). The class and its characteristics are indicative of a second coin, the people who produced the assemblages (a, top) and that people's total culture (b, top), which has to be reconstructed from the assemblages. The hatched area symbolizes the diagnostic complex of types and modes that is used to identify the people and its culture.*

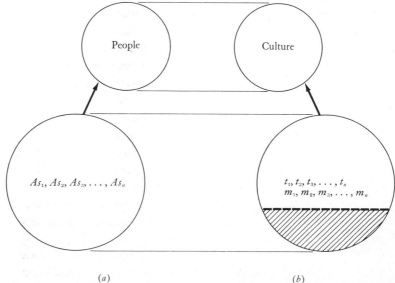

(a) (b)

assemblages into classes, each of which is indicative of a single people, as shown in Figure 7.

The prehistorian must take care in selecting the assemblages he uses for cultural classification. Most importantly, he should concentrate on assemblages from residential sites, if at all possible, since they yield the greatest range of a people's activities and are therefore most representative of its culture. Assemblages from purely burial or ceremonial sites should be used only as a last resort.

In Section 2.6, we saw that some assemblages are pure but others may be mixed, it being impossible to determine which part of a mixed assemblage has been produced by one people and which part by another. The materials excavated from a typical New England rock shelter provide a good example of a mixed assemblage. They have normally been laid down through occupation by a succession of peoples, none of whom stayed long enough to build up an appreciable deposit, with the result that it is impossible to distinguish the remains of one people from the deposits made by another. Mixed assemblages such as these must be avoided when doing cultural classification. It is advisable to work only with assemblages from single-component sites or from sites in which multiple components are physically separated, for example, by sterile deposits. In the case of multicomponent sites, one should also eliminate those assemblages that come from disturbed areas.

Another important factor to be considered in selecting assemblages for cultural classification may be approached obliquely by considering a problem of linguistic classification. If one studies the variations in two languages from place to place, one generally finds that they differ most in their respective centers of distribution and become more alike as one approaches the boundary between the two. They tend to be mutually intelligible along the boundary, even though the speakers of the two languages who live at any distance from the boundary cannot understand one another. As a result of this phenomenon, one can move from Portugal through Spain and France to Belgium, or from southern to northern China, without, even while crossing linguistic boundaries, ever encountering two adjacent villages that are unable to understand each other. Because languages are transitional in this manner, linguistic classifiers must be careful to work with typical examples of each language, avoiding examples from along linguistic boundaries.

The same care must be taken in classifying archeological assemblages, with the added proviso that transition in assemblages takes place not only along the dimension of space but also through the dimension of time. The prehistorian must select for cultural classification only those assemblages that come from the central part of a people's distribution, avoiding those from along its boundaries, whether in space or in time (Fig. 8a). Like so much of archeological and prehistoric research, this selection is a matter of intuitive judgment, for which no general rules can be stated, but at that later stage in the strategy of prehistory after one has turned from the question "Who?" to "Where and when?" one can easily check one's judgment by laying out one's assemblages in the order of their relative positions in time and space, delineating the boundaries between the assemblages of different peoples, and thereby determining which assemblages must be considered transitional, because they lie along the boundaries. If, after checking in this manner, the prehistorian finds that he has based his cultural classification on transitional assemblages, he will have to redo it, using more typical assemblages (e.g., Rouse, 1952, p. 341).

This checking procedure is another example of the need for feedback between the successive parts of the strategy of prehistory.

FIGURE 8. *Distribution of typical and transitional assemblages of cultural (a) and morphological (b) remains: TyCA = typical cultural assemblage. TrCA = transitional cultural assemblage. TyMA = typical morphological assemblage. TrMA = transitional morphological assemblage. The figures assume no geographic or ethnic barriers to the diffusion of traits; such barriers would cause skewing, as shown in Clarke (1968, fig. 53).*

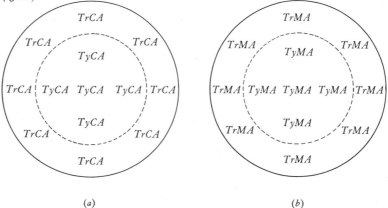

(a)   (b)

The conclusions reached in answering one question—in this case, "Who?"—should be regarded merely as working hypotheses, to be tested while answering other parts of the strategy—in this case, the question "Where and when?"

A final problem in selecting the assemblage for cultural classification results from the fact that no people carries out all of its activities at a single site. It is probably no accident that the procedure of cultural classification was first worked out and has been most widely used in dealing with the Neolithic age in Europe and with the Formative stage in the New World, for these peoples tended to carry on more of their activities at a single place, with the result that their assemblages are more representative of the artifacts used in all of their activities. This concentration of activities at one place was not so true of the Paleolithic and Mesolithic ages in the Old World, or the Lithic and Archaic stages in the New World, when the practice of seasonal nomadism caused many peoples to deposit different kinds of tools in the sites that they occupied at different times of the year, or of the Bronze and Iron Ages in the Old World and the Classic and post-Classic in the New World, when many peoples were divided into urban and rural dwellers, each of whom deposited different kinds of assemblages.

In cases such as these, it is advisable to select the kind of assemblage that appears to be most typical of the people under study and to limit one's classification to it. In the case of seasonal nomads, for example, one should use the assemblages from the places in which the people carried on the greatest number of their activities, and in the case of an urban–rural continuum, the assemblages from the cities, since the major advances in culture took place there.

Alternatively, one may choose to reverse the normal strategy by answering the question "What?" before "Who?" One will then begin with activity rather than cultural assemblages, use them to reconstruct activity patterns (Sec. 5.10), and thereby learn about the potential variations in each people's cultural assemblages before distinguishing the people itself by classifying the cultural assemblages. Here again, we see that it would be a mistake to consider the strategy of prehistoric research inviolable. The investigator must ultimately answer all four questions, since agreement among the answers serves to validate them, but he may vary the order of the answers to fit the circumstances.

In summary, the procedure of cultural classification should be applied primarily to residential assemblages that are pure (rather than mixed) and typical (rather than transitional). One's sample should also include assemblages resulting from as many as possible of the activities in which the peoples have been engaged. The success of one's classification will depend to a considerable extent upon one's selection of assemblages.

In this selection of assemblages we see a major difference between the prehistorian and the archeologist. The prehistorian naturally concentrates on those asemblages that best enable him to attain his goals—answers to the questions "Who?", "Where and when?", "What?", and "How and why?" To the archeologist, on the contrary, one assemblage is as good as another. He studies them for their own sake rather than for what they can tell him about prehistory. If he thinks at all about their relative value, he will prefer to excavate those which provide him with the greatest variety of classes of artifacts and other remains, since this variety advances him toward *his* goal—determination of the nature of the remains.

It is for this reason that the prehistorian often finds it necessary to do his own archeological research instead of simply relying upon the archeologist to supply him with all the data he needs. He cannot expect the archeologist to be aware of all his requirements in recovering assemblages, since the archeologist views assemblages in a different way. Hence, he must undertake his own excavations in order to obtain the classifiable assemblages that he needs (Fig. 6).

After the prehistorian has obtained enough cultural assemblages of the proper kinds, he proceeds to group them into classes. We have seen that these classes are called "foci" by the midwestern taxonomists (Sec. 3.5). We shall instead term them *classes of assemblages,* in order to stress the fact that they are the prehistorian's counterpart of the archeologist's classes of artifacts (Sec. 2.9).

The same alternatives are available in forming classes of assemblages as in forming classes of artifacts: either taxonomic or typological classification. The taxonomic approach must be ruled out because cultures, like artifacts, do not develop furcately (Brew, 1946). Hence, the prehistorian proceeds typologically. He formulates a series of trial patterns, each composed of types, modes, and other cultural norms, and classifies his assemblages in terms of these patterns. Then he compares the assemblages he has put into each class in order to see just how alike they are and revises the classes in an effort to achieve greater homogeneity, repeating the process until he is satisfied that each class is as homogeneous as possible. If it seems desirable, he may also test the classification by statistical manipulation of its types, modes, and other cultural norms (e.g., Kroeber, 1940; Spaulding, 1960b).

It is customary, as we have seen, to name each class after a typical site, often with the addition of the suffix "-ian," for example, Aurignacian (Chard, 1969b, pp. 130–132). Alternatively, a class may be named after the area or period in which it was produced, for example, Early Dynastic (Chard, 1969b, pp. 240–241). A third possibility is to use the name of a characteristic of the class, for example, Kurgan (Russian for mound; Chard, 1969b, pp. 305–306).

Prehistorians have been less than systematic in their use of these alternatives and as a result have frequently coined new names for peoples already in the literature under old names. Biologists, who also are faced with this problem, have established the rule that the first name to be published has priority, and prehistorians would do well to follow their example, as recommended by Colton, Sellers, and Hargrave (1937, pp. 21–27).

7
Cultural
complexes

Classes of assemblages, then, are formed by grouping one's assemblages in terms of patterns of types, modes, and so forth. What are we to call these patterns? In the literature they have variously been termed "complexes," "industries," and "styles" (Rouse, 1965b, p. 4). Here they will be called *cultural complexes,* the term "cultural" being used to distinguish them from the morphological complexes that result from classification of morphological assemblages (Sec. 3.15). The individual traits within each complex may similarly be termed *cultural diagnostics.* (Midwestern taxonomists refer to them as determinants; see Sec. 3.5.)

It is important to note that each cultural complex includes only a portion of its people's types, modes, and so forth (Fig. 7). This point has been well stated by Kluckhohn (1962, pp. 75–76) as follows:

> *Observation of the actual operation of [prehistorians] suggests that in many cases the classification of [assemblages] is actually*

made on the basis of pottery complex or architectural style (including masonry type). If this fact is explicitly stated, the procedure may well be the most convenient and quite unobjectionable. If, however, there is assertion or implication that the classification has been made on the basis of the total cultural complex, this is misleading, for what occurs is that other cultural elements found associated with the critical pottery complex or architectural style are simply dragged in after the crucial step has been taken. If we are really operating with pottery or masonry-architectural complexes (or a combination of these two) only, it would be in the interests of clear thinking to bring this circumstance into the open, either through terminology or explicit statement. It seems possible that classificatory operations based solely upon these apparently somewhat more sensitive and more consistent criteria would be the most useful. The associated cultural elements (not used in classification) could then be studied apart from the prejudice of a question-begging nomenclature, and, after the trends towards uniformity had been unequivocally ascertained, the operations for definitions in terms of total culture ... could be rigorously set up.

Kluckhohn was referring in this passage to the late prehistory of the southwestern United States, but his words would apply equally well to the late prehistory of other parts of the world, such as the Near East (e.g., Braidwood, 1952, figs. 26 and 27).

As Kluckhohn indicates, the cultural norms not used as diagnostics can best be studied at a later stage in the strategy of prehistory, when answering the question "What?" Therefore, we shall defer consideration of those norms until we come to that question (Sec. 5.8). At present, we need only concern ourselves with the norms needed to define a people.

Barth (1969, p. 14) draws a similar conclusion from his studies of contemporary cultural groups:

It is important to recognize that although ethnic categories take cultural differences into account, we can assume no simple one-to-one relationship between ethnic units and cultural similarities and differences. The features that are taken into account are not the sum of "objective" differences, but only those which the actors themselves regard as significant.

In discussing the classification of artifacts, we made a distinction between intrinsic, extrinsic, and cognitive types (Sec. 2.10). Since a type and its class of artifacts is paralleled by a complex and its class of assemblages, we might expect also to be able to distinguish intrinsic, extrinsic, and cognitive complexes. An "intrinsic complex" is a contradiction in terms, however, for complexes are not formulated in order to express the nature of their classes, as intrinsic types are. Instead, they express the nature of the peoples that produced the classes. Kluckhohn's passage, then, refers to *extrinsic* rather than intrinsic *complexes*. Barth, on the other hand, is discussing the peoples' own diagnostics, which constitute *cognitive* rather than extrinsic *complexes*. To convert Barth's statement from cognitive to extrinsic complexes, it would be necessary to change the last phrase from "features...which the actors themselves regard as significant" to "features which the prehistorian finds to be archeologically significant."

In Section 2.10, we also noted the need to distinguish between those cognitive types that are in the minds of the artisans, as parts of their cultures, and those which are in our own minds, as parts of our culture, and we warned against imposing the latter upon archeological remains. This warning also applies to cultural complexes. It is where the pre–World War II German prehistorians went astray (Sec. 3.5). They were imposing the cognitive complex diagnostic of their own cultural group on the archeological remains instead of deriving extrinsic complexes from the remains and, where feasible, correlating those extrinsic complexes with their own cognitive complex.

The prehistorian's selection of the diagnostics that comprise an extrinsic complex is not a matter of free choice (as I erroneously assumed in a previous article, Rouse, 1965b, p. 6). It should arise out of his classification of assemblages. He should seek the types, modes, and other cultural norms that appear to be most diagnostic of the class he has formed and is attempting to define. These diagnostics will normally consist of extrinsic types and stylistically significant modes, since those are the most likely to be indicative of the people that produced the assemblages in the class under study. The diagnostics must also be relatively frequent, or else they will not be reliable indicators of the class and its people, and they must be relatively widespread, or else it will not be possible to use them to identify additional occurrences of the people under study. Types and modes of chipped stone artifacts best meet these requirements in the case of Paleolithic and Paleo-Indian remains, and types and modes of pottery in the case of Neolithic and Neo-Indian remains, but there are exceptions. Specialists in Eskimo prehistory have come to rely primarily upon harpoon heads (Bandi, 1969) and Polynesian specialists upon fishhooks and adzes (Emory et al., 1959). As for civilized peoples, monumental architecture and art are perhaps the best source of diagnostics, because people tend to regard them as civic and ethnic symbols. It does not really matter what sort of norms are used so long as they do the job they are supposed to do: define a class of assemblages and the people who produced it.

In conclusion, let us return to the parallel between a class of assemblages and its complex, on the one hand, and a class of artifacts and its type, on the other hand. A class of assemblages is an objective entity, like a class of artifacts, in that it consists of specimens that can be laid out on tables in a laboratory or museum, whereas the complex, like a type of artifacts, has to be abstracted from the specimens. The class is constantly being expanded by excavation of new assemblages produced by the same people, whereas the complex, being the common denominator of all the assemblages in the class, should remain unchanged, providing that the classification was properly done in the first place and was based upon a representative sample of all the assemblages in the class.

8
Peoples and their cultures

The name that a prehistorian coins for a class is also applicable to the people that produced the class. Thus, we may speak not only of a Single Grave class, when referring to the assemblages that are characterized by single burials in graves, but also of the Single Grave people, when discussing the creators of the assemblages. A class and the people that produced it are often confused, if only because they have the same name, but we must differentiate them here if we are to think clearly about prehistory.

By definition, each class consists of all the assemblages that have been laid down by a single people. It follows that the class is indicative of the people and that its diagnostic complex can be used to identify the people. A people consists of all the human beings who deposited the assemblages marked by a particular complex.

We have made a distinction between extrinsic complexes, which are obtained by classifying assemblages, and cognitive complexes, which are obtained by questioning informants. Since peoples are defined by their complexes, peoples too can be either *extrinsic* or *cognitive*. The distinction between extrinsic and cognitive peoples is an important one, which the beginner in prehistory often overlooks. The beginner is likely to assume that he can make a one-to-one correlation between an extrinsic and a cognitive people, but this correlation is not probable, since the extrinsic people is defined in terms of archeological evidence and the cognitive people in terms of its own choice of criteria, which may include morphological, social, and linguistic traits as well as the cultural traits to which extrinsic complexes are limited (Sec. 1.2). For example, prehistorians have found it very difficult to identify the remains of the Carib Indians of the Lesser Antilles because this group defined itself in terms of criteria that are not represented in the local archeology (Rouse, 1964b, p. 512).

We have seen that a class of assemblages and the characteristics of that class, including its complex, form two sides of the same coin (Fig. 7). This coin is paralleled by another one consisting of the people and its culture (Sec. 1.2). Just as the class is indicative of the people that produced it, so also the characteristics of the class provide a basis for reconstructing the people's culture. And just as the name of the class is applicable to the people that produced the class, so also that name is applicable to the complex diagnostic of the class, to the remaining characteristics of the class, and to the people's entire culture, which is reconstructed from the class.

Reading the literature on prehistory, one finds a tendency to shift at will among phrases such as the "Single Grave class," the "Single Grave complex" (or one of the synonyms for "complex," such as "industry," "style," or "determinants"), the "Single Grave people," and the "Single Grave culture." There is nothing wrong with this variation, since the four entities are opposite sides of related coins (Fig. 7). It is only necessary to be clear about the meanings of the four nouns: *class* refers to the assemblages that have been grouped together; *complex* to the traits diagnostic of the class; *people* to the individuals who produced the class; and *culture* to all the cultural traits shared by those individuals.

9
Magnitude of
peoples

Since peoples are the primary units of prehistoric research, formulated at the beginning of the strategy, they can hardly be considered an end in themselves. On the contrary, one's peoples must be designed in such a way as to be most serviceable in answering the subsequent questions in the strategy, "Where and when?", "What?", and "How and why?" Indeed, an advantage of the tactic of starting with a later stage in the strategy and working back to the question "Who?" is that this approach ensures the serviceability of one's peoples. But the prehistorian who begins with the question "Who?" should have no difficulty anticipating the demands to be placed upon his units at later stages in the strategy, for he will have training and experience with the demands. (Since this anticipation will not be true of an archeologist who lacks training in prehistory, it is a strong reason for making a distinction between the two disciplines.)

The most important problem in designing one's peoples is how large to make them. In doing cultural classification, as in other kinds of classification, it is possible to be either a "lumper" or a "splitter"—to pay so little heed to the differences between one's assemblages that one groups a relatively large number of them into a single class, or to be so obsessed by the differences among them that one puts them into a relatively large number of classes, each containing a relatively small number of assemblages. In the former case, one's result will be small complexes, delineating large groups of people, whereas in the latter case there will be larger complexes, delineating smaller groups of people. The difference between these two results is well illustrated by the now abandoned hierarchical levels of the midwestern taxonomic method. If one is a lumper in doing cultural classification, one will end up with peoples on the order of magnitude of the aspects, phases, or even patterns in the midwestern taxonomy (Table 3), while if one is a splitter, one will end up with peoples on the order of foci.

The midwestern taxonomists resolved this problem by concentrating on foci at the expense of the larger units in their abandoned hierarchy, and hence they became splitters—though, as always, there is considerable variation from author to author. The specialists in European prehistory, on the contrary, have tended to be lumpers. The European practice will be followed in the present study for two reasons. First, it is more appropriate for a world survey, since it reduces the number of units with which the reader must cope and the number of proper names that he must learn. Second, it provides a better basis for substantive, as opposed to systematic, study, by producing larger units than in the case of splitting. When one's units are made larger, more archeological data become available for the reconstruction of each culture and for the study of its changes, and there is less duplication of changes from culture to culture.

On the other hand, if this book were concerned with a single region and if it stressed the systematics of the region at the expense of substantive knowledge, it would be more appropriate to use a splitting approach (as in Rouse and Cruxent, 1963). In other words, one should design one's peoples to fit the purposes of one's study. Biologists and physical anthropologists have been quicker to recognize this principle than prehistorians as a result of their experience in working with the parallel concept of race (e.g., Dobzhansky, 1966, pp. 266–269; Washburn, 1963, pp. 10–13).

10
Dividing peoples

Having chosen to use a lumping approach, we must expect to encounter a relatively great number of differences in culture among the individuals we group together as a single people—differences that the splitter would handle by distinguishing separate peoples. How are we to handle these differences?

We may conceptualize them by dividing our peoples into two or more *subpeoples*. These may be either successive or contemporaneous. If they are successive, it is the practice to designate them by prefixing chronological adjectives to the names of the peoples, as in the case of Early, Middle, and Late Minoan (Finley, 1970, pp. 30–46), or to append numbers to the name of the people, as in the case of Ubaid 1 to 4 (Porada, 1965, pp. 149–152). If they are contemporaneous, the names of the peoples are modified by prefixing geographic terms, as in the case of the African and European Acheulean (Chard, 1969b, p. 109), or else points of the compass, as in the case of Western and Eastern Gravettian (G. Clark, 1969, pp. 53–56).

Just as a people is defined by a diagnostic complex of cultural traits, so each of its subpeoples is defined by a diagnostic *subcom-*

plex. This subcomplex normally consists of details of style, which serve to differentiate the members of one temporal or geographic subgroup from the others.

We have seen that each people possesses its own distinctive culture, the two being opposite sides of the same coin. Similarly, each subpeople may be said to have its own distinctive *phase* of the culture (Willey and Phillips, 1962, pp. 22–24). A subpeople and its phase form opposite sides of the same coin, the phase consisting of all the cultural traits possessed by a particular subpeople. Hence, the term "phase" corresponds to "focus" in the midwestern taxonomic system (Table 3).

11
Combining peoples

Whether one is a lumper or a splitter, there will be similarities in culture among the peoples one distinguishes. These are taken into consideration by grouping together all peoples who share a considerable proportion of their diagnostic traits, that is, of their complexes. We may call such a grouping a *series* of peoples (Rouse and Cruxent, 1963, pp. 23–26) and shall refer to the diagnostics shared by the peoples of a series as the *diagnostic tradition* of the series (Willey and Phillips, 1962, pp. 34–39).

Each series is named after a feature of its archeology in accordance with the rule prohibiting the use of historic names for prehistoric cultural groups. A common practice is to select the name of a typical people—often the one first distinguished—and to add the suffix "-oid." Thus, the Aurignacioid series of the Western World is named after the Aurignacian people (Chard, 1969b, pp. 128ff.) Alternatively, the series may be named after the region in which it existed, for example, Danubian, or after its diagnostic tradition, for example, the Megalithic series, referring to the peoples of western and northern Europe who built megalithic monuments (Chard, 1969b, p. 302). One may also speak of the peoples of the Aurignacioid, Danubian, or Megalithic tradition.

A series and its diagnostic tradition are sometimes considered to be two sides of the same coin, with one side referring to human individuals and the other side to the totality of the individuals' cultural characteristics, as in the case of a people and its culture or a subpeople and its phase of culture (Secs. 3.8 and 3.10). This is a false analogy, for a tradition includes only a small proportion of the traits present in a culture or phase of culture. The proper analogy is with a complex or subcomplex. Like them, a tradition comprises only diagnostic traits.

The other side of the coin formed by a series of peoples may be termed a *series of cultures*. Each such series is a heterogeneous unit, its constituent cultures being linked together only by the few traits that we call their tradition. A series of cultures can be given the same name as its corresponding series of peoples and its tradition, since the three are related concepts. Thus, we may speak of the Megalithic [series of] peoples, the Megalithic tradition, and the Megalithic [series of] cultures, provided that we limit the first to human beings, the second to diagnostic traits, and the third to cultural wholes.

12
Hierarchies of
cultural units

The discussion to this point is summarized in Table 4. We began with peoples, since they are the basic units of prehistoric research; then considered division of those units into subpeoples; and finally took up combination of the units into series. The diagnostics of the three kinds of units are known respectively as complexes, subcom-

TABLE 4   *Hierarchies of ordinary peoples*[1]

Hierarchical levels	Cultural groups	Diagnostics of the groups	Characteristics of the groups [2]
Basic units	People	Complex	Culture
Divisions of the basic units	Subpeoples	Different subcomplexes	Phases of a culture
Combinations of the basic units	Series of peoples	Common tradition	Series of cultures

[1] These hierarchies are called hierarchies of ordinary peoples in order to distinguish them from the hierarchies of civilized peoples shown in Table 5.
[2] See Clarke, 1968, p. 234 for a similar formulation.

plexes, and traditions, and we are calling the characteristics of the units cultures, phases of a culture, and series of cultures respectively.

Thus, we shall be dealing in this volume with a three-level hierarchy of cultural groups: subpeoples, peoples, and series of peoples. The procedure of forming peoples has already been discussed (Sec. 3.6). Subpeoples and series of peoples are formed in a similar manner. One begins by setting up a trial set of subcomplexes or traditions and uses them to classify one's cultural assemblages. If the trial set of subcomplexes or traditions does not produce a homogeneous set of classes, then the diagnostics must be revised and the classification repeated. This procedure is continued until the classes do become homogeneous. Each of the final classes will be indicative of a subpeople or a series—those who produced the assemblages assigned to the class—and each subcomplex or tradition will consist of the diagnostics that define the class.

As in the case of artifactual classification (Sec. 2.11), this procedure should be applied to individual assemblages, not to the classes of assemblages that are indicative of peoples. Only after classes indicative of subpeoples and of series of peoples have been formulated should they be correlated with the classes indicative of peoples. In this way, one will be able to avoid the taxonomic fallacy by establishing hierarchies that incorporate transitional subpeoples and peoples (as in Fig. 5b).

We shall see later (Secs. 6.1 and 6.8) that cultural hierarchies are ways of answering the question "How and why?" They establish continuities within a people or among peoples and thereby set the stage for study of the changes that have taken place along these continuities. The formulation of hierarchies in answer to the question "Who?" is thus preliminary to the subsequent study of change in answer to the final question "How and why?" (Fig. 6).

So far as the question "Who?" is concerned, the effect of placing two subpeoples within the same people or two peoples within the same series is only to indicate that they share a complex or tradition. So placing them does not tell us how or why this relationship happened. There are a number of possible ways in which any particular hierarchy may have arisen. In the case of a series, for example, the original people may have changed so many of its diagnostics that it transformed itself into a new people, while at the same time retaining enough of the diagnostics that it remained in the same tradition. Alternatively, the original people may have migrated to another area and have changed so much in adaptation to the new conditions that it became a new people, linked with their previous state only by a common tradition. A third possibility is that the original people's tradition was adopted by a neighboring people, causing the second people to become enough like the first people that it must be included in the same series. A decision among possibilities cannot be made until later in the strategy of prehistory, when answering the question "How and why?"

Viewed from this standpoint, the hierarchy of cultural phases, cultures, and series of cultures is a heuristic device that raises problems to be investigated during subsequent parts of the strategy of prehistoric research. In any particular instance, it may be advisable to reverse the strategy, for example, by postulating a migration from one place to another. One will then adopt the tactics of working back from the question "How and why?" to the question "Who?" It will still be necessary, in answering the latter question, to establish subpeoples, peoples, and series by means of cultural classification as a final check upon the validity of the postulated migration.

13 Co-peoples and co-cultures	Thus far, we have assumed that all prehistoric peoples were simple and homogeneous in culture. During most of prehistory they were, but some late prehistoric peoples had reached the stage of civilization and, as a result, had become culturally more complex. We must develop a special set of terms to deal with them.

A people may be said to have reached the stage of civilization when it has become divided into two coordinate residential groups, one consisting of agriculturalists who supply food for both groups and the other of specialists who focus upon nonessential activities, such as religion, burial, and trade (Rouse, 1971). For example, as the Classic Maya Indians of Yucatán advanced to civilization, their farmers apparently became so proficient and so well organized that they were able to supply not only their own needs, but also those of a developing group of specialists who lived in religious centers. The specialists were thereby enabled to develop a new configuration of cultural traits different from that among the farmers, including writing, astronomy, mathematics, monumental architecture, and sculpture, none of which seems to have been practiced in the farmers' villages (Willey, 1956, pp. 109–112).

We may refer to the farmers and the specialists as co-peoples, since they formed coequal divisions of the Classic Maya people, that is, of the group of individuals who possessed Classic Maya civilization. The farmers will be called a *sustaining co-people,* because they served to support the entire people, supplying it with the necessities of life. The specialists will be termed a *professional co-people,* since they included priests, scribes, merchants, craftsmen, and the members of other professions that developed in the religious centers (Sec. 5.10).

Despite the differences between the two Classic Maya co-peoples, they shared many cultural traits, such as pottery types, styles of clothing, and religious beliefs. Consequently it is possible to treat all the Classic Maya assemblages as a single class and to set up a complex of pottery traits that is diagnostic of that class (Fig. 7). The assemblages in the class are easily divided between the two co-peoples by separating those which contain evidences of sustaining activities from those with evidences of professional activities.

We may refer to the configuration of cultural traits possessed by each co-people as its *co-culture,* for each forms a coordinate part of Classic Maya civilization. A co-people and its co-culture comprise two sides of a coin, one referring to individual persons and the other to the cultural traits possessed by those persons, as in the case of an ordinary people and its culture (Sec. 3.8). Hence, we may say that the Classic Maya were divided into sustaining and professional co-peoples/co-cultures, which together constituted the Classic Maya people/civilization.

As the Classic Maya developed into the post-classic Maya, they began to increase in population, and eventually Mayapán, one of their ceremonial centers, became so heavily populated that it may be called a city (Willey, 1956, p. 113). This population increase, of course, changed the nature of the professional co-culture but did not affect the dichotomy between the professional and sustaining co-cultures; the former now became urban while the latter remained rural. Subsequently, the Spaniards destroyed the professional co-culture, replacing it with their own, but the Maya Indians still retain their original sustaining co-culture in a modified form.

Co-peoples/co-cultures such as these should not be confused with plural peoples/cultures, which were discussed earlier in the chapter (Sec. 3.4). Plural peoples/cultures are characterized by a common social structure, not by a common cultural complex. For example, the Amerinds of the United States are united only in their allegiance to the federal government. Each group has retained its own culture instead of adopting Western civilization. Such a situation is practically impossible to distinguish archeologically, since the cultures involved are linked by a social structure and not by common cultural traits.

Similarly, immigrants to the United States do not per se constitute distinct co-peoples/co-cultures. Sociologists customarily refer to immigrant groups as "subpeoples," but they use the term differently than in prehistory (Sec. 3.10). From the standpoint of the present volume, immigrant groups must be regarded as intrusive peoples/cultures, unless and until they are assimilated.

Hierarchies of co-peoples, co-cultures, and civilizations can be formulated in the same manner as hierarchies of ordinary peoples and cultures. Table 5 gives the terms that will be used for the purpose in this book.

14
Cultural
identification

When discussing archeological procedures in Section 2.7, we made a distinction between classification of artifacts or other remains, which the archeologist does in order to discover new classes, and identification, which is the process of assigning the remains to already established classes. This distinction is also applicable to the classification of assemblages. Thus, one may speak of cultural classification, whereby one distinguishes new classes of assemblages, and of cultural identification, whereby one assigns additional assemblages to already established classes.

But there is more to cultural classification and identification than the assignment of assemblages to classes. If they were no more than this, they would qualify as archeological procedures and should have been discussed in Chapter 2. The reason for discussing them here is that assemblages are assigned to classes, not for their own sake, but in order to discover and identify the peoples, co-peoples, or other kinds of cultural groups that made them (Fig. 7). It is this concern with cultural groups rather than the assemblages themselves that makes cultural classification a procedure of prehistory rather than archeology.

Doing cultural classification is a job for the prehistorian or for the archeologist who has been trained to practice prehistory, since it requires special knowledge and experience. Cultural identification, on the other hand, can easily be done by any archeologist, with or without special training in prehistory, and often is. It is a simple job for anyone with a good knowledge of the local archeology to attribute assemblages to established subpeoples, co-peoples, or other kinds of cultural groups by ascertaining that they have the proper subcomplexes, complexes, or traditions.

Cultural identification, then, is the procedure of finding out which cultural group produced a particular assemblage by noting the presence of the diagnostics of a previously recognized cultural group. Theoretically, it should be possible to construct a key for this purpose, like the keys constructed from types of artifacts (see Sec. 2.11). As another aid to identification, one might prepare an exhibit or an illustration of artifacts of each of the types and modes that distinguish a particular cultural group. Braidwood (1952, figs. 26, 27) has done this for the Uruk people in Mesopotamia. He calls it a "partial assemblage," but, as Goodwin (1953, p. 21) has pointed

TABLE 5   *Hierarchies of civilized peoples*

Hierarchical levels	Cultural groups		Diagnostics of the groups	Characteristics of the groups	
	Wholes	Coordinate parts		Wholes	Coordinate parts
Basic units	Civilized people	Co-people [1]	Complex	Civilization	Co-culture [2]
Divisions of basic units	Subpeoples	Co-subpeoples	Different subcomplexes	Phases of a civilization	Phases of a co-culture
Combinations of basic units	Series of peoples	Series of co-peoples	Common tradition	Series of civilizations	Series of co-cultures

[1] Each civilized people is divided into two or more co-peoples, only one of which is shown here as an example.
[2] Each civilization is similarly divided into two or more co-cultures.

out, it is not an assemblage in the sense in which the word is being used here, since it is not limited to material from a single site. The objects illustrated are taken from several sites—assemblages, in our terms—in order to illustrate the types of artifacts, including monuments, that recur from assemblage to assemblage and thus enable the prehistorian to attribute all of the assemblages to the Uruk people.

15
Morphological
groups

While the major part of the answer to the question "Who?" is provided by the superorganic groups known as subpeoples, co-peoples, peoples, and series, the prehistorian also needs to distinguish organic groups wherever and whenever it is feasible to do so. As we have seen (Sec. 3.3), these include not only the contemporary morphological groups known as races, but also higher units in the biological taxonomy: species, which are groupings of races, and genera, which are groupings of species.

Races differ fundamentally from species and the higher units in the biological taxonomy. They are enough alike that the members of one race can interbreed with the members of all other races belonging in the same species, unless prevented from so doing by a geographic barrier, such as a sea, or a superorganic norm, such as a taboo against miscegenation. In the absence of such obstacles to interbreeding, races tend to merge or to become indistinct. By definition, the members of different species do not interbreed, and this fact makes them sharply distinct and competitive, contrary to races.

All contemporary human beings belong to races within the so-called human species, *Homo sapiens*. However, as one moves back into the early part of prehistory, one encounters increasingly greater differences within mankind, and, at the beginning of prehistory, the differences are so great that all authorities assign the various finds of man to different species, if not genera. Unfortunately, there is no way to determine which forms of early man actually do belong in different species, since all these forms are now extinct and cannot be tested for interbreeding. As Buettner-Janusch (1966, Table 10.2) has noted, some of the authorities are "lumpers" and others are "splitters," just as in the case of cultural classification (Sec. 3.9).

The procedure used by prehistorians to distinguish races has changed in recent years. Previously, human races were formed by selecting a single skeleton to serve as the "type" and grouping with it all similar skeletons, regardless of their provenance. Now, however, students of man (as well as students of the other animals) work with populations rather than with individual skeletons (Garn, 1965). They sample the local population by obtaining a number of skeletons from each of several different site-components. The skeletons from each site-component comprise an assemblage of morphological remains. Prehistorians group together the assemblages that look alike, thus establishing a class of assemblages, and define the class by listing its distinctive attributes.

This procedure for distinguishing races is identical to the procedure for distinguishing peoples, except that it is applied to morphological rather than cultural remains (see Table 2). Indeed, Figure 7, which illustrates the results of cultural classification, can also be used to illustrate the results of morphological classification simply by making three substitutions: "morphological" for "cultural" in the explanation of the bottom two circles, "race" for "people" in the upper left circle, and "morphology" for "culture" in the upper right circle.

The procedure may be called *morphological,* as opposed to cultural, *classification.* Similarly, we may refer to the traits diagnostic of each class of assemblages as its *morphological complex.* The morphological complexes serve to identify additional assemblages of the class, and hence of the race, just as cultural complexes are used to identify additional assemblages of a people (Sec. 3.14).

Morphological classification and identification are subject to the same limitations as the corresponding cultural procedures. Neither of them should be applied to single skeletons (although they often are, for lack of better evidence); they will yield valid results only when applied to sufficiently large assemblages of skeletal materials. They should not be applied, either, to mixed assemblages, resulting from the mingling of two different racial groups, or to transitional assemblages, situated on the boundary between two racial groups, where interbreeding across the boundary is likely to have produced a combination of racial traits quite different from those in the centers of distribution of the two races (Fig. 8b). As in the case of cultural classification, mixed or transitional assemblages may not be noticeable until the prehistorian has continued on to answer the questions "Where and when?" and "What?" However, he must correct for these conditions when he discovers them. Finally, the prehistorian must be wary of applying the names of contemporary or historic races to prehistoric races, just as he is wary of applying the names of contemporary or historic peoples to prehistoric peoples, because he cannot be sure until he has completed his study by answering the question "How and why?" whether the prehistoric group is, in fact, the same as any historic or contemporary group.

The nomenclature for races parallels that for peoples. The name of a race may refer either to its geographic or temporal location, as when we speak of the Caucasoid or European race; to a diagnostic of the members of the group, as when we refer to the Negro race; or to a typical site, often the one in which the race was first distinguished, as in the case of the Neanderthal race (Garn, 1965; Pilbeam, 1970, pp. 186–190).

Just as peoples are divided into subpeoples and grouped into series, so races may be divided into *subraces* and grouped into *series of races*. There is a parallel nomenclature, too; for example, series are commonly designated by the suffix "-oid." All these units should be formulated typologically in order to avoid the taxonomic fallacy (Sec. 3.12), and one should take care not to confuse the units with cognitive races, based upon contemporary conditions (Sec. 3.7).

The procedures used to distinguish and name species and larger morphological groups need not be discussed, since these have been adopted from biology. They may be studied in the standard textbooks on biological taxonomy.

The prehistorian's task is to identify the subraces, races, series of races, species, and genera to which each of his peoples belong and, if necessary, to distinguish new morphological groups by means of the classificatory procedures discussed above. The importance of this task is greatest when one is studying the early part of prehistory, for that was the period during which man evolved into the species *Homo sapiens*. When one is concentrating on the period after this species had become universal, when the only physical differences were racial, there is less to learn by studying morphological groups. The specialist in the late prehistory of Europe or the Americas pays relatively little attention to races, since the populations he studies were morphologically quite homogeneous. On the other hand, races do play a role in the late prehistory of Africa, Asia, and Oceania, for there the populations were morphologically as well as culturally heterogeneous.

SUPPLEMENTAL READING

BEATTIE, JOHN, *Other Cultures* (1964), pp. 34–64.

CHILDE, V. GORDON, *Piecing Together the Past* (1956), pp. 111–134.

GARN, STANLEY M., *Human Races* (1965).

GREENBERG, JOSEPH H., *Anthropological Linguistics: An Introduction* (1968).

PIGGOTT, STUART, *Approach to Archaeology* (1965b), pp. 76–100.

TAYLOR, WALTER W., *A Study of Archaeology* (1967b), pp. 111–149.

WAINWRIGHT, F. T., *Archaeology and Place-names and History* (1962).

WILLEY, GORDON R., AND PHILIP PHILLIPS, *Method and Theory in American Archaeology* (1962), pp. 21–24, 29–40.

4

CHRONOLOGICAL ORDERING

After distinguishing cultural and morphological groups, the prehistorian is faced with the problem of arranging these units in a systematic manner. Since cultural groups are so much better grounded in fact, he uses them as the basis for his ordering system and fits morphological groups into the system after it has been established. Hence, in the present chapter we shall deal primarily with cultural groups, deferring consideration of morphological groups to the end of the chapter.

The immediate problem is how to order the three kinds of cultural groups—subpeoples, peoples, and series. The prehistorian is governed in his solution to this problem by the fact that he approaches our cube of knowledge through its front face (Fig. 1). He organizes the groups according to their positions on this face, fitting them into a chronology based upon space and time, the dimensions of the face (Kroeber, 1962). Thus he shifts from the question "Who?" to the question "Where and when?"

The prehistorian's use of chronology as his ordering device runs counter to the practice in natural history of fitting organic groups on the level of species and above into phylogenies, consisting of branching lines of development. As we shall see later (Sec. 6.7), phylogenies are not delineated on the front face of the cube, in the dimensions of space and time, as chronologies are; instead they are delineated on the side face, in the dimensions of form and time. In effect, the natural historian uses the dimensions of form and time, rather than space and time, as his ordering devices.

The natural historian is able to do this because species and the larger units in his hierarchy have developed along independent lines, kept distinct by the lack of interbreeding among organisms that belong to different lines, so that space per se cannot be a factor in development of the lines (Sec. 2.11). A few prehistorians in the United States have attempted to emulate the natural history procedure by arranging subpeoples, peoples, and series phylogenetically, but they have failed (Brew, 1946). Cultural groups are not kept distinct by barriers against interbreeding, as are species and genera; instead, cultural groups exchange norms with neighboring groups, often to such a degree that they lose their separate identities and merge to form new groups (Sec. 6.7). As a result, space *is* a major factor in their development and must be used as an organizing principle.

The natural historian himself has to forego the phylogenetic approach when he moves below the level of species to that of race. Interbreeding does occur among races, and so they, like cultural groups, cannot be fitted into phylogenetic lines (Sec. 6.7). Races, whether of the lesser animals or of man, must instead be fitted into chronologies (e.g., Brace, 1967).

The chronological approach is also used by the historian, since he, too, is dealing with divisions of the human species (*Homo sapiens*). The ethnologist follows suit, except that he concentrates on the dimension of space, since for him the dimension of time is zero. He fits his groups into systems of cultural areas (e.g., Wissler, 1923, pp. 55–61), and, if he deals with time at all, he takes it up at the close of his strategy by turning to historical reconstruction, in which case he moves out of the role of ethnologist and into that of prehistorian (Sapir, 1951, pp. 392–393).

The prehistorian, then, orders his systematic units by fitting them into chronologies instead of combining them to form phylogenies. He may work solely with subpeoples, peoples, or series of peoples (Table 4), or with a level of the corresponding hierarchy of co-peoples (Table 5). Alternatively, he may use any combination of the foregoing categories. These options would not be available to him if he were setting up a phylogeny, for in that case he would have to use his hierarchies as the basis for ordering his cultural groups.

In order to simplify the following discussion, we shall proceed as if only peoples are organized into chronologies. The reader should bear in mind, however, that it is equally possible to work with subpeoples, with co-peoples, or with any other kind of cultural group. (If this book were concerned with a single region, it would be better to give priority to subpeoples, for reasons that have been noted in Sec. 3.9.)

2
Relative and absolute dating

The first part of our question "Where and when?" may be answered either by saying that a particular people lived in such and such places or by plotting the people's distribution on a map. In the former case, one gives a verbal answer to the question and in the latter case, a graphic answer.

"When?" may be answered in the same two ways. One may either say that a people lived in such and such times, or one may plot the people's distribution on a chronology.

Maps and chronologies are comparable devices. A map consists of features and other entities plotted with respect to the two dimensions of geographic space. A chronology, as the term will be used here, is simply a modification of a map in which the dimension of time has been substituted for one of the dimensions of space, as in our Figure 1. The distribution of peoples can therefore be plotted on a chronology in the same way as on a map.

Maps are subject to distortion because the convex surface of the earth has to be adapted to a flat surface. Chronologies are subject to a different kind of distortion, depending upon whether one uses an absolute or a relative method of dating.

Absolute dating is that which places a people in its exact position in time with reference to a universal time scale, applicable throughout the world. It follows from this definition that all events that are given the same absolute date will actually be contemporaneous, regardless of the parts of the world in which they took place.

Absolute dates are usually expressed in terms of the local calendar. If, for example, a historian is studying Christian peoples, he will be able to obtain absolute dates B.C. or A.D. from their documents. If, on the other hand, the people under study were Jews, the dates would be given in years since the Creation (3761 B.C.), and if Arabs, in terms of years before or after the Hegira, or flight of Muhammad from Mecca (622 A.D.). Such dates can either be converted into Christian dates or can be expressed in terms of the number of years before the present (B.P.). The latter practice is favored by many scientists, because it provides a cross-cultural measure of time. Nevertheless, the Christian calendar continues to be used by European and American historians, because their readers are accustomed to it, and this practice will be followed here. For us, as for the historian, absolute time will be expressed in years B.C. and A.D.

The reason the Christian calendar can be used as an expression of absolute time is that it is based upon astronomical events, such as the movements of the earth and the moon, which take place more or less simultaneously throughout the world. Hence, dates expressed in the Christian calendar are equally applicable to all parts of the world and can be used as a universal measure of time.

Relative dating, on the contrary, gives the time of an event such as the deposition of an assemblage with reference to another event that is not worldwide, as when we say that a particular assemblage was deposited during the Renaissance or the Ice Age. By "Renaissance" is meant the time of revival of Greek and Roman learning after the Middle Ages. But this revival took place some years later in France than in Italy and was later still in England. Conversely, the Ice Age began earlier and lasted longer in northern than in central Europe, because the continental ice sheet originated in Scandinavia and advanced to and retreated from central Europe at a very slow rate. All relative dates vary in absolute time from place to place, because they are based upon innovations that have spread from one place to another, and spreading takes time.

Another characteristic of relative dates is that they are limited to parts of the earth's surface. For example, we can speak of the age of the Renaissance in relation to Europe but not in relation to Africa, Asia, or the New World. Similarly, the Ice Age can be distinguished only in northern latitudes. One of the problems in working with relative dates is to correlate those based upon innovations or other events that took place in different parts of the world.

It is sometimes assumed that all chronological charts are relative, because they show the temporal position of one people's assemblages relative to the assemblages of other peoples. This relativity is not the significant point, however. What matters is the manner in which the dimension of time has been marked off on the chart. If there are dates B.C. and A.D. along the side, providing a calendrical measure of the dimension of time, then the chart is absolute. If, instead, the dimension is marked off by means of innovations or other less than universal events, such as the Bronze Age, then the chart is relative.

The historian works primarily with absolute time expressed verbally by means of calendrical dates, as in the examples given above. Relative dating is less important to him, but he uses it, as we have seen, expressing it verbally rather than graphically.

In the absence of written records, from which a verbal expression of dates can be obtained, the prehistorian must work graphically. He starts with a graphic chronology, on which he plots the temporal positions of his peoples in the same way that he plots their geographic positions on a map. He must base the plotting of temporal positions on inference, however, whereas he is able accurately to measure geographic positions.

When prehistorians first began to work with graphic chronologies, they made them relative; that is, they expressed the dimension of time in terms of relative periods such as the Bronze and Iron Ages. Eventually, they developed absolute charts, with dates B.C. and A.D. along the sides. Now it is customary to work primarily with absolute charts and to use relative ages in a supplementary manner, as in the case of historians (e.g., Ehrich, 1965, p. v). The calendrical dates, like the charts to which they are attached, are still inferential, though, and will never be able to equal historic dates in accuracy and reliability.

The inferential nature of these chronologies is the reason for placing the question "Where and when?" second in the strategy of prehistoric research and not first. It is more logical to carry out the empirically based operation of cultural classification before proceeding to the inferential one of working out a chronological chart. Nevertheless, it may be good tactics to reverse this strategy and start with the question "Where and when?" if good chronological evidence happens to be available.

Here also is the reason why the second question is "Where and when?" rather than "When and where?" Either order would be equally possible for the historian, but it is advisable for the prehistorian to begin with the part of the question that he can answer empirically before proceeding to the part that requires inference.

3
Development of
chronological
research

The first attempt to work out prehistoric chronology took place simultaneously among the classical peoples of China and the Mediterranean region during the first millennium B.C. In China, Feng Hu Tzu, a philosopher of the Eastern Chou period (ca. 770–221 B.C.), theorized that man had passed through four "ages," in which he had successively learned to make artifacts of stone, jade, bronze, and iron (Chang, 1968, p. 2). The Chinese did not, however, test this hypothesis by means of archeological research.

Simultaneously, several Greek and Roman authors began to think along similar lines. In the eighth century B.C., for example, Hesiod, a Greek, postulated a sequence of golden, silver, bronze, heroic, and iron peoples, characterized by a steady decline in the conditions of life. The Roman poet Lucretius (98–55 B.C.) modified Hesiod's technological sequence and rejected his theory of decline. In *De Rerum Natura,* Lucretius theorized that man had at first made tools only of stone and wood, then had advanced to the use of bronze and to a more complex form of society, and finally had learned to make tools and weapons of iron (Phillips, 1964).

In effect, the classical writers divided the front face of our cube into three horizontal layers, consisting respectively of Stone, Bronze, and Iron Ages (Fig. 9a). They had no archeological basis for this division, so far as we know, but they had noticed that only bronze weapons are mentioned in the Homeric legends referring to the preclassical period. They also based their speculations on descriptions by Herodotus (ca. 480–425 B.C.) and others of the barbarians around the fringes of the classical world. Undoubtedly they tended to assume, like modern prehistorians and ethnologists, that conditions among the barbarians approximated those among their own predecessors.

These speculations were temporarily forgotten after the fall of the Roman empire, along with the rest of classical scholarship.

FIGURE 9. *Development of cultural chronologies: (a) classical, (b) medieval, (c) Renaissance, (d) Victorian, (e) modern. (a) to (d) are relative chronologies; (e) is absolute. In (e), A_{1-3} = local areas, P_{1-5} = peoples, and I–III = general periods. Each general period consists of three contemporaneous local periods, which are demarcated by combinations of dotted and (where the boundaries of periods and peoples coincide) solid lines.*

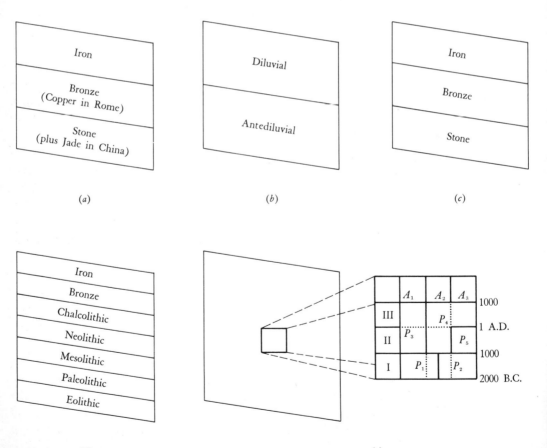

(a)   (b)   (c)

(d)   (e)

Medieval Europeans based their ideas of man's past on a strict interpretation of the Bible, dividing prehistory into only two epochs, antediluvial and diluvial, before and during Noah's flood (Fig. 9b).

With the coming of the Renaissance, a number of writers revived the Stone-Bronze-Iron sequence (Fig. 9c). Michael Mercati, superintendent of the Vatican Botanical Gardens in the late sixteenth century, was the most convincing of these writers. He supported Lucretius' classical sequence by citing the Biblical account of the introduction of iron into Bronze Age Palestine by the Philistines and by noting the variable occurrences of stone, bronze, and iron tools in the ethnographic collections that were being sent to the Vatican from Asia and America (Clarke, 1968, pp. 6–7).

It remained for Christian J. Thomsen, a Dane, to document the classical sequence archeologically. In 1816–1819 he arranged the artifacts that had accumulated in the Royal Danish Museum of Antiquities (now the National Museum of Denmark) in order of the Stone, Bronze, and Iron Ages (Ellesmere, 1848, p. 69). For this action, he justly deserves the title of "father of prehistory." His system of ages still forms the basis of the local chronology, though, as we shall see, it has been superseded in much of the rest of the world.

Beginning in the 1830s, a Frenchman named Boucher de Perthes began to collect stone axes of a more primitive kind than the celts from the terraces along the river Somme. These axes were roughly chipped into shape, lacked the grinding that is characteristic of the celts, and were so much larger and thicker as to suggest that they had been held in the hand instead of being hafted like celts. Hence, Boucher de Perthes called them *"coups de poing,"* or "hand axes." He concluded that they had been deposited during the formation of the river terraces, at a considerably earlier time than that of the deposition of the celts. His conclusions were summarily rejected by the savants of the early nineteenth century, who could not conceive of the existence of man before Biblical time. Nevertheless, Boucher de Perthes persisted and gradually gained converts. By the middle of the century it had become clear that the hand axes belonged to a part of the Stone Age earlier than that of the celts. In 1865, John Lubbock (later Lord Avebury) proposed that the term "Paleolithic" (literally "Old Stone") be applied to the age when only hand axes and other chipped stone tools were made and the term "Neolithic" ("New Stone") to the age when celts and other ground-stone tools became dominant (Avebury, 1900, pp. 2–3).

Subsequent finds led to further revision of the system of ages. A controversial Eolithic (Dawn of Stone) age was placed before the Paleolithic to account for stones that seemed to have been used by man with little or no modification; a Mesolithic (Middle Stone) age was inserted between the Paleolithic and the Neolithic to take care of remains transitional between the two; and a Chalcolithic (Copper Stone) age was put between the Neolithic age and the Bronze Age in order to account for other transitional remains, characterized by tools of copper but not of bronze. This produced the sequence shown in Figure 9*d,* which became standard during the first part of the twentieth century (Daniel, 1943, pp. 24–28).

Up to this point, prehistoric research had been concentrated in western and northern Europe. The only other parts of the world that had been intensively excavated were Argentina and the United States, and the finds there appeared to be so recent as to have no chronological significance. It was assumed that when earlier remains would be discovered in other parts of the world, they would fit into the European sequence. In other words, the European chronology was thought to extend all the way across the front face of our cube of knowledge. The lines had to be slanted somewhat, in order to account for the slowness of cultural development among the more remote, non-Western peoples, but nevertheless it was taken for granted that all peoples of the world had passed or would pass through the succession of periods shown in Figure 9*d.*

World War I and its aftermath provided an opportunity to test this hypothesis. Archeologists accompanied the Allied troops into the Middle East and the Balkans in a pioneer effort to conserve remains, and they continued to work there after the war. At the same time, the new governments established after the war, especially the Soviet Russian and Nationalist Chinese regimes, developed programs of prehistoric research, and the British and French extended their own programs into their African and Asian colonies. As a result, archeological material became available in many hitherto neglected regions.

Contrary to expectation, the new material did not fit into the system of ages that had been established during the Victorian era.

For example, it proved difficult to distinguish between the Chalcolithic age and the Bronze Age in Egypt. The two do not occur anywhere else in Africa, and they also are lacking from Northeast Asia and Oceania. Similarly, the flint blades that characterize the late Paleolithic age of Europe are replaced by different kinds of tools in sub-Saharan Africa, the Far East, Australia, and the New World. Consequently, prehistorians have had to abandon the assumption that the Victorian chronology is generally applicable, though they continue to use it in Europe and in adjacent regions. They have belatedly recognized the principle that relative dates must be geographically delimited (Sec. 4.2).

There is one exception. Soviet prehistorians and their followers in eastern Europe continue to regard the Victorian scheme as a general, and hence absolute, chronology. They are obliged to maintain this point of view by their belief in Marxian theories of cultural evolution. Marx himself was a Victorian and, like his contemporaries, assumed the unilinear development of culture. He regarded communism as the latest stage in the development, succeeding capitalism, and considered it inevitable that all peoples of the world, including those of the United States, would eventually progress from the stage of capitalism to that of communism. If the Soviet prehistorians were to admit that some peoples have passed through a different set of ages than others, they would be conceding that no cultural development is inevitable and hence that communism is not a necessary consequence of capitalism. This concession would be heresy. To avoid it, Soviet and East European prehistorians continue to adhere to the Victorian conception of chronology. Fortunately, they are saved from conflict with their archeological evidence by the fact that their own countries are within the region to which the Victorian chronology is applicable.

Conflicts with the data do arise, however, in connection with subdivisions of the Victorian chronology. For example, the Victorians had divided the Paleolithic age into a series of periods: Chellean, Acheulean, Micoquean, Mousterian, Aurignacian, Solutrean, and Magdalenian. Eastern prehistorians continue to regard these as universal categories, whereas the Western prehistorians have found it necessary to reformulate them as peoples, each with a relatively limited distribution in space as well as time, in order to account for the new data that have accumulated since World War I.

This necessity illustrates a second change in the Western approach to chronology. Having recognized that ages are an expression of relative time, Western prehistorians now relegate them to a secondary position, as historians do, and devote most of their time to new methods, based upon the study of peoples, that are designed to produce estimates of absolute, rather than relative, time.

The British prehistorian V. Gordon Childe pioneered the new approach in a classic study, originally published in 1925, of the spread of civilization from the Near East into Europe (Childe, 1964). First he distinguished the late prehistoric peoples of Europe and identified their assemblages. Then he delimited the peoples' boundaries by plotting the distribution of their assemblages and determined their temporal succession, relative to one another, by working out the order of deposition of their assemblages, using techniques to be discussed later in this chapter. Finally, he was able to draw up a chronology of the kind diagrammed in Figure 9e, in which a part of the earth's surface—Europe in Childe's case—is divided into a series of local areas, A_1, A_2, A_3, . . . ; the resident peoples, P_1, P_2, P_3, . . . , are placed in these areas in their temporal order relative to one another; and the peoples are then moved up and down in terms of various criteria until they reach their presumed absolute positions. Childe placed a sequence of arbitrary periods, I, II, III, . . . , on the left side of the chart as a measure of absolute time. (These took the place of calendrical dates, which he was unable to calculate with any accuracy.) He supplemented the chronological chart with a series of maps showing the distribution of peoples period by period (Childe, 1964, pp. 346–352).

Childe's chart and maps set the pattern for subsequent chronological research by West Europeans. Childe himself applied the approach more systematically and in greater detail in his *The Danube in Prehistory* (1929), and he extended it to the Near East in a study of the rise of civilization there (Childe, 1952). His great contribution was that, in searching for absolute time, he reversed the procedure that had prevailed during the Victorian era (and is still followed in communist countries). Instead of ascribing absolute values to the Victorian chronology and using these values to determine the ages of archeological assemblages, he started with the assemblages and inferred absolute time by ordering them in terms of the peoples that had produced them. Thus he applied to chronological research the principle that prehistoric interpretation must be derived from archeological evidence (Sec. 2.1).

Nevertheless, Childe did not completely abandon the Victorian approach. Being a Marxist, he believed in the uniformity of cultural evolution, assumed that the Victorian sequence correctly expresses the way in which culture has evolved throughout the world, and refined and elaborated it from this point of view in a number of publications (e.g., Childe, 1946b, 1951, 1963). For him, Paleolithic, Mesolithic, Neolithic, and so forth, were not only "ages," but also "stages" (Childe, 1956, p. 85), to be used not only as a measure of time, but also as an expression of the degree of cultural development among all mankind.

Other West Europeans have preferred to continue the use of the Victorian sequence solely as a measure of relative time. Some have put the names for the ages along the left side of their chronological charts, thereby converting the charts from absolute to relative time (e.g., Mellaart, 1965, fig. 1). Others have explicitly or implicitly inserted the names in the body of each chart, so that the ages are marked off in absolute time. The latter procedure is recommended here (Fig. 10).

Let us now look at the manner in which prehistorians south of the Sahara have answered the question "Where and when?" L. S. B. Leakey pioneered in that area with his *Stone Age Africa* (1936). Like Childe in Europe, he worked with peoples (he called them "cultures"). He divided the continent into areas, laid these out across the top of a chronological chart, and placed the names of the peoples in the body of the chart in the order of their appearance. On the side of the chart he put geologic rather than cultural periods; but he and the other Africanists subsequently decided that cultural periods were also needed. They rejected the European ages because they do not fit the African evidence and in their place developed a new and purely African sequence: Earlier Stone Age, First Intermediate, Middle Stone Age, Second Intermediate, and Later Stone Age. These ages are now placed on the left side of the African charts, along with the geologic periods. Here, we shall instead move the ages into the bodies of the charts in accordance with the model shown in Figure 10. This model gives a better picture of the overlaps in time that are inherent in a relative chronology; for example, in the body of a chart it is possible to show the survival of the Later Stone Age alongside the Iron Age in South Africa and to outline the geographic as well as the temporal boundary between the two.

In the New World, chronological research began during the late nineteenth century with attempts to apply the Victorian sequence of ages to archeological remains in the United States and Argentina. The attempts failed, and as a result the Americanists concluded that man had only been in the western hemisphere for a few thousand years—not long enough to produce remains like those of

FIGURE 10. *The kind of ethnic chronology recommended in the present volume: A_{1-3} = local areas. P_{1-6} = peoples. $R_{1,2}$ = races. Absolute time is expressed by the calendrical dates on both sides of the chart. Relative time is expressed by Ages$_{1-3}$, which are delineated by the dotted lines. Each dotted line marks the first appearance of the innovation used to define an age. The solid lines indicate the maximum extent of a people's distribution in the dimensions of space and time. (Subpeoples, series of peoples, or co-peoples may be substituted for peoples, and societies or speech communities may be substituted for races.)*

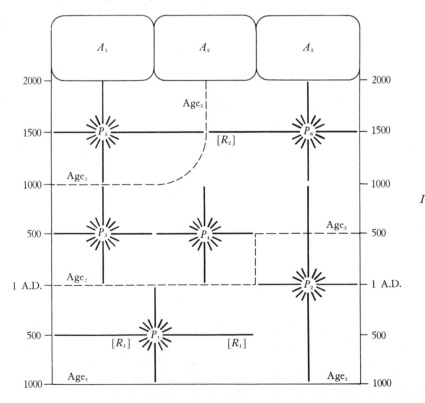

the prehistoric European ages. It never occurred to Americanists to question the assumption on which they were operating—that earlier remains would have to be like those in the Old World because cultural development is unilineal—and to look for earlier remains of different kinds in accordance with the principle of relativity in cultural development.

Belief in the recency of the American Indian persisted throughout the first part of the twentieth century, precluding any attempt to formulate an overall set of ages, comparable to the Victorian chronology. When Americanists turned again to chronology, after World War I, they worked with peoples in an effort to infer absolute time, as in Childe's contemporaneous European research. A. V. Kidder initiated this approach in 1924 with the publication of his *An Introduction to the Study of Southwestern Archaeology* (Kidder, 1962). A conference in 1927 at Pecos, the site he was digging, systematized his efforts as the so-called Pecos classification, consisting of a series of eight "stages": Basketmaker I-III, followed by Pueblo I-V. Several of these stages have since had to be redefined, but the overall sequence has been well substantiated, especially by the technique of dendrochronology (tree-ring analysis) that will be discussed later in this chapter. In addition, the southwesterners have come to realize that the Pecos classification applies only to a single "basic culture," Anasazi. They now recognize other basic cultures in the Southwest, each with its own set of stages (Rouse, 1962, pp. 4–9).

In our terminology, each southwestern stage is a people or a culture and each basic culture is a series of peoples or a tradition, depending upon the side of the coin that is under study (Sec. 3.8). The southwesterners have gone on to distinguish subtraditions, which they call "branches," and subpeoples, which they call "phases" (Olson, 1962), but these are too detailed to be considered in the present book. For our purposes, it is enough to know that the southwestern peoples (stages) and series (basic cultures) are now being fitted into chronological charts, with areal subdivisions across the top and calendrical dates along the sides (e.g., Rouse, 1962, figs. 1, 3). The midwestern "foci" and southeastern "phases," which were discussed in Section 3.5, are being treated in a similar fashion.

Despite the recent discovery of early remains in the New World, which push the time of man's first arrival back from the last few millenniums to a period contemporaneous with the latter part of the Paleolithic age in Europe, American prehistorians have not yet attempted to set up a system of ages like those in Europe, based upon single technological innovations. They have only worked with stages, expressing the degree of cultural development, as Childe did in Europe (see, e.g., Willey and Phillips, 1962, fig. 2).

Our abbreviated survey of the development of chronological research has shown that once again, as in the case of ethnic classification, different procedures and different terminologies have arisen in Europe, Africa, and sections of the United States. If we were to continue into other parts of the world, we would find even more variation. We have sketched out a single, standardized procedure that will be used throughout the present book in an effort to keep the reader from being confused by the local variations. It remains to explain this procedure and to develop a standard terminology for use with it.

4
Cultural
chronologies

First, we need a name for the charts constructed to show the geographic and temporal distributions of peoples (Fig. 10). They will be called *cultural chronologies*. The term "cultural" indicates that the purpose of each chart is to date cultural groups. The term "chronology" signifies that each chart is, in effect, a section of the front or chronological face of our cube of knowledge (Fig. 1).

Ideally, we ought to draw up a single chart covering the entire prehistoric part of the front face, but the situation is much too complex for such a chart. Instead, we shall have to deal successively with sections of the face. These will be so delimited that each is restricted to the peoples most closely interrelated by prehistoric events, as was the case when Childe drew up a cultural chronology in order to facilitate his study of the spread of civilization into Europe (Sec. 4.3).

In our overall cube of knowledge, the dimensions of space and time are absolute; that is, space is divisible into finite areas that can be measured in square miles and time into finite periods that can be dated in years B.C. and A.D. If these dimensions were not absolute, the lines marking the first appearance of man and the beginning of written history would be horizontal. They are slanted in order to indicate that each innovation took place at a different time in different parts of the world.

It follows that our partial chronologies must also express absolute time. They are made to perform this function by fitting peoples into them with reference to more than one innovation. If, for example, peoples were to be arranged in a sectional chronology only in terms of the invention and spread of writing, they would form a sloping horizon, lowest where writing was invented and increasingly higher along the route of diffusion from that place, as in Figure 1. If, then, the peoples were rearranged in order of a second innovation, such as bronze working, the horizon would slope in a different direction, since bronze metallurgy originated among a different people than writing and spread by other routes. Arrangement of the peoples in terms of a third innovation, such as painted pottery, would produce a horizon inclined in still another way. If, then, all these arrangements were combined, their various inclinations would cancel one another out, leaving the peoples in a level horizon approximating absolute time.

This arrangement of peoples in terms of a number of innovations is the principle underlying cultural chronologies. The names of individual peoples are placed in the proper geographic columns of a chart in their chronological order and are moved up and down the columns in terms of cultural innovations that appear to have spread from one to another until they are in positions that approximate absolute time. To be sure, the positions are only approximate, but they are the best the prehistorian can do in the absence of written records.

Positioning a people in a cultural chronology is like plotting that group on a map. Just as a map indicates the points on the earth's surface occupied by the people, so a chronology shows the people's successive occurrences through time, and just as the map is provided with a scale in yards or meters with which to measure the distances between the people's sites, so the chronology is provided with a scale in years B.C. and A.D. with which to date the people's occurrences.

A fivefold sequence is required to set up a cultural chronology: (1) The prehistorian distinguishes a series of local areas, each of which will ultimately be represented in the chronological chart as a single column. (2) He arranges the peoples of each local area in chronological order; that is, he fits them into a local sequence. (3) He puts the local sequences into the columns of a chronological chart and moves the constituent peoples up and down in terms of the innovations that have affected them until all the contemporaneous peoples are on the same level, insofar as can be determined, and until the vertical distances between peoples most closely approximate elapsed time. In other words, he synchronizes the local sequences by moving them into their proper positions in absolute time. (4) He places estimates of years B.C. and A.D. alongside the chart in order to date the peoples' occurrences as shown in the body of the chart. (5) Finally, if he desires, he may show the relative ages of the peoples by drawing lines along the points in time when each age gave way to its successor. These lines will normally be curved, since the absolute value of an age varies from place to place.

The above five steps will be described in turn. First, however, let us consider several possible alternatives to cultural chronologies.

5
Other kinds of
chronologies

It is not uncommon for the layman to speak of dating sites or, if he is more sophisticated, assemblages. This is a logical impossibility. We cannot date a site or assemblage because it is still in existence. (If it were not, we would be unable to study it.)

To say that we date a site or assemblage is like saying that we date a person who is still alive. We can give the date when that person was born, the date when he married, and the dates of other events in his life, but we cannot ascribe a single date to him because he has lived through a series of dates. To be sure, we can say how old he is, but even his age cannot be determined without first establishing the date of his birth.

So it is with a site, an assemblage, or any other purely archeological unit. We cannot determine when it existed; we can only say when various events associated with it took place and, from these events, calculate its age. This is the reason dating was not discussed in connection with archeology (Chap. 2). What is dated is not assemblages per se but the various acts that produced and modified them. These involve people, and hence dating is, by our definition, a part of prehistory rather than archeology.

The acts that have produced an assemblage are many and varied

(Rouse, 1967, table 1). The all-inclusive act is that of occupation of a site, either by a single people or by successive peoples, but occupation subsumes a number of more specific acts such as burial, consumption of materials, and manufacture and use of equipment. Natural acts such as stream deposition, glaciation, and occupation of the site by wild plants and animals may also have left an imprint on the assemblages.

A cultural chronology serves to date the peoples' acts in occupying their sites. We might instead want to date the peoples' activities, such as the manufacture of artifacts of a certain type, in which case we should have to set up a chronology of another kind, which may be called an *artifactual chronology*.

Artifactual chronologies could be set up in the same way as cultural chronologies. One would start with individual cultural norms, rather than peoples, put them into local sequences, and then synchronize the local sequences within a chronological chart (Ford, 1962). The first part of this procedure, working out local sequences, is a common practice, especially when dealing with pottery types, and, indeed, sequences of pottery types are often used as a basis for setting up local sequences of peoples. The second half of the procedure, synchronization of the types, is a more questionable practice, since it sharply limits the number of cultural innovations that can be used as the basis for synchronization. We have seen that every synchronization should be based upon as many innovations as possible in order to factor out the relativity inherent in each one and thereby arrive at the closest approximation of absolute time (Sec. 4.4). In synchronization of types the number of usable innovations can best be increased by converting the local sequences of types into sequences of peoples, for all the innovations will then be brought into consideration as parts of the peoples' cultures. To be sure, diagnostics will be emphasized at the expense of other aspects of culture, but there will be an opportunity to correct this imbalance later in the strategy of prehistory, after reconstruction of the peoples' cultures in answer to the question "What?" At that time, the synchronization can be checked against the reconstructed cultures, in accordance with the principle of feedback in the strategy of prehistoric research.

If there were better evidence of morphological, social, or linguistic groups, we could date the occurrences of such groups by constructing a *morphological, social,* or *linguistic chronology.* So poor is the evidence, however, that chronologies of this kind are only attempted by physical anthropologists, who project the evolution of the primates forward from geologic time into the early part of prehistory, and by ethnologists, who project social or linguistic groups of historic time back into prehistory. While one is working on the main part of prehistory, between these periods of transition, it is preferable to fit morphological, social, and linguistic groups into cultural chronologies. Once these groups have been added, we may say that the cultural chronologies have been converted into ethnic chronologies. An *ethnic chronology,* then, is a cultural chronology into which other kinds of ethnic groups have been inserted.

Geologists and biologists also have their own chronologies, which are known to prehistorians as *geochronologies* (G. Clark, 1960, pp. 138ff.). Since these date natural events, which may have affected the lives of peoples, it is often possible to correlate geochronologies and cultural chronologies. For instance, Pleistocene geologists have drawn up a series of charts with which to date glacial events in various parts of the world (Flint, 1971), and biologists have worked out a comparable series of climatic charts, based primarily upon the evidence of changes in temperature and moisture provided by pollen analysis (e.g., Movius, 1942, Table 6). Such geochronologies are helpful in setting up and synchronizing the local sequences within a cultural chronology; for example, the peoples of some local areas can be arranged in the order of the faunal succession in their areas. Conversely, cultural or artifactual chronologies are sometimes used as an aid in constructing geochronologies. A summary of the geochronology is often placed alongside a chart of cultural chronology, or vice versa, in order to indicate the relationship between the two, as in the case of Leakey's African chronology, cited above (Sec. 4.3).

It may be concluded that artifactual, morphological, social, linguistic, ethnic, and geo- chronologies are all useful adjuncts to cultural chronologies but cannot be used in their place. The fact is that the act of occupation by a people is the only event that is common to all prehistory and to all kinds of sites and that at the same time is well-documented archeologically. Certain events, such as the manufacture of pottery, are limited to particular regions and periods, while others, such as burials, tend to be found only in special sites. Still others, like a change in society or a natural event, are difficult to discern in the remains. It would be impossible, therefore, to use any of these kinds of events as the basis for chronological ordering. Only occupation by peoples can serve this purpose, and we shall therefore concentrate upon cultural chronologies in the following pages. Subsequently, at the close of the chapter, we shall discuss the procedures for converting cultural chronologies into ethnic chronologies.

6
Distinguishing
local areas

Distinguishing local areas is the logical first step in constructing a cultural chronology because it is the only part of the procedure that can be empirically carried out. One plots the distribution of one's sites on a map of the region chosen for study and demarcates the areas by drawing their boundaries on the map. Each area will then constitute a finite division of space and can serve as the basis for working out finite divisions of time within a chronological chart.

When one plots the geographic distribution of sites, one often finds that they fall into clusters, in which case each cluster may be treated as a separate area. If there is no clustering, the division into areas may be based upon features of the environment; for example, island groups, river valleys, or sections of coasts may be utilized as separate areas. These are more satisfactory than modern political units because the latter depend upon conditions that may not have been present during prehistoric time.

As in the case of cultural classification, one's choice of areas is a matter of judgment. The aim is to eliminate all geographic variation in the times of the local peoples' occurrences. Experience with historic peoples indicates that a people may vary in time from area to area. Thus, the Romans were earlier in Italy than in France and survived longest as a classical people in the Byzantine region.

It is also advisable to make the area small enough to eliminate variations in the time of occurrence of cultural norms. This objective will be a necessity if one is going to base the local sequence of peoples on a sequence of pottery types or other cultural innovations. The area must then be small enough to ensure that new modes, types, and so forth, were able to spread through it without any appreciable time lag.

In case of doubt, it is better to make the area smaller in order to reduce the possibility of local variation. One can always lump areas together at a later stage in the procedure if it turns out that they have been made too small.

7
Establishing
local sequences

After delineating local areas, the prehistorian proceeds to determine the order of occupation of each area by its respective peoples. There are three alternative ways in which he may determine this order: (1) he may work directly with the peoples' cultural assemblages, arranging them in a sequence; (2) he may work with individual types, modes, or other cultural norms, using them to establish an artifactual sequence with which to date the assemblages and thereby establish a cultural sequence; or (3) he may correlate the assemblages with a chronology of some other kind, such as a geochronology. Let us consider these three alternatives in turn.

CULTURAL DATING. The simplest and most reliable procedure is to search for a site that was successively occupied by all the local peoples, in the hope of being able to find their cultural assemblages lying on top of one another, in the order of their deposition. This situation is known as *stratigraphy.*

Geologists originated the stratigraphic method, and prehistorians have adopted it from them. If an assemblage deposited by People A is found overlying an assemblage deposited by People B, then it may be concluded that People A was later than People B—unless, of course, the stratigraphy has been reversed by subsequent disturbance of the site or there is reason to believe that the two peoples lived side by side, alternating at the site.

The method works best if assemblages of all the peoples under study can be found in a single stratigraphic column or in contiguous columns that can be empirically related. This configuration happens only among peoples who were permanently attached to their sites or kept coming back to them. For instance, the Neolithic, Bronze, and Iron Age peoples of the Near East rarely moved and, as a result, built up huge mounds, known as "tells," which contain assemblages deposited in stratigraphic succession over thousands of years. To construct a local sequence of late prehistoric peoples in the Near East, it is only necessary to trench a tell, distinguish its assemblages, work out their stratigraphic sequence, and identify the peoples who produced them. The same procedure can be used in studying the late Paleolithic peoples of western Europe, because those peoples were accustomed to take shelter in the mouths of caves, kept coming back to the same caves for thousands of years, and hence built up a more or less complete series of assemblages in stratigraphic order (G. Clark, 1960, pp. 121–125).

Once one has determined the stratigraphic sequence of peoples in a tell or cave, one can use this sequence to date the other remains in the local area. One need only identify the people that produced each assemblage and arrange the assemblages in order of the sequence of their peoples that has been stratigraphically demonstrated at the master site.

Unfortunately, most prehistoric peoples were not strongly attached to their sites, and hence long stratigraphic sequences are a rarity—much more so than in geology. Short sequences are the rule, and when found they must be related to one another by a different method, which is known as *seriation*.

This method is applicable only to peoples that belong to a single series. If they do, they will exhibit a distinctive pattern of cultural development. The prehistorian reconstructs this pattern and then proceeds to fit the cultures of the local peoples into the pattern, thereby determining the order in which they developed.

In reconstructing local patterns of cultural development, the prehistorian relies upon his knowledge of the ways in which cultures have developed in other parts of the world. If a pattern has already been established for a neighboring area, he may base his reconstruction upon it, on the assumption that the cultures in two adjacent areas are likely to have changed in a similar manner because of mutual influence.

A. V. Kidder used the technique of seriation in his pioneer attempt to set up a local sequence in the southwestern United States (Sec. 4.3). He assumed that the local Indians had developed through three "stages" characterized successively by (1) cave dwelling, a gathering economy, and the absence of religious structures; (2) simple, single-story masonry dwellings, an agricultural economy, and the beginnings of the religious structures known as "kivas"; and (3) fully developed, multistory dwellings, agriculture, and elaborate kivas. Subsequent research has proved him right, though only with reference to the Anasazi series of peoples.

It is important to note that seriation reveals only the order of peoples, not the direction of their order. Kidder happened to be dealing with peoples who had advanced in culture, but peoples do not always advance in culture. For instance, the late prehistoric peoples of the Indus Valley first advanced from copper metallurgy and village life to bronze working and urban life but then relapsed into their previous state (G. Clark, 1969, p. 216). Hence, it is not enough simply to seriate peoples in their order of development; one must also determine whether the order was progressive, regressive, or cyclical. One can make this determination by finding the remains of several peoples in stratigraphic succession; by correlating the developmental sequence with another kind of local sequence, whether it be typological, racial, social, or geochronological; or by obtaining absolute dates for a part of the series. In the Southwest, for example, Kidder had evidence that the people of stage 3 had been in existence since the arrival of the Spaniards in 1540, and hence he was justified in concluding that the series had proceeded in the direction of that stage. If the historic stage had been stage 1, he would have had to reverse the seriation.

Seriation is thus the opposite of stratigraphy. In stratigraphy, one builds up a sequence of peoples by inference from the superimposition of their assemblages. In seriation, on the contrary, one starts with the hypothesis of a sequence and must test this hypothesis against stratigraphy or other evidence. The validity of a seriation depends upon how well it has been tested out by means of other methods.

As we have already seen (Sec. 3.11), the concept of series and that of tradition, which is the other side of its coin, are answers to the question "How and why?" When the prehistorian resorts to seriation he is in effect using a special tactic in place of the normal strategy of prehistoric research, as it is diagrammed in Figure 6. He is entering the strategy at its end and must work backward by subsequently testing the seriation in terms of stratigraphy or other approaches that provide a direct answer to the question "Where and when?"

Quite apart from this observation, Kidder's southwestern seriation was effective only because the Anasazi peoples had a strong sense of tradition, which caused them to remain distinct as a series for nearly 2,000 years. If they had been more susceptible to influences from other peoples, they would have disappeared some time ago and it would then have been impossible to establish the local sequence of peoples solely by means of seriation. Shorter series are more common and, like short stratigraphies, have to be correlated by other means in order to work out entire sequences of peoples.

ARTIFACTUAL DATING. The procedure used in the absence of long stratigraphies or series of peoples is to set up a local sequence of types, modes, or other cultural norms. It is hoped that this sequence will cut across all stratigraphies, series, and unattached peoples in the area and so provide a basis for putting all of them in chronological order.

The artifactual approach is also useful in situations where prehistorians have not yet gotten around to the classification of assemblages in answer to the question "Who?" or where assemblages are difficult to distinguish. Among the Anasazi peoples, for example, it was customary to sweep out the houses regularly and deposit the sweepings in trash heaps. When one excavates these heaps, one finds good stratigraphy, but of pottery rather than assemblages, since potsherds are the principal component of the trash.

Artifactual dating is better done in terms of the category of type rather than mode, because types contain larger numbers of attributes and are therefore more reliable indicators of differences in time (Ford, 1962, p. 16). The types should be extrinsic, rather than intrinsic, since the aim is to elicit chronologically significant attributes (Sec. 2.10).

Potsherds and stone tools are most commonly used as time-markers because of their frequency, variability, and stylistic qualities. (Future archeologists will doubtless find automobiles to be the best time-markers for our own civilization.) The same two techniques can be applied to these artifacts as to assemblages, namely, stratigraphy and seriation.

If, for example, one decides to work with the stratigraphy of stone projectile points, one will search for deep sites where the local types occur in stratigraphic succession and will study the distribution of the types layer by layer or level by level. Normally, each of these units will yield projectile points of several different types, and the combination of types will vary from layer to layer or from level to level. One may then proceed to correlate each layer or level with those in other sites that have yielded similar types of projectile points, on the assumption that deposits that are marked by the same types must be contemporaneous. By continuing the procedure, one should eventually be able to build up a sequence of all the available deposits in the area, which can then be converted into a cultural sequence by identifying the peoples who made the deposits.

This procedure is similar to the one used by paleontologists to correlate natural deposits. They refer to the animal or plant species that characterize their layers as "type fossils." Childe (1956, p. 59) has applied the same phrase to the artifact types that distinguish cultural periods, but it would be more appropriate to call them "time-markers," since their function is to provide a measure of time. Within the limits of the local area, the types indicate absolute as well as relative time; that is, all deposits that are marked by the same types can be considered absolutely contemporaneous so long as they come from the local area, where, by definition, there should have been no time lag in the spread of the types.

In dealing with potsherds, which normally occur in large numbers, prehistorians have found that the relative popularity of types provides a more sensitive measure of time than presence versus absence. The percentages of pottery types normally vary from level to level in a stratigraphic column, and each level has its own distinctive set of percentages, indicating the relative popularity of each type at the time the level was laid down. Where this situation exists, the prehistorian proceeds to correlate each level with the ones at other sites that contain similar percentages of the same pottery types.

The assumption behind this procedure is that, other things being equal, the frequencies of pottery types vary in the same way throughout a local area, because the potters in that area have been led by the dictates of fashion to make pottery of the same types and frequencies at the same time. This assumption has been tested by studying the relative popularity of precisely dated historic and modern types of pottery and other artifacts, such as grave stones, and the technique has been found to be valid (Goggin, 1968; Deetz, 1967, pp. 26–33).

To this point, we have been concerned with the stratigraphic succession of types, whether in terms of occurrences or frequencies. Unfortunately, types are not always in stratigraphic succession, nor are all stratigraphies complete enough to be used as the bases for establishing the entire sequence of peoples within an area. Under such circumstances, the prehistorian is forced, as in the case of cultural dating, to fall back on the technique of seriation.

As we have seen, seriation is the reverse of stratigraphy. One starts by postulating a pattern of typological change, often by analogy to one already worked out for a neighboring area, and then tests this pattern against the archeological record. In effect, one shifts one's tactics. Instead of attempting directly to answer the question "Where and when?" by working with stratigraphies, one enters the strategy via the final question, "How and why?" One establishes a pattern of typological change in answer to that question and then uses it to answer the question "Where and when?" The pattern may be one of occurrences, of frequencies, or of development (Rouse, 1967). An example of each follows.

Christian Thomsen used a pattern of occurrences to establish the pioneer Danish chronology. He assumed that all the deposits that had yielded only stone artifacts were earliest, that those with both stone and bronze tools were intermediate in age, and that those which also contained iron tools were the latest (Sec. 4.3). This seriation was subsequently confirmed by correlating the deposits with the pollen sequence in Denmark, among other evidence (e.g., Klindt-Jensen, 1957, p. 10).

The late James A. Ford, of the United States, was the leader in working with frequency patterns. He collected potsherds from the surfaces of sites, identified their types, and calculated the frequencies of the types for each site. He plotted these frequencies as bar graphs on strips of paper, one for each site, arranged the strips in the order that gave the most consistent picture of changes in frequency, and assumed that this arrangement was the order in which the sites were occupied (Ford, 1962). He then had to check this order, and particularly its direction, by the use of other techniques such as stratigraphy.

Petrie (1899) employed a developmental pattern to "sequence date" the predynastic graves of Egypt. He arranged samples of the graves in the order of their presumed development from simple trenches to large, multichambered tombs—a development that, incidentally, continued into historic time and culminated in the great pyramids of Egypt. Then he checked and refined his arrangement of the graves by seriating the grave pottery in terms of such modes as kinds of handles. The general outline of his seriations has stood the test of time, but parts of it have had to be revised in the light of more recent discoveries (Arkell and Ucko, 1965, p. 151).

Just as a developmental seriation of peoples will work only if all the peoples belong to the same series, so a developmental seriation of types or modes will work only if they all form part of a single pattern of development or, as Kubler (1962, pp. 32–39) has put it, of the same "formal sequence." Developmental seriation is the procedure of utilizing a formal pattern or sequence to arrange archeological remains in chronological order, and it will fail if the pattern is broken.

CORRELATION WITH OTHER SEQUENCES. Cultural and typological sequences are not the only kinds of local sequences that can be used to arrange peoples in their proper chronological order. Theoretically, it should also be possible to order peoples in terms of sequences of human species or of races, societies, or linguistic groups, but such ordering is practically impossible, for lack of evidence. On the other hand, geochronologies can often be used for the purpose, either directly or by interposing an artifactual sequence, as the following examples will illustrate.

One reason Boucher de Perthes' theory about the antiquity of hand axes was slow to gain acceptance (Sec. 4.3) was that he based it on the succession of river terraces in the Somme Valley, which the geologists had not yet recognized. We now know that the uppermost terraces of any river system are the earliest and were formed before the river began to erode out its present valley. The river produced successively lower terraces while working its way down to its present level. As a result, remains in the uppermost terrace, where Boucher de Perthes found hand axes, must be the earliest and remains in the lowest terrace the latest—providing, of course, that it was the river that incorporated the remains in the terraces. One has to eliminate the possibility of subsequent deposition by man.

More specifically, when one finds human bones in a terrace, one needs to know whether they were laid down by the river or buried by man at a later date. The answer can be determined by comparing the amounts of certain substances, especially fluorine and nitrogen, that both the human and animal bones have taken on since their deposition. Similar amounts are an indication that both were deposited at the same time, presumably by the river. This technique of *chemical dating* can only be applied to bones from the same locality, since the rate of absorption varies from place to place, depending upon local conditions (Oakley, 1963).

The same principle is now being used to set up local sequences of obsidian artifacts. These are arranged in order of the depth to which ground water has penetrated from their surfaces, a technique that is called *hydration dating* (Michels, 1967).

In parts of the world that have experienced marked changes of climate, botanists have been able to obtain a record of the changes by studying variations in the pollen from plants and trees that increased or decreased in frequency as the climate changed. In effect, they have worked out patterns of change in the pollen. Like patterns of change in assemblages and artifacts, these can be used to date archeological remains, whenever a sufficient sample of pollen is found in association with the remains. The technique is known as *pollen analysis.*

Finally, hunting peoples tend to deposit large numbers of animal bones in their assemblages. If these include extinct forms, the forms can be identified and used to relate the people to a paleontological period, defined by its type fossils.

SUMMARY. It will be apparent that no single method suffices to set up a local sequence, except under extraordinary circumstances. Normally, the data are so fragmentary that the prehistorian must utilize all available facts, whatever the kind, and fit them together like a jigsaw puzzle. Stratigraphic facts are the most reliable, whether these be cultural, artifactual, or geologic, and therefore should be utilized as fully as possible. Ultimately, one hopes to be able to set up a stratigraphic sequence for each local area, so that one's cultural chronology will be based primarily upon that kind of evidence.

8
Synchronizing the sequences

The procedure of synchronizing the local sequences has already been outlined. One draws up a chronological chart, containing a column for each local area, inserts each local sequence in its own column, and moves its constituent peoples up and down until they are in the proper absolute position, insofar as this position can be determined.

Since peoples are culturally defined, it is logical to order them in terms of their cultural norms. We have seen that the peoples are frequently arranged in local sequences by working with their types or, less commonly, with their modes. When synchronizing the sequences it is better to use modes, which, because they affect only parts of the artifacts, tend to spread more rapidly and widely than types, which affect the total appearances of the artifacts (Sec. 2.12).

The modes and types that remain constant throughout a local sequence are said to constitute a *local tradition* because they link together the peoples of a local series (Sec. 3.11). Traditions are of no use in synchronizing sequences, unless the local peoples happen to have migrated widely, which is rarely the case. The prehistorian instead looks for modes and types that have spread from the people of one area to the people of another so widely that they link a large number of areas and so rapidly that there has been relatively little time lag. Such modes and types frequently occur in complexes, which are known as "horizon styles" (Willey and Phillips, 1962, pp. 29–40).

Horizon styles, then, are complexes of modes, types, and other cultural norms that have a relatively horizontal distribution when their occurrences are plotted upon a chronological chart and that therefore can be used to position contemporaneous peoples on the chart. They consist mainly of design motifs, often having religious significance; many are believed to have spread as parts of religious cults. They can occur on pottery, textiles, buildings, or any other kind of artifact.

Single modes, types, and other cultural norms are also worth using to position peoples if they have spread widely and rapidly enough. The more diverse their origins the better, since diversity of origin will help to cancel out their time lags.

Other things being equal, the peoples in adjacent areas who are most alike in culture should be placed on the same time level, since they may be assumed to have influenced one another if they did not previously share many of the same cultural trends. Peoples who are completely dissimilar belong on different levels, since they could hardly have lived side by side without exerting some influence upon one another.

Peoples in the same environment who have produced relatively thick deposits are assigned more space in their respective columns than peoples with thin deposits, and peoples who show more changes in culture may likewise be assumed to have had a longer lifetime. Too much should not be made of such impressionistic judgments, however, since rates of deposition and of cultural change vary greatly from place to place.

Special attention is paid to relationships among the peoples, for example, warfare and trade. Objects of trade, in the form of potsherds and ornaments, are not uncommon in archeological sites and can be distinguished from the local artifacts by differences in material and in style, though this procedure requires detailed techniques of analysis, which are not infallible. Such objects provide an especially good basis for synchronization, since trade can take place only between contemporaneous peoples.

Finally, peoples can be synchronized by relating them to widespread geologic or biological events. For example, all peoples with sites on a raised shoreline, higher than the present one, may be assumed to have been in existence during the time when the sea was at the higher level.

All of these procedures involve assumptions of cultural, social, or ecological change, which the prehistorian will not study per se until he reaches the final stage of his research—providing that he follows the logical strategy—and attempts to answer the question "How and why?" At the present early stage in his procedure, he can only hypothesize that the assumptions are correct and reserve a final decision about them until he is able subsequently to test the hypotheses.

9
*Estimating
calendrical dates*

While calendrical dates are occasionally used in establishing and synchronizing local sequences, their main function is to provide a scale for the dimension of time in chronological charts. They are placed along the sides of the charts for this purpose.

There are several different ways of obtaining them. Prehistorians who work in the twilight zone between prehistory and history, that is, after the invention of writing but before it was widespread enough to serve as the basis for written history, may be able to obtain calendrical dates from documents or inscriptions. However, these will be rare and will probably have to be supplemented by other methods of dating.

Several techniques of estimating calendrical dates have been developed in recent years. The most reliable is *dendrochronology,* or the study of tree rings. A. E. Douglass, an astronomer in the southwestern United States, originated this method as a by-product of research on the way the earth's climate has been affected by sunspot activity. Needing an indicator of climatic change, he turned to tree rings, on the assumption that differences in moisture have affected the growth of trees and hence the thickness of their annual rings.

Douglass began by making borings in living trees, in order to be able to count the rings from the present back into the past. Seeking to extend the record further into the past, he began to make borings into the roof beams of Pueblo Indian ruins. He was able to match up the innermost rings of the living trees with the outermost rings of the latest roof beams by comparing their characteristic patterns of thick and thin rings, resulting from variations in yearly rainfall. Eventually he was able to build up a master pattern of relative thicknesses, extending back beyond the time of Christ. Now, when a beam is brought into the laboratory from a Pueblo Indian ruin, it can be dated by laying out its rings on a strip of graph paper, moving the strip up and down the master pattern until it reaches the part with the same succession of thick and thin rings, and reading off the date of the outermost ring of the beam, which should be the time when it was cut (Stokes and Smiley, 1968).

Dendrochronology gives accurate dates only if the trees were used immediately after being cut. Unfortunately, the Pueblo Indians were sometimes faced with a shortage of trees, in which case they pulled beams out of abandoned ruins and reused them. It is therefore necessary to check each tree-ring date by another method of dating.

The tree-ring method also suffers from technical problems. For instance, the outermost rings, from which the date must be read, are sometimes indistinct or obliterated. Growth patterns differ from place to place, making it necessary to set up a new master pattern for each area. The method will work only in areas where there is a delicate balance between moisture and dryness, or else warmth and coldness, for otherwise there will not be sufficient differences in the widths of the rings. So far, the technique has been little used outside the upland parts of the southwestern United States, the central

Plains area, and Alaska, but it is potentially applicable to many other parts of the world.

A comparable technique of *varve analysis* is employed in sub-arctic areas. This technique depends upon the fact that, as the water from melting glaciers slows down upon entering lakes, it deposits silt in the form of annual layers, known as "varves." These have a characteristic pattern of thickness, depending upon the summer temperature; more and larger particles of silt are deposited during warm than during cold summers. As a result, varves can be studied in the same way as tree rings. Unfortunately, they are more subject to disturbance and are not always annual. Also, they are rarely found in direct contact with archeological remains, as timber is, and must be correlated via some kind of geochronology, with consequent loss of reliability (Flint, 1957, pp. 293–297).

Several more generally applicable, though less precise, methods have recently been developed as a by-product of atomic research. These are based upon the study of radioactive isotopes. The American chemist Willard F. Libby originated the first of them, called *radiocarbon analysis,* in the 1940s. He worked with carbon 14, a radioactive isotope formed by the action of cosmic rays on nitrogen in the atmosphere. Plants acquire carbon 14 from the atmosphere by photosynthesis, and animals obtain it from plants. Libby found by experimentation that all living organisms retain the same proportion of radioactive carbon 14 to inert carbons 13 and 12 so long as they are alive. When they die, carbon 14 decays into inert carbon at a constant rate, giving off radioactivity in the process. Libby extracted the carbon from organic material and measured its radioactivity in order to determine how much of its carbon 14 had decayed. Dividing this amount by the rate of decay gave him the time that had elapsed since the organism had died. He converted this time into time B.C. or A.D. by subtracting 1,950, which has become the accepted standard of reference for radiocarbon dating (Libby, 1955).

Charcoal is the best material to use for radiocarbon analysis, because it is least likely to have been contaminated by chemicals in the soil. Other organic materials have varying degrees of reliability. Bone is worst, not only because it is most likely to soak up chemicals, but also because it contains a relatively small proportion of carbon.

The amount of radioactivity present, even in large samples of relatively recent carbon, is so small and so difficult to measure that the dates must be given to us with an appreciable margin of error, which may range from ±50 to ±1,000 years, depending upon the size of the sample and its radioactivity. We cannot even be sure that any particular date actually falls within the limits of its margin of error; there is one chance in three that it does not. Radiocarbon dates are therefore like throws of the dice; we cannot assume that the first one will be close to actuality, but a series of them will average out properly. By contrast, every tree-ring date should be correct, unless there is some technical or correlational problem.

Radiocabon analysis of timbers that have been dated by the tree-ring method shows that even averaged radiocarbon dates differ somewhat from actual tree-ring dates (Stuiver and Suess, 1966). It would seem that the radiocarbon determinations are biased by variations in sunspot activity, which have affected the intensity of the cosmic rays and, through them, the amounts of carbon 14 in the atmosphere and in living organisms. There is no need to abandon the method, however. The differences between radiocarbon dates and actual dates are no greater than the distortion that results when the earth's round surface is projected against the flat surface of a map. Radiocarbon-dated chronologies, like maps, are useful despite their distortions.

Radiocarbon analysis is most effective when the sample is younger than the half-life of carbon 14, that is, younger than the time when one-half of the carbon 14 will have decayed into inert carbon, which is approximately 5,570 ± 30 years according to the original Libby calculation. (More accurate calculations have since been made but have been withheld pending resolution of the differences among them.) As one moves further back into the past, the amount of radioactivity becomes progressively smaller until, finally, it can no longer be measured. The practical limit of the method is about 60,000 B.C. (e.g., Deevey, Flint, and Rouse, 1967).

For earlier periods, it is necessary to shift to other isotopes that decay more slowly. The most promising of these is potassium 40, which came into existence during the formation of the earth and is still present in measurable amounts because its half-life of 1.3×10^9 years is comparable to the age of the earth. The method is known as *potassium-argon analysis,* because it measures the amount of potassium 40 relative to argon 40, a decay product (Getner and

Lippott, 1965). The sample must have originally contained only potassium 40, so that the amount of argon 40 in it will be a true measure of the time since the sample was formed. Volcanic rock meets this requirement because the heat of its formation eliminated all previous argon 40. Subsequent contamination by atmospheric argon or older rock fragments may bias the results, and it is therefore important to select fresh, uncontaminated material (Rosenfeld, 1965, pp. 228–233).

What is actually dated, then, is the time of the volcanic eruption that produced the rock. In order to correlate this time with archeological remains, it is necessary to find material from a volcanic eruption overlying a human deposit, a condition that fortunately occurs in Olduvai Gorge, East Africa, where the potassium-argon method has been used to date early traces of man at about 2,000,000 B.C. (Howell, 1962).

Once an absolute chronology has been established in a particular locality by studying tree rings, varves, or isotopic decay, it can be transferred to other events that occur with enough regularity within that locality to have absolute validity there but that vary so much from locality to locality that they do not have interareal validity. Hydration dating, already mentioned as a technique of relative dating, is one example (Sec. 4.7). Another is *archeomagnetism*, which is based upon the movements that took place in the position of the earth's magnetic pole during prehistoric time. The direction to the magnetic pole during the time of occupation of a site may be determined by measuring the remnant magnetism in objects of baked clay, such as kilns, hearths, and fired floors or walls of houses. In the southwestern United States, where this technique has met with considerable success, such measurements are used to establish the directions to the magnetic pole during the times when sites dated by dendrochronology and radiocarbon analysis were in existence. A master curve showing movements in the directions to the north magnetic pole has been built up in this way and is being used to date sites of unknown age from which baked-clay objects have been obtained (Weaver, 1967).

Glottochronology, or lexico-statistic dating, is a less reliable method of estimating calendrical dates that depends upon the observation that a language's basic vocabulary, consisting of words for parts of the body, pronouns and other terms not subject to borrowing from another language, tends to change at a constant rate. This rate, as calculated by studying the divergence of historic languages such as French and Italian, is applied to comparable prehistoric languages in order to determine the time that has elapsed since they split apart (Swadesh, 1952). The method is by no means foolproof; for example, the rate of change may have been slower when the speakers of the two divergent languages remained in contact than when they became isolated. But at least it gives us some idea of elapsed time.

Positive correlation of glottochronological dates with prehistoric peoples is impossible in the absence of written records. Nevertheless, comparison of linguistically and ethnically derived dates is often useful, not only in order to check the two, but also in an effort to correlate linguistic and cultural groups of people. If it can be shown that there were only a single linguistic and a single cultural group in a particular area at any particular period, then the two groups can be considered one.

10
Delimiting ages

Up to this point, we have been concerned with the absolute chronological positions of peoples. We have seen how prehistorians attempt to work these out graphically, by fitting peoples into cultural chronologies, and conceptually, by estimating calendrical dates. Now we turn to the practice of fitting peoples into relative sequences of ages.

Here, we must focus upon single cultural innovations, instead of working with all possible innovations in order to cancel out differences in temporal distributions. We need to select key innovations, each of which has been accompanied by a number of other innovations, so that the key innovation will serve to demarcate a major division in the chronology of a region, which is what we mean by an age. At the same time, the key innovations must be clearly identifiable in the archeological record, or else we will not be able to use them to date peoples. Each age is frequently named after a key innovation, although a term for the age's sequential position may be used instead, as in the historian's phrase "Middle Ages."

We have seen that the ancient Chinese, Greek, and Roman peoples focused upon stoneworking and metallurgy in setting up the

Stone-Bronze-Iron-Age sequence, with its various subdivisions (Sec. 4.3). They were undoubtedly impelled to do so by the values of their own civilizations, which emphasized technological development, and their divisions have withstood the test of time, so far as these civilizations are concerned.

To be sure, Childe (1946b, 1951, 1963) has reformulated the Neolithic, Bronze, and Iron Ages of the Middle East in terms of food production and civilization. This practice has complicated the issue, for technology, food production, and civilization appeared at different times in different places. As a result, it has been necessary to define the three ages in different ways in dealing with different regions. Thus, the Neolithic age in the Middle East is the time of development of intensive agriculture; ground stonework had already appeared there during the previous Mesolithic age (Mellaart, 1965). On the contrary, the Neolithic age in Siberia is the time of first appearance of ground stonework; agriculture did not develop there until the Bronze Age (Mongait, 1961). These differences need not be confusing if it is recognized that, because ages are units of relative time, their definition must be varied from region to region.

In other parts of the world—Asia and Africa beyond the sphere of Western influence, Oceania, and the New World—it has been necessary to formulate completely different sequences of ages, which reflect the divergent courses of cultural development in these regions. In the New World, for example, metallurgy is not a key invention, because the American Indians did not attach the same importance to it as in the Western World. The Western peoples developed a complex economic system by means of which to secure metals, process them, and distribute the finished products; and this economic system also served as a vehicle for the spread of many other cultural innovations (e.g., Childe, 1958a). In the New World, the appearance of metallurgy did not have this consequence. Trade continued to be primarily in pottery, stonework, and shellwork, which, not being innovations, cannot serve to delimit ages. New World prehistorians have turned instead to the stylistic treatment of these materials, with the result that the final two ages in the New World are called Classic and Post-Classic respectively (Willey and Phillips, 1962).

It is important not to reify an age by attributing a definite time and content to it wherever it occurs. As the term "relative" implies, each age varies from place to place, both in its temporal position and in its cultural content. Thus, it is necessary to plot the beginning of an age as a curved line in order to account for time lag in the diffusion of the innovation by which it is defined (Sec. 4.3). As for content, the Bronze Age in Mesopotamia was marked by a rise from towns to cities, but in neighboring Palestine the first men of the Bronze Age advanced only from villages to towns (cf. Childe, 1946b, pp. 82–105, with Albright, 1960, pp. 72–74).

The only feature of an age that remains constant is the key innovation or set of innovations by which it is defined, and this feature remains so only within a single chronological chart. When we plot an age on such a chart, we are only noting the time between the first appearance of the key set of innovations and the first appearance of the set diagnostic of the subsequent age. In this respect, the age lines on a chronology are comparable to contour lines on a map. Just as the contour lines mark the space between one height above sea level and another, so the age lines mark the time between the first appearances of two key innovations or sets of innovations. The only difference is that contour lines, being on a map, are drawn in two dimensions of space, whereas age lines, being on a chronology, are drawn in the dimension of time and in only one dimension of space.

The function of the concept of age is to provide a baseline, such as bronze working, against which we can view the variable appearances of other cultural innovations. Thus it helps to synthesize our picture of the bewildering variety of peoples and cultures that have been distinguished in recent years. It enables us to look at the forest without losing sight of its individual trees.

11
Converting cultural into ethnic chronologies

To this point we have been concerned only with cultural groups. To complete his chronological research, our prehistorian must also date the morphological groups he has been able to formulate. He may do so by correlating his human skeletal assemblages with the cultural assemblages he has already dated. This correlation is easy enough when the people who produced the assemblages had the custom of burying their dead in the places where they carried out other activities or of including grave objects with the deceased, but it is more difficult when the human skeletons are completely isolated.

Under these circumstances, the best the prehistorian can do is to assume that skeletal and cultural material that occur in the same area and period belong together.

If the prehistorian is following the logical order of the strategy, when he answers the question "Where and when?" he will not have studied social and linguistic groups, since they have to be dealt with in the substantive rather than the systematic part of the strategy. If, however, he has reversed the strategy, he may have already been able to distinguish social or linguistic groups and will want to date them. Here again, his procedure is to correlate the groups with the cultural assemblages he has already dated. This job is easier than correlating morphological and cultural assemblages, since the evidence for the presence of social and linguistic groups is in itself cultural.

Having made the correlation, the prehistorian can then place the names of the morphological, social or linguistic groups in his cultural chronology alongside the names of the peoples with which they are associated. The two sets of names should be handled differently, for example, by enclosing the names for noncultural groups in brackets in order to distinguish them from the names for peoples (Fig. 10). The number of names inserted in this manner will be relatively small, however, because of the difficulties in distinguishing morphological, social, and linguistic groups during prehistoric time.

SUPPLEMENTAL READING

CLARK, GRAHAME, *Archaeology and Society* (1960), pp. 121–168.

DEETZ, JAMES, *Invitation to Archaeology* (1967), pp. 21–42.

FORD, JAMES A., *A Quantitative Method for Deriving Cultural Chronology* (1962).

HOLE, FRANK, AND ROBERT F. HEIZER, *An Introduction to Prehistoric Archaeology* (1969), pt. IV.

KUBLER, GEORGE, *The Shape of Time: Remarks on the History of Things* (1962).

MICHAEL, HENRY N., AND ELIZABETH K. RALPH, *Dating Techniques for the Archaeologist* (1971).

PIGGOTT, STUART, *Approach to Archaeology* (1965b), pp. 51–75.

WILLEY, GORDON R., AND PHILIP PHILLIPS, *Method and Theory in American Archaeology* (1962), pp. 24–29.

5

RECONSTRUCTION
OF ETHNIC SYSTEMS

1
The conjunctive
approach After distinguishing cultural and morphological groups by means of ethnic classification and placing the groups within a chronology, the prehistorian is finished with the systematic part of his research and is ready to turn to substantive problems. He has learned who produced the remains under study and has found out where and when the producers lived. Now he attempts to discover what the producers were like (Fig. 6).

Answering the question "What?" requires a twofold procedure. Working separately with each cultural or morphological group, the prehistorian *infers* the group's cultural or morphological traits from its remains. He must also *articulate* each group's traits by fitting them together and finding out how they function in relation to one another, that is, as parts of an ethnic system. Thus he shifts his attention from the cultural and morphological groups upon which he had focused during his systematic research to the cultural and morphological systems possessed by those groups.

We have seen that neither social nor linguistic groups can be included in the systematics of prehistory because neither is distinguishable on the basis of archeological evidence (Sec. 3.3). By the same token, the prehistorian cannot expect to be able to reconstruct social and linguistic systems on the basis of archeological (as opposed to historic and ethnographic) evidence. Nevertheless, he can infer some social and linguistic traits from the archeological evidence, can project others back from historic into late prehistoric time, and can make a partial articulation of the traits. Therefore, in answering the question "What?" he should aim toward full reconstruction of cultural and morphological systems and partial reconstruction of social and linguistic systems.

The cube of knowledge (Fig. 1) illustrates the logic of this procedure. Our prehistorian must begin with ethnic groups because he is entering the cube through its front face. He distinguishes peoples and races in order to obtain manageable and consistent units of study. Then he determines each group's position on the front face of the cube, with respect to the dimensions of space and time. Next he moves from the groups' positions into the body of the cube, along the dimension of form, in order to find out about the characteristics of each group: its cultural, morphological, social, or linguistic system.

Persons with a purely archeological interest are likely to assume that they have learned all there is to know about the dimension of form when they have recovered and described an area's cultural assemblages, but they have only begun to acquire knowledge. The knowledge continues to accumulate during the course of cultural classification, when certain traits are singled out to serve as diagnostic complexes, and during the construction of cultural chronologies, when other traits become known as time-markers. This skeletal knowledge must subsequently be fleshed out by drawing inferences from the remains about the rest of each people's cultural traits and by articulating the traits so as to reconstruct the people's cultural system, or, as Benedict (1959) calls it, the people's "pattern of culture."

But one's task is not completed when one has reconstructed a people's culture (Fig. 1). Continuing along the dimension of form, one should infer morphological traits from one's morphological assemblages and should articulate these traits by reconstructing the appearances of the people. It is also desirable to work out the local environment, social structure, and language, insofar as possible in the absence of written records.

We saw in Section 1.4 that the study of the dimension of form among contemporary nonliterate peoples is termed "ethnography." Ethnographers, too, attempt to distinguish a people's cultural, morphological, social, and linguistic traits and to articulate these traits within their proper systems. It is obvious that the ethnographer and the prehistorian cannot be equally successful in these tasks. The ethnographer has the good fortune of being able to study the dimension of form at firsthand. Unless the subjects of his study are in the process of losing their indigenous way of life, he can find out about all parts of their life by observation and by questioning informants. The prehistorian must instead rely primarily upon archeological evidence (Sec. 2.1), most of which is cultural, and hence the prehistorian is able to learn much more about cultures than about the rest of the dimension of form (Sec. 3.3).

The ethnographer, then, is able to present a balanced, holistic picture, covering all parts of the dimension of form, whereas the prehistorian is forced by the nature of his data to emphasize culture. Because of this limitation, many prehistorians prefer to speak of "cultural reconstruction" rather than the reconstruction of ethnic systems, but the latter phrase is used here to indicate that the prehistorian's goal should be holistic, even though he rarely succeeds in attaining that goal. He should obtain as much information as possible about the local morphologies, social structures, and languages, as well as about the local cultures. Following Taylor (1967b, p. 5) and Friedrich (1970, pp. 2–3), we shall call this approach the *conjunctive approach*.

Knowledge of the dimension of form is needed not only for its own sake, but also as a check upon the previous parts of the strategy of prehistoric research. More than once, for example, assemblages from dwelling and burial sites have been classified separately as the remains of distinct peoples when, in fact, both kinds of assemblages were produced by a single people accustomed to dwell in one place, to bury in another, and to furnish their dead with artifacts of different types from those which they left in their dwelling sites. Under these circumstances, the prehistorian is not likely to realize that the dwelling and burial sites were produced by the same people unless and until he looks for the burials of the people who lived in the dwelling sites and for the dwellings of the people in the burial sites, as he must do in order to answer the question "What?" (e.g., Rouse, 1968, p. 10).

Knowledge of the entire dimension of form is likewise needed in order to answer the final question in the strategy of prehistory, "How and why?" For instance, one may encounter a striking similarity between the ritual objects deposited in two areas and seek to explain it. One will have to decide whether the similarity is because of (1) spread of a religious cult from one area to the other, (2) conquest of one area by the inhabitants of the other area, or (3) a situation in which the peoples of both areas gave allegiance to a religious center and obtained from it the objects themselves or the idea of making them. One cannot make an adequate choice from among these various alternatives without first learning as much as possible about the cultures, morphologies, social structures, and languages of the two areas. Alternative 1 is investigated by comparing the local cultures, in order to determine how much one affected the other. Alternative 2 can best be tested by finding out whether the morphology of one area intruded into the other area—assuming, of course, that the two areas differ significantly in their morphologies. To determine the probability of alternative 3, one must study the nature of the social relationships that linked the two areas. Finally, if the peoples of the two areas happen to have differed in language, a study of the linguistic effects they have had upon each other will yield evidence about the relative validity of all three hypotheses.

2 Development of conjunctive research

The early prehistorians were quick to develop an interest in the lives of the peoples they studied. When Sir John Lubbock (later Lord Avebury) wrote his pioneer synthesis of prehistory in 1865 he discussed not only the cultural, but also the physical finds of early man and appended three chapters on "Modern Savages" in order, as he put it, to "throw light on the ancient remains found in

Europe, and on the condition of the early races which inhabited our continent" (Avebury, 1900, p. 408). In *Ancient Hunters,* originally published in 1911, W. J. Sollas (1924) similarly prefaced his discussion of the Paleolithic age with an account of the natives of Tasmania and then juxtaposed chapters on the subdivisions of the Paleolithic and chapters on modern peoples as follows: Mousterian and the Australian aborigines, Aurignacian and the Bushmen of South Africa, and Magdalenian and the Eskimo. In each case, his aim was to fill out our knowledge of the prehistoric peoples with information about the modern peoples that most closely resemble them, morophologically as well as culturally.

By the first decades of the twentieth century enough archeological data had accumulated to make possible inference of certain aspects of prehistoric life from the remains themselves. Toolmaking was the obvious subject for inference but was largely bypassed because of the discovery of Upper Paleolithic art in western Europe. This discovery stimulated the local prehistorians to reconstruct both the artistic and the religious life of the time, on the assumption that the Upper Paleolithic art had had magical and religious significance, as among modern nonliterate peoples (Ucko and Rosenfeld, 1967, pp. 116–138). The German prehistorian R. R. Schmidt subsequently extended the reconstruction to the entire Paleolithic in his *The Dawn of the Human Mind* (1936).

During the period between the two world wars, the Soviet prehistorians developed quite a different approach to ethnographic reconstruction. They possessed a ready-made reconstruction in the form of Marxian theories of evolution and needed only to apply these to the various divisions of the Victorian chronology. Following Marx, they emphasized economics and their sociological implications at the expense of art and religion, but they were careful to cover the entire range of the dimension of form, even including language (M. W. Thompson, 1965).

This was the time when West European prehistorians were shifting from the Victorian chronology to the discovery of cultural groups and the chronological ordering of the groups. Paleolithic specialists began to pay special attention to the techniques of flint chipping, because they found them to be the best basis for distinguishing Paleolithic peoples—so much so that the specialists still use the term "industry" in place of our "diagnostic complex" (e.g.,

Burkitt, 1963). Paleolithic art and religion, as well as the types of fossil man, were now correlated with particular industries—our peoples—and inferences were drawn from the remains about other aspects of the peoples' lives, especially their subsistence. This line of research culminated in *Beyond the Bounds of History* (1949), in which the Abbé Henri Breuil, then the leading Paleolithic specialist, presented a series of thirty-one sketches of scenes from the lives of particular peoples, each with an accompanying textual explanation.

As for post-Paleolithic studies in western Europe during the period between the two world wars, the task of defining peoples and placing them chronologically took so much time that little was left for interpretation. The available time was devoted mainly to the question "How and why?" rather than "What?", since the West Europeans were primarily interested in historical problems, such as the spread of civilization from the Near East to Europe (Sec. 6.10).

V. Gordon Childe was an exception. His strong interest in historical problems (Sec. 4.3) did not blind him to the need for ethnographic reconstruction, and he drew all the inferences he could about the economic and sociological life of the peoples he studied. Reviewing his career in *Retrospect* (1958b), he attributes his interest in these subjects partially to Marxism and partially to the influence of British social anthropology. He was greatly impressed by the extent to which the Soviet prehistorians had been able to reconstruct the dimension of form, and he experimented with their approach in *Scotland before the Scots* (1946a). He could not use the Victorian chronology, as they did, because it had been abandoned in the West. For it, he substituted a succession of six "stages," each consisting of a single Scottish people or several contemporaneous peoples, and applied Marxian theories of evolution to them. He did not not consider the experiment a success, and in a subsequent series of lectures on social evolution given at the University of Birmingham in 1947–1948, he limited himself to inferences from the remains and avoided the temptation to fill these out with Marxian theories (Childe, 1963). Again, though, he chose to use local periods rather than individual peoples as his units of study.

The present generation of West European prehistorians continues to recognize the need to infer ethnographic traits, and has also begun to pay attention to articulation, especially through the use of geographical and anthropological models (Ucko, Tringham, and Dimbleby, 1971). Interest has centered on culture and social structure at the expense of morphological and linguistic traits. Thus, in France André Leroi-Gourhan (1957, p. 45) states the aim to be "an overall view" of (1) a people's means of sustenance, (2) its houses, clothing, and other protective devices, (3) its social organization, and (4) its religious and artistic pursuits; and in England Grahame Clark (1960, fig. 25) has formulated a diagram showing the interrelationships between environment and various aspects of culture as a model of ethnographic reconstruction. Both men agree that reconstruction and articulation must be based upon the facts of archeology. Leroi-Gourhan is loath to use ethnographic parallels, since they have to be drawn from peoples who are far removed in both place and time from prehistoric Europe. On the other hand, Clark (1951, 1967) does employ them, especially parallels in European folk culture that can be assumed to have survived from prehistoric time.

Given these restrictions on the use of evolutionary theory and ethnographic parallels, contemporary West Europeans fall far short of their ideal for both reconstruction and articulation. They are able to approach the ideal only in the rare case of a site containing evidence about an exceptionally broad range of human activities under unusual conditions of preservation. Such a site is Star Carr in England, where Grahame Clark (1954) was able to reconstruct an unusually full picture of life among the early Maglemosian people. Ordinarily, however, the evidence is so fragmentary that, when Clark wrote *Prehistoric Europe: The Economic Basis* (1952), he had to discuss each aspect of culture separately, instead of articulating the cultural traits of each people, as advocated in his ideal model.

Conditions are different in the New World. American prehistorians are able to work back from the present into prehistory without having to pass through thousands of years of history, as in Europe. Moreover, no remains more than a few thousand years old were known before World I (Sec. 4.3). It was therefore feasible to project conditions among the modern Indians back into prehistory and to use them to interpret the remains, especially in areas such as the southwestern United States, where direct connections can be established between modern and prehistoric peoples (Parsons, 1940). The close professional association between archeol-

ogists and prehistorians, on the one hand, and cultural, physical, social, and linguistic anthropologists, on the other hand, led to more
of a knowledge of general ethnographic analogies than in Europe
and a greater inclination to use them in interpreting the remains
(Sec. 1.5). Finally, Americans had more time to spare for reconstructing the dimension of form, since they had not yet developed
ways of distinguishing peoples and constructing chronologies.

For all these reasons, the conjunctive approach received considerable attention in the United States around the turn of the century.
For instance, Harlan I. Smith (1899) advocated arranging museum
exhibits in an ethnographic manner, and in 1910 he entitled a field
report *The Prehistoric Ethnology of a Kentucky Site*. A number of
other early-twentieth-century prehistorians included conjunctive reconstructions in their site reports (e.g., Harrington, 1924, pp. 246–
280). These were on a relatively superficial level, however; they
consisted mainly of the obvious inferences to be drawn from artifacts and cultural materials by visualizing how they might have
been used, along with projections of present social and linguistic
groups back into prehistory.

Between World Wars I and II, attention was diverted from conjunctive reconstruction by the development of techniques for cultural classification and chronological research and by the discovery
of early remains, which pushed the origin of the American Indian
back into the remote past (Secs. 3.5 and 4.3). Nevertheless, the conjunctive approach still had its champions. Steward and Setzler
(1938, p. 7) urged that descriptions of archeological materials—
archeology proper in our terminology—be supplemented by "more
information about . . . the general features of a culture," including
sustenance, environmental relationships, social groups, and the distribution of population. The midwestern taxonomists stressed the
need to cover the entire range of a people's activities (e.g., Fairbanks, 1942, pp. 228–229) and formulated a concept of "community"
by means of which to link together the sites in which a particular
social group carried out its various activities (McKern, 1939, p. 311).
Reconstruction of cultures continued, though still on a rather superficial level (e.g., Martin, 1939, pp. 461–471; Rouse, 1941, pp. 24ff.).

Interest in the reconstruction of traits has increased since World
War II and, as in Europe, it is now accompanied by attempts at
articulation. Walter W. Taylor made a strong plea for reconstruc-

tion in *A Study of Archeology* (1967b), in which he criticized the prewar leaders of American prehistory for having spent too much time on the systematic pursuits of distinguishing peoples and organizing them chronologically. He coined the phrase "conjunctive approach" to refer to the reconstruction and articulation of ethnic traits, but he was unable to devise a method for accomplishing these objectives and so they remained an ideal, like the European models of the postwar period.

A new method of reconstruction that enables us to attain the conjunctive ideal was developed during the 1960s under the name of "settlement archeology" (Trigger, 1967). In it, inferences are drawn not only from artifacts and other cultural materials per se but also from a people's settlement pattern, and that pattern is further used to articulate the people's cultural system and to study its adaptation to the environment (Sec. 5.4). The Steward and Setzler article cited above had foreshadowed this approach, and the lead in its development was taken by a colleague of theirs in the Smithsonian Institution, Gordon R. Willey. In doing ethnographic research on the seminomadic Indians of the Great Basin in the western United States, Julian H. Steward had followed the Indian bands from place to place and had observed them depositing their remains in different sites. Accordingly, he suggested to Willey that, instead of focusing upon the remains left by a people in a single site, he make a study of the distribution of the people's remains from site to site. In other words, he advised Willey to approach the people's remains in terms of its settlement pattern.

Willey first applied this approach in a study of the prehistory of Viru Valley, Peru, and it enabled him to make an unusually successful reconstruction of the local cultures (Willey, 1953). It was soon adopted in other parts of the New World (e.g., Willey, 1956); and was subsequently improved through use of the geographical models developed in Europe, as mentioned above.

Finally, as American ethnographers and ethnologists have become more concerned with social, as opposed to cultural, phenomena, American prehistorians have likewise begun to stress the study of social rather than cultural groups. Sears (1961) proposes that both settlement patterns and artifactual remains be used to infer the social and religious systems of the North American Indians. Binford (1964, p. 440) argues that prehistorians "are faced with the ... task of isolating extinct sociocultural systems as the most appropriate unit for [explaining] cultural similarities and differences," that is, for answering our question "How and why?". He also suggests how excavations might be designed to do this job. Chang (1967a and 1967b) has devised a conceptual scheme for doing it; he would focus upon individual "settlements" and "articulate" each one's internal and external social relationships, which he terms its "microstructure" and "macrostructure" respectively.

If we were to turn to other parts of the world, we would find parallel developments in conjunctive research, but enough has been said to indicate the range of variation, from the relatively limited inferences drawn by West European prehistorians to the relatively full and detailed reconstructions that the Soviet prehistorians have been able to achieve by use of Marxian theories. American prehistorians fall somewhere between these two extremes, but they also differ among themselves as to the relative importance of cultural and social phenomena. Let us now attempt to find common ground among the various points of view.

3
The dimension
of form

First, we need to distinguish between the ideal of conjunctive research and the practice. When we speak of the dimension of form, we are referring to the answer we would like to be able to give to the question "What?" Ideally, this answer should include all the information that would be available if the people under study were still in existence and could be observed and questioned by an ethnographer. The answer should furnish a complete, holistic picture of the people's life, not limited to art, biology, sociology, technology, or any of the other specializations into which the study of our own civilization is divided (Sec. 1.4).

Contrasting with this ideal is the practice—the amount of information that can actually be inferred from the remains without exceeding the limits of reliability. It is never possible to reconstruct the entire dimension of form. The proportion that can be recovered varies from place to place and from time to time. In general, the more recent a people is, the more one can learn about its life, for several reasons. First, there will have been less time for destruction of its remains. Second, as a people evolves in culture it produces a greater variety of artifacts specifically designed for particular purposes, and these furnish a better basis for reconstructing the people's activities. Finally, the closer a people is to the present, the greater is the opportunity to project the findings of history or ethnography back to it, as in the studies of American prehistory mentioned above.

The prehistorian's task is not ended when he reconstructs those parts of the dimension of form for which evidence is available. He must also take note of those parts for which he has no evidence. Only if he is aware of the gaps in his knowledge will he be able intelligently to plan further research with which to close the gaps. Recognition of his own ignorance is also essential if he is properly to answer the final question, "How and why?" In answering this question, he must be sure to take into consideration the deficiencies in his answer to the previous question, "What?"

The dimension of form may be compared in both these respects to the dimensions of space and time, as they are expressed in an ethnic chronology. One function of such a chronology, which has not yet been mentioned, is to indicate gaps in our systematic knowledge. It reveals the places and times for which we have not yet been able to distinguish peoples, races, and so forth, and thus spurs us to search for new sites with which to fill the gaps. It also helps us to keep the gaps in mind while answering the subsequent questions "What?" and "How and why?"

An ethnic chronology is able to perform these functions because it portrays both the goal of research—full coverage of space and time—and the extent to which that goal has been achieved. We need a comparable representation of the full dimension of form, against which to measure the actual extent of our ethnographic knowledge. This representation may take the form of either a diagram or an outline portraying the total range of information we would like to have. Several such diagrams or outlines have been proposed by prehistorians—the most recent is that of David L. Clarke (1968, fig. 13)—but none has gained general acceptance, nor have ethnographers been able to agree upon a single outline that we might follow (cf. Anonymous, 1952, and Murdock et al., 1950). This lack of consensus is not surprising, since the formulations are based upon differing aims and experiences with ethnographic research. It will be necessary for us to develop our own diagram and outline, based upon the aims of this book and upon the experiences of prehistorians around the world.

The major divisions in our outline of the dimension of form have already been presented on the top face of the cube of knowledge (Fig. 1). There are five of them: (1) the inorganic and organic environments which we may group together in the present context; (2) peoples and their cultures; (3) races and their morphologies; (4) societies and their social structures; and (5) speech communities and their languages. We shall consider each of the divisions in turn, but first we must decide how to select and organize the pertinent archeological data.

4
Settlement patterns

In answering the two systematics questions "Who?" and "Where and when?" we found it necessary to work primarily with cultural groups rather than with morphological, social, or linguistic groups, because most archeological remains are cultural (Secs. 3.3 and 4.1). This situation also holds true in answering the question "What?"

It is advisable to work primarily with peoples, rather than with smaller or larger units in cultural hierarchies (Tables 4 and 5). Subpeoples and co-peoples are too small to provide the entire range of data needed for the reconstruction of ethnic systems, and series of peoples are too large and too variable to be used for that purpose.

But a people is not a functioning unit. It consists of a number of individuals who have been arbitrarily grouped together because they share cultural traits. Some way must be found to articulate these traits, so that we may see how they functioned in relation to one another and how they fulfilled the needs of the people who possessed them.

The conceptual device that prehistorians use for the purpose is a *settlement pattern,* by which is meant the manner in which either a people's activities or a society's institutions are distributed over the landscape (Trigger, 1968b, p. 55). This concept provides a means of articulating three of the five parts of the dimension of form listed above: environment, culture, and social structure.

If we are to think clearly about settlement patterns, we must distinguish the distribution of activities, which is cultural, from the distribution of institutions, which is social. We shall call the former the *activity pattern* and the latter the *residential pattern.* (The latter is so called because the most important institutions are those based upon the principle of residence; Table 6.)

In studying the activity pattern of a contemporary people, one determines the nature of the people's activities, such as tool making, food production, warfare, art, and religion, and then plots the manner in which the different kinds of activities are distributed over the landscape. Thus one obtains a network of loci and a record of the activities that took place in each locus.

In studying the residential pattern of a contemporary society, one similarly observes the range of the society's residential institutions, such as households, villages, and tribes, and determines the manner in which they are distributed over the landscape. Thus one obtains a second network of loci that is less extensive than the first, since a community does not normally carry out all of its activities in the places where it lives. The second network is also smaller, since there are fewer kinds of residential institutions than there are kinds of activities.

The prehistorian has to work primarily with activity rather than residential patterns, for his remains are the product of activities rather than institutions. (To be sure, institutions carry out the activities, but the nature of the institution does not determine the nature of the activity.) What survives are remnants of the activities, deposited in the loci where the activities were carried out. If only a single activity was performed at a site, as in the case of an isolated burial mound, we may refer to that site as an activity locus. If several different activities took place at the site, as is normally the case when people lived there, the site has to be divided, insofar as possible, into a number of activity loci (Binford, 1964, p. 424). Hence, an *activity locus* may be defined as any spot where a minimum number of activities took place.

A prehistorian who wishes to recover the surviving traces of an activity pattern must first find loci covering the entire range of a people's activities and then collect remains from representative loci. We may refer to the remains obtained from each locus as an *activity assemblage*.

What the prehistorian obtains, then, is a network of activity loci, some of which consist of whole sites and others of parts of sites, together with an activity assemblage from each locus. We shall call the combination of network and assemblages a *remnant activity pattern* in order to distinguish it from the full pattern that is observed by the ethnographer. A remnant activity pattern is to a full pattern as a fossil skeleton is to its living counterpart.

The prehistorian bases his reconstruction of the full pattern on its remnant in the same way that the paleontologist bases his reconstruction of an animal on its fossil remains.

A similar procedure is followed in recovering the remnants of a society's residential pattern and in reconstructing the original pattern. The prehistorian distinguishes a series of residential sites or components of sites, collects an assemblage from each one, and determines the pattern of distribution of the assemblages (Sec. 5.16).

Here again, we encounter a point of difference between archeology and prehistory. The archeologist's basic unit of study is the site, for it is the natural division of the remains, which are his primary interest. The prehistorian, on the contrary, does not have a single kind of unit; he uses a different one in answering each of the questions in his strategy. When seeking to answer the question "Who?" he focuses upon typical assemblages, to which he can apply the procedure of ethnic classification (Sec. 3.6). In answering the question "Where and when?" he concentrates instead upon stratigraphic sequences, since they are the most reliable means of working out local sequences (Sec. 4.7). When he comes to the question "What?" the remnant settlement patterns become his basic units, because they help him to articulate ecological, cultural, and social traits.

Ethnic assemblages, stratigraphic sequences, and remnant settlement patterns are all heuristic devices that enable the prehistorian to seek the kinds of data he needs to answer a particular question in the strategy of prehistory, instead of simply accumulating all kinds of data, as is the case in purely archeological research. Each of the three concepts serves as a screen, which filters out the kinds of data not pertinent to a question and retains the kinds needed to answer that question. As we shall see later (Sec. 6.2), the concept of a "remnant pattern of change" performs a similar function in answering the fourth question, "How and why?"

5
A model of
ethnic
relationships

In the preceding section, we discussed selection of the evidence needed to answer the question "What?" Now, let us return to the anthropological knowledge used to interpret that evidence (Fig. 6), that is, to the dimension of form. A model diagramming the relationships among the five parts of the dimension of form is pre-

sented in Figure 11. It consists of an outer rectangle, symbolizing
the environment in which a particular people lives, an inner circle
symbolizing the local population of human beings that inhabits that

FIGURE 11 *A model of ethnic systems: The numbers refer to the four "coins":*
(1) people/culture, (2) race/morphology, (3) society/social structure, and (4)
speech community/language. In each case the egg-shaped figure represents one
side of the coin and the triangle the other side. The arrows indicate the normal
order in which ethnographers study the characteristics of each group, and the let-
ters indicate the order in which prehistorians reconstruct these characteristics.

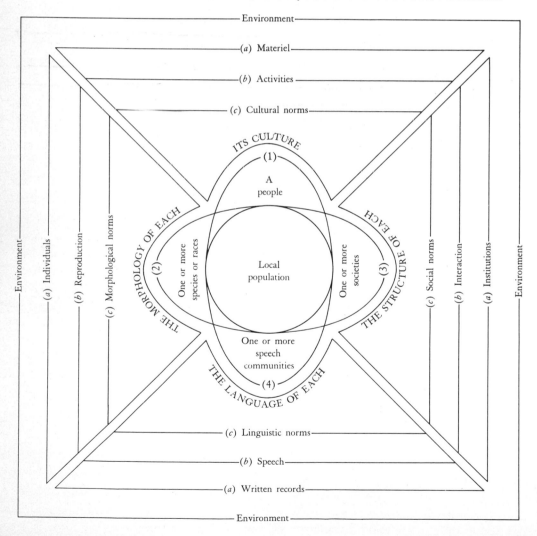

environment, and, between them, a series of figures referring to the four kinds of ethnic groups and their characteristics.

Four egg-shaped figures extend out from the inner circle. The first symbolizes the people (cultural group) to which the inhabitants belong. The other three represent the inhabitants' species or race(s), society(ies), and speech community(ies) respectively. (The plurals are added in parentheses to signify that a single people often includes individuals belonging to several different races, societies, and speech communities.)

The egg-shaped figures, then, refer to the different kinds of ethnic groups. As we have seen (Sec. 1.2), each may be regarded as one side of a coin. Extending out from each one is the other side of its coin, consisting of an inverted, truncated, and layered triangle, which symbolizes the traits characteristic of the group. The first triangle represents the people's culture and the other three signify respectively the morphology of each species or race to which the people belong (if more than one), the structure of each society, and the language of each speech community.

Each triangle is divided into three parts, symbolizing different kinds of characteristics, and these parts are connected by arrows, indicating the order in which an ethnographer studies the parts.

1. In the case of a cultural group or people, the ethnographer begins by observing the activities of daily life, by means of which the people maintains its existence. He also studies the norms that mediate the activities and the materials and artifacts resulting from them, which collectively may be termed "materiel." The combination of activities, norms, and materiel constitutes the people's *culture*.

2. In dealing with a morphological group, whether a species or a race, the investigator begins with the individuals in the group and studies their characteristics. In order fully to understand these characteristics he must also study the behavior of reproduction, by means of which new individuals were born, and the morphological norms that affected that behavior. Again, therefore, we have a combination of behavior (reproduction in place of activities), norms, and products (offspring in place of materiel). Taken together, the three comprise the *morphology* of the species or race, corresponding to the culture of the people.

3. The student of a society begins by distinguishing its institutions, that is, the overlapping groups of individuals into which it is organized. He observes the ways in which the members of each institution interact toward one another and studies the norms that mediate the behavior of interaction. To this third combination of behavior, norms, and the products of behavior in the form of institutions we may apply the term *social structure*.

4. Finally, the speech of each linguistic group is connected by arrows with the norms that determine the way its members speak and enable the speakers to understand one another, and with the records of speech, if any. Here again, we have a triad of behavior (speech), norms, and the products of behavior (records), which we call *language*.

The four triads are obviously interconnected. Thus, reproduction produces not only new offspring (2), but also, as a secondary effect, new families (3). The construction of a house (1) may require the organization of a new and perhaps evanescent work group (3) for the purpose. A word may be coined (4) or an insignia manufactured (1) in order to symbolize and thus help to maintain a social class (3). Such interconnections are symbolized by the parallel lines extending between the corresponding parts of each triad.

Despite the interconnections, the four triads are resonably distinct. The cultural triad is a people's means of adapting to its environment. It provides the people with uniquely human ways of obtaining food, shelter, defense, medication, and the remaining things it needs in order to survive and to compete successfully with other peoples. The morphological triad produces offspring to replace individuals who die, and hence it, too, is essential for survival of the group.

The other two triads govern the ways in which human beings adjust to one another. The triad of social structure regulates interpersonal relations by organizing societies into institutions. The triad of language provides the means of communication within speech communities.

Nevertheless, triads are often combined. For example, some authorities argue that culture includes language, while others consider them to be distinct phenomena (cf. Linton, 1936, p. 83, and

Sapir, 1939, p. 233). Actually, both views are correct. Culture and language may logically be grouped together because both consist of behavior (activities or speech) that frequently produces objects (materiel or records), whereas the other two triads consist of individuals (singly or in groups) who are the product of interaction (sexual or social). Nevertheless, language is so complex that the persons who study it have been forced to distinguish it from culture and to treat it as a separate system.

Parts of the cultural and social triads are often lumped together as "socio-cultural" units (e.g., Binford, 1962, p. 219). This lumping is appropriate on the level of norms, for cultural and social norms are the same kind of phenomenon. It is inappropriate on the levels of behavior and products, however. Cultural activities and social interaction are distinct kinds of behavior, and it is absurd to lump together materiel and institutions.

Each culture, morphology, social structure, and language may be regarded as a separate system, arbitrarily distinguished by the investigator because all four systems together would be too complex to study as a unit. It is a matter of historic accident that the totality of human traits has been divided in this fourfold manner, but there is also a certain logic to the division, as we have just seen.

Up to this point, we have portrayed the four systems in abstract terms, as they appear to the ethnographer who is able to observe and question a people and thus to obtain full information about its norms and behavior and the products of behavior. Unfortunately, the prehistorian does not have access to the people themselves, unless he is working so close to the present time that descendants of the people he is studying are still alive. Hence, he is forced to reconstruct the people's culture, morphology(ies), social structure(s), and language(s). He must start with remains, in accordance with the principle that all his research has to be based primarily upon archeological evidence (Sec. 2.1). This requirement means that he must change the direction of the arrows in Figure 11, proceeding from the outer to the inner part of each triad, that is, from (*a*) to (*c*).

Changing the direction of the arrows also means that the prehistorian must work with fragmentary evidence, for two reasons: (1) All products of behavior, whether materiel, individuals, institutionally organized groups, or written records, are subject to destruction. As a result, one is only able to base one's reconstruction on surviving traces of the products. (2) Not all behavior, whether cultural, reproductive, social, or linguistic, results in the production of objects that can survive archeologically. When it does not, the chances of reconstructing the behavior and its norms are negligible.

6

The environment

Let us now consider the five parts of Figure 11 in more detail. We shall begin with the environment and then discuss the four kinds of ethnic systems that operate within it.

Biologists refer to units of the environment as ecological systems, called *ecosystems* for short. By an ecosystem is meant a community of organisms considered in relation to its inorganic surroundings. The concept of an ecosystem applies only to wild plants and animals; domesticated organisms, including man, belong instead to one or more of the kinds of ethnic systems to be discussed below.

We are here concerned with the relationships between ethnic systems and their environments, including not only ecosystems, but also individual features of the environments. Every ethnic group has to make some adjustments to the setting in which it lives. This necessity is particularly noticeable in studying the early part of prehistory, when the environment in many parts of the world differed greatly from today's conditions (Butzer, 1966). For example, the succession of glacial periods in Europe and North America forced man, who is essentially a tropical animal, to adapt to arctic conditions (Chard, 1969b, pp. 98–100). In addition, the glaciers formed barriers that prevented the dispersal of man in certain directions and facilitated migrations in other directions by causing the sea level to fall and thereby exposing land bridges between areas that are now separated by the sea (Chard, 1969b, pp. 140–142).

As we move forward through prehistory toward the present, conditions become more and more like our own, but at the same time man becomes increasingly adept at taking advantage of particular features of the environment, such as the existence of fertile soil with which to grow crops and of minerals that can be smelted to produce metal artifacts. Even when the environment is familiar to us, therefore, we must examine it in detail in order to learn the features that may or may not have been exploited by the inhabitants.

No people lives in a completely uniform environment. Instead, a people has access to several *microenvironments,* each differing somewhat in climate, topography, drainage, rocks, soils, flora, and fauna (Coe and Flannery, 1964). A people tends to exploit several microenvironments, moving from one to another at different seasons of the year or else visiting each when in need of one of its resources. The greater the diversity of the environment and the broader the variety of the resources that are exploited, the more a people expands its activities in this way.

Remnant activity patterns are used to study the manner in which a people exploited its various microenvironments. As we have seen (Sec. 5.4), such an activity pattern is an expression of the manner in which the remains of a people's activities are distributed over the landscape. From it, the prehistorian is able to find out which activities, if any, were carried on in each microenvironment and thereby to obtain an idea of the extent to which the people utilized that microenvironment (e.g., Flannery, 1968).

It is not enough simply to note which resources a particular people utilized or ignored in each of its microenvironments. In addition the investigator should study the limitations imposed on the people by its microenvironments, for example, the absence of mineral resources and the lack of enough moisture to carry on agriculture efficiently. Knowledge of these limitations is essential for an understanding of the people's culture.

Societies, too, must adapt to the environment. Prehistorians study a society's adaptation by reconstructing its residential pattern and correlating it with features of the environment (Sec. 5.4). In so doing, they make use of the theoretical models for the distribution of residential institutions that have been developed by geographers (Chorley and Haggett, 1967).

7
Cultures: activities

In approaching the ethnic components of Figure 11, we must focus not upon ethnic groups per se, as we did in Chapters 3 and 4, but upon the systems of traits that characterize the groups. In the case of each kind of system, we shall first consider the nature of its parts, proceeding in order of the arrows in Figure 11, and shall then discuss how to reconstruct the parts, proceeding in order of the letters from (*a*) to (*c*).

Let us begin with cultural systems, since they offer the greatest possibilities for reconstruction. Behavior is the key to cultural systems, since it forms the connecting link between norms and materiel (Fig. 11). Human beings do not behave randomly; they tend to organize their behavior around activities that are designed to fulfill specific needs, such as the manufacture of tools, acquisition of food, and burial of the dead (Linton, 1936, p. 397). We may refer to these activities as subsystems within the overall system that constitutes the culture.

It will be advisable to organize our discussion of behavior around the activity subsystems (Table 6). Let us begin with the activities that man shares with the other animals and would carry out even if he did not possess cultural norms. We shall call these *sustaining activities,* since they are necessary for the maintenance of life. They may be grouped into eight broad categories, as follows:

1. *Toolmaking.* The production of tools is basic because tools function in so many other kinds of activities. In effect, man uses tools to extend his own organic capabilities. For example, knives improve upon the cutting man can do with his teeth, and hammers intensify blows with his hands. As we have already seen (Secs. 2.4 and 2.5), some lesser animals also make tools, but their procedures are rudimentary and they work only with their limbs and other parts of the body. Man has been able to develop more elaborate procedures, in which he uses tools to make tools, because his technological activities are mediated by cultural norms.

2. *Food.* No organism can survive without food. Man is able to produce a much larger and more varied food supply than the lesser animals can by using specialized tools and more intricate procedures, based upon cultural norms. In addition, he has learned how to domesticate plants and animals and thus to ensure himself a more reliable and more stable supply than is available to the lesser animals.

3. *Sleep.* This is another basic activity; we devote up to one-third of our time to it and, as a result, are accustomed to reside where we sleep. Many animals construct shelters for the purpose; for example, birds build nests and rabbits dig burrows. But only man is able to use tools and thus to produce more complex structures.

Only he, in addition, is able to use fire to heat the places where he sleeps.

4. *Clothing.* Some animals grow fur to protect themselves against the winter and shed it when summer comes. Man, of course, can-

TABLE 6 *Cultural and social subsystems*

Ethnic systems	Categories of subsystems	Subsystems
Culture or civilization	Sustaining activities	Toolmaking Food Sleep Clothing Transportation Recreation Warfare Education
	Intellectual activities	Burial Religion Esthetics Government Commerce Science Medicine Philosophy
Social structure	Residential institutions	Communities: bands, villages, towns, cities, etc. Divisions of communities: households, wards, suburbs, etc. Groups of communities: tribes, states, etc.
	Activity institutions	Work groups: hunting parties, workshops, pilgrimage groups, etc. Sustaining and professional enterprises: farms, estates, churches, factories, markets, etc. Professional associations: trade unions, guilds, scientific institutions, etc.
	Relational institutions	Interaction groups: political parties, committees, police, etc. Descent groups: families, clans, moieties, etc. Rank groups: age grades, classes, castes, etc.

not grow fur naturally, but he has developed specialized tools with which to remove it from animals and make it into clothing. He also employs other materials to produce clothing and ornaments. His unique skills in the manufacture of clothing and structures have enabled him to move out of the tropics, to which all other primates are limited, and to become the only animal who can live in every ecological niche—even on the moon!

5. *Transportation.* Other animals must move about solely by means of their legs, wings, and other organic equipment. Man alone has developed cultural equipment with which to increase his mobility. This equipment enables him to transport himself and, equally important, to transport the tools, clothing, and other artifacts he has accumulated as part of his culture.

6. *Recreation.* The lesser animals pass the time by playing among themselves or with natural objects. Man is able to develop more elaborate equipment and procedures for the purpose.

7. *Warfare.* Both the lesser animals and man are faced with the need to defend themselves against attacks by other animals, including members of their own species. Man has achieved the greatest success in defense because of his ability to produce more efficient weapons and because he has been able to devise elaborate fighting techniques, mediated by cultural norms.

8. *Education.* Among the lesser animals (and probably also early man), education is primarily a matter of example. Advanced peoples have developed special procedures for the purpose of education, which are based upon cultural norms.

We come now to man's unique activities, which are not merely mediated by norms but are dependent upon them and would be impossible without them. We may call these *intellectual activities,* since they are dependent upon the ability to think conceptually. They are listed in the approximate order of their appearance in the archeological record:

1. *Burial.* This activity is of greatest importance to prehistorians because it produces a frequent constituent of archeological remains. Intentional burial presupposes a belief in afterlife, in the super-

natural power of the deceased person, or in something else beyond
the range of a people's experience, and hence it can only develop in
the presence of human thought.

2. *Religion.* Mankind has other beliefs in supernatural powers and
beings that are the basis for religious activities. The beliefs take the
form of cultural norms, and the activities are mediated by other
norms. Lacking such norms, the lesser animals are incapable of
religious beliefs and activities.

3. *Esthetics.* Only man has developed humanistic values, as part of
his cultural norms, and is able to express these in the form of art,
architecture, literature, and music. We see the beginning of esthetic
activity in the attention that Lower Paleolithic man paid to the
shape of his artifacts (G. Clark, 1970, pp. 70–72). This activity
reaches an early climax in the cave art of Upper Pleistocene time
(G. Clark, 1970, pp. 120–124).

4. *Government.* Studies of the lesser primates have shown that
each band is led by one or more males, who have gained authority
by fighting the other males or by facing them down (Eimerl, De-
Vore, et al., 1965, pp. 104–114). Human leaders, on the contrary,
obtain their authority from custom or law and have recourse to their
more advanced fighting techniques only in the case of emergency.

5. *Commerce.* A few wild organisms live together in symbiotic
relationships, each contributing materials to the other, but only man
is able to exchange both materials and equipment over long distances, by virtue of his possession of norms for the purpose. As a
result, he is able to live in environments that lack the resources
necessary for survival.

6. *Science.* Man alone has been able to accumulate knowledge
about his environment, himself, and the development of the two.
The earliest archeological evidence of this knowledge dates from
Late Pleistocene time (Eimerl, DeVore, et al., 1965, p. 128).

7. *Medicine.* Man's scientific knowledge has enabled him to devise
remedies for diseases, an achievement of which the lesser animals
are incapable.

8. *Philosophy.* Finally, the ability to think abstractly and logically
is limited to man because only he can use words to express ideas.

We do not know when he acquired this ability, since it does not appear in the archeological record until after the development of writing.

Having surveyed the various kinds of activities, let us inquire what they have in common to justify calling all of them cultural behavior and contrasting them with morphological, social, and linguistic behavior. The common factor is that they are directed toward the environment, rather than toward fellow human beings. To be sure, not all are directed toward the natural environment as it is viewed by the lesser animals. Religion and parts of other activities are oriented toward the supernatural environment, which man has created as a result of his unique ability to think and to imagine unreal conditions. In addition, techniques and weapons developed to cope with the environment are sometimes used to defend oneself against other human beings. These are exceptions to the rule, however.

8

Cultures: norms

Norms are a creation of the investigator. They consist of regularities that he observes in a people's activities and in the resultant materiel and that he abstracts from the activities and materiel for purposes of study (Fig. 12). We saw how he establishes norms, so far as materiel is concerned, in discussing the formulation of types and modes, both of which are cultural norms abstracted from materiel (Secs. 2.9, 2.11, and 2.12).

Norms are a way of expressing the essential nature of a people's activities and materiel. In this respect they may be compared with the symbols used by chemists to refer to elements, for example, H for hydrogen. Like such a symbol, a norm is a shorthand way of referring to the particular qualities under study.

In the previous section, we found that activities include both actions and thoughts. The ethnographer observes a people's actions and learns its thoughts from its speech and writings. Actions, thoughts, and materiel mutually affect one another (Fig. 12). For example, a potter is guided in making a vessel partially by the way in which he conceives of the vessel, partially by the need to perform techniques such as firing, and partially by his remembrance of the appearances of other vessels. The vessels he produces reflect all three of these factors, and the norms that are abstracted from the potter's thoughts, actions, and products should cover all three of them, in all their interrelationships (Fig. 12).

The regularities in thoughts, actions, and materiel that we conceptualize as norms may come into existence in two different ways. Individuals may repeat the same behavior instinctively, out of habit, or in adaptation to something in their environment, as among the lesser animals. Alternatively, the individuals may conform to agreed-upon laws or rules, to unwritten customs or taboos, or to moral or esthetic standards. The term "norm" does not discriminate among these sources of behavioral regularities; it simply indicates the existence of the regularities.

Nevertheless, every regularity has the potentiality of being conceptualized as a law, rule, custom, taboo, or standard. In effect, the investigator so conceptualizes a regularity when he calls it a norm. This fact does not necessarily mean that the individuals from whose behavior or materiel he has abstracted a regularity were themselves aware of its existence. For example, the speakers of a language are

FIGURE 12 *Relations among a people's behavior* (left, top *and* bottom), *materiel, and norms: The solid arrows show how actions, thoughts, and materiel influence one another* (left) *and how perceptual, procedural, and conceptual norms are consequently related* (right). *The dashed arrows show the manner in which the ethnographer abstracts regularities or norms from the three kinds of observed data, and the dotted arrows symbolize the prehistorian's attempt to infer norms from the remains of a people's materiel.*

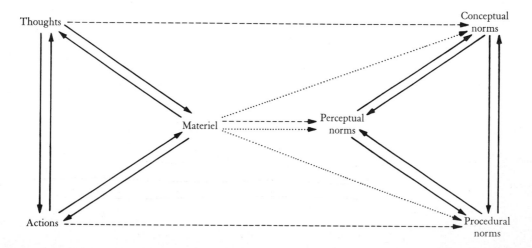

rarely conscious of the grammatical rules inherent in their language. Similarly, studies of Pueblo Indians have shown that potters are aware of only part of the design motifs with which they decorate their vessels (Bunzel, 1929). No speaker of a language or maker of pottery will know more than a small portion of the norms to which his behavior conforms unless he has been trained to think like an anthropologist and has analyzed his own behavior anthropologically.

We may say, then, that norms are potentially definable laws, rules, customs, taboos, or standards to which a people conforms in carrying out its activities and in producing its materiel. In effect, the people's behavior is mediated by the norms. It is through the process of mediation, or conformity to past practice, that a people's activities and materiel acquire the distinctiveness that enables us to identify them as parts of a particular culture.

The process of mediation is made possible by man's unique ability to think conceptually, if often unconsciously, about what he is doing (Lorenz, 1966, pp. 238ff.). Man alone is able to plan ways of doing things by putting together sequences of cultural norms, as when making an artifact, or by constructing patterns of norms, as when designing a building (Homans, 1950, pp. 122–130). It is the existence of these sequences and patterns that makes it necessary for us to use the procedure of articulation.

Once established, the norms and their patterns have an existence apart from the people that originated them. They may spread to other peoples—witness the diffusion of Americanisms around the world at the present time. They may also be adopted by outsiders who enter the local group, as when a foreigner learns the language and customs of the country in which he is residing. Most importantly, they are handed down from generation to generation. Over the period of man's evolution the norms have tended to persist and accumulate as part of our total fund of knowledge about the world around us and the ways of coping with it. Indeed, education is for the most part a process of inculcating our own cultural norms into the next generation.

Cultural norms, then, are on a higher level of abstraction than behavior itself and must be derived from it. They are conceptual units, existing in our thoughts, whether consciously or unconsciously. In any particular instance an individual must decide whether to conform to a norm, that is, to custom, to disregard it, or to act contrary to it; he may make this decision either consciously or unconsciously. Whatever the decision, his behavior will have been affected by the norm but will not in itself be the norm (Taylor, 1967a).

9
Cultures: materiel

Cultural materials and equipment have already been discussed at length in the chapter on archeology (see especially Table 2). Here, we need only summarize that discussion, in order to complete our survey of the nature of cultural systems. (We shall consider only raw materials and worked equipment, that is, artifacts, omitting the intervening categories of processed materials and unworked equipment for the sake of simplicity.) We must also consider aspects of the subject that only the ethnographer is able to study, because his data are so much fuller than the archeologist's.

We saw in Chapter 2 that archeologists assign raw materials to natural-science classes similar to the genera and species used to identify organic remains. Ethnographers are able in addition to query the peoples who used the materials about their own ways of classifying them. The term *ethnoscience* has been coined to distinguish the peoples' own classifications of materials from those of natural science. In effect, ethnoscientific classifications are learned from the peoples under investigation, whereas natural-science categories are created by the investigators (e.g., Arnold, 1971).

As for artifacts, we have already noted three different kinds of classification, each distinguished by a different kind of type: (1) intrinsic types, each of which expresses the nature of the artifacts in its class; (2) extrinsic types, which express qualities of the people that produced the classes—that people's nature, chronology, activities, or development; and (3) cognitive types, by means of which the people themselves categorize their artifacts, as in the ethnoscientific approach to materials (Sec. 2.10). We have also noted that the features of artifacts can be classified in all three ways, so as to produce intrinsic, extrinsic, and cognitive modes (Sec. 2.12).

Each type or mode, whether intrinsic, extrinsic, or cognitive, may be said to consist of a pattern or cluster of attributes that the artisan has built into his artifacts in accordance with the norms of his culture. In effect, the attributes *are* the norms, for an artisan may be presumed to have been guided by his memory of previous procedures and of previously completed artifacts—if, indeed, he did not actually copy the attributes of previous artifacts. The various kinds of materials may likewise be considered indicative of cultural norms, insofar as they appear to have been selected in accordance with custom.

10
Cultures:
reconstruction

Heretofore, we have been discussing the nature of cultural systems as they appear to ethnographers, who are able to study them in their entirety. Now let us turn to the reconstruction of extinct systems by prehistorians.

In this discussion, we shall assume that intrinsic types and modes have already been established by archeologists and that it is impossible to reconstruct cognitive types and modes, unless one is working so close to the present or to the dawn of history that one is able to project ethnographic or ethnohistoric categories back in time to the people one is studying. As a result, we shall be concerned here only with the use of intrinsic types and modes and with the formulation and use of extrinsic types and modes.

We have seen that activities are the key to cultural systems (Sec. 5.7). The prehistorian must therefore focus upon them, even though his evidence consists entirely of types, modes, and other categories of materiel.

The reconstruction of activities has often been likened to detective work. Just as a detective searches for all possible clues with which to reconstruct a crime, so the prehistorian must seek all possible evidence about a people's activities; and just as a detective reconstructs the crime from his clues by utilizing his knowledge of, and experience with, other crimes, so the prehistorian must reconstruct a people's activities in terms of his knowledge about other peoples' activities. Hence, we may distinguish two parts to the reconstructive process: the search for evidence and the interpretation of that evidence in terms of the activities of better-known peoples.

THE SEARCH FOR THE EVIDENCE.   The key concept in the search for evidence is that of remnant activity pattern, by which is meant the manner in which the remains of a people's activities are distributed over the landscape and among its sites (Sec. 5.4). This concept focuses, not upon the remains per se, but upon the manner in which the remains were made and used. It is thus a concept of prehistory rather than archeology.

A remnant activity pattern may be said to consist of a series of loci, in each of which the local people carried out one or more of its activities (Sec. 5.4). The remains obtained from each activity locus comprise an activity assemblage, so called to distinguish it from the cultural assemblage obtained from a site or a component of a site (Sec. 2.6). The specimens from a single-locus site or component are an exception. In such a case, the activity assemblage, from the locus, and the cultural assemblage, from the site or component as a whole, will coincide.

The remnant activity pattern should not be thought of merely as an accumulation of activity loci, each with its own assemblage. It also involves the distribution of the loci, as the term "pattern" implies. In this respect it resembles the structure of a site. A remnant activity pattern is to its collective assemblages as the structure of a site is to its contents.

In studying remnant activity patterns, the prehistorian is guided by the knowledge about the distribution of activities that ethnographers have acquired by studying contemporaneous communities (e.g., Vogt, 1956). He may expect to find one of three main kinds of patterns.

1. *Dispersed pattern*. The community under study may have moved from place to place, in search of game if it lived by hunting, of other wild foods if it also practiced gathering and fishing, or of pastures if it lived by herding. Such a community's activity loci will be scattered among a number of sites, and the prehistorian will have to dig many of them in order to obtain the total range of the community's activities. This kind of pattern was most prevalent during the early part of prehistory (Sec. 3.6).

2. *Concentrated pattern*. The community under study may instead have remained in the same dwelling site throughout the year, traveling elsewhere only to procure raw materials or for purposes of trade. In such a case, the prehistorian can expect to find the same set of activity loci in each site he digs. This condition is most characteristic of the middle part of prehistory, when the develop-

ment of agriculture fostered a sedentary or shifting form of residence.

3. *Sustaining and professional co-patterns.* As agricultural peoples evolved toward civilization, their constituent communities gradually ceased to be uniform in culture. Some continued to maintain their former peasant way of life, while others began to specialize in nonessential activities, such as religion, burial, or commerce. Eventually, this trend resulted in the differentiation of two kinds of residential communities: sustaining communities, which produced food and other essential materiel, and professional communities, which specialized in nonessential activities. The sum total of the sustaining communities may be called a "sustaining co-people" and the totality of the professional communities, a "professional co-people" (Sec. 3.13).

Each of the co-peoples has its own activity co-pattern. Among the early Sumerians of Mesopotamia, for example, the sustaining co-people apparently divided its activities between the outskirts of the cities, where it lived, and the surrounding countryside, where it practiced agriculture, while the professional co-people concentrated its activities in the temple precincts at the centers of the cities (Frankfort, n.d., pp. 57–58). Among the early Maya Indians of Yucatán, on the contrary, the sustaining co-people lived in the jungles and carried out its activities there, whereas the professional co-people lived in separate ceremonial centers (Willey, 1966, pp. 117–124).

As the co-peoples developed further, their sustaining and professional activities were often transferred from residential communities to other kinds of institutions, such as farmsteads and factories. Nevertheless, the fundamental distinction between co-peoples who performed different activities in terms of separate co-patterns continued to exist; thus, our own sustaining co-people is rural, whereas our professional co-people is predominantly urban and suburban.

When studying a dispersed activity pattern (1), the prehistorian has to begin with a survey of sites, designed to identify those in which different kinds of activities were carried out. Then he looks for a cluster of sites that includes as many different kinds of activity loci as possible and appears to have been produced by a single residential community. If this cluster appears to be typical of the people he is studying, he uses it as the basis for reconstructing the people's activity pattern. If he is unable to find a cluster of sites in which all possible activity loci are represented, he will have to piece together the pattern by studying several incomplete clusters. In either case, he will need to recover assemblages from the loci in order to learn about the activities that took place there. His final pattern should include all possible activities in the dimension of form (Table 6).

When studying a concentrated activity pattern (2), the prehistorian usually begins his search for its loci at a typical dwelling site. He attempts to distinguish areas in that site that were used for different purposes, such as house sites, workshops, and graves. Each of these areas constitutes an activity locus. Many will be self-evident, but others will be discoverable only by statistical analysis of the distribution of the remains, designed to reveal concentrations of artifacts destined for use in a single activity (Tugby, 1965, p. 11) Each of these concentrations may be treated as an activity assemblage.

This kind of research requires more intensive excavation than when one is working in systematics, that is, answering the question "Who?" or "Where and when?" (Chaps. 3 and 4). It is desirable to sample all parts of the site, in order to be sure of obtaining evidence of all the activities carried out there. One should also sample other dwelling sites to discover activities that were performed but may have left no traces at the first site.

While seeking to recover an adequate sample of activity assemblages from a people's dwelling sites, the prehistorian should keep in mind a list of the people's potential activities, that is, the cultural part of the dimension of form (Table 6). He should constantly be on the lookout for additional activities that the people may be expected to have undertaken. If he cannot find them, he must assume that they were carried on away from the people's dwelling places and must search elsewhere for the loci of these activities. In some cases, he will find the missing loci grouped together in a single site, but in other cases each will occur by itself, as when a burial mound was constructed some distance away from a place of residence and a cave was used only for religious purposes. The search for the missing loci should continue until the entire range of potential activities has been covered.

The investigator who is working with activity co-patterns (3) follows a similar procedure. He normally begins his search for activity loci in sites occupied by the professional co-people, to which he is attracted by the wealth of its remains if he is an archeologist or by the opportunity for studying the development of civilizations if he is a prehistorian interested in answering the question "How and why?" All too often, he confines his research to that site and others like it, becoming so preoccupied with the professional co-pattern that he completely overlooks the sustaining co-pattern.

This neglect of the sustaining co-pattern is a mistake. The question "What?" is our present concern, and if the investigator is to provide a satisfactory answer to that question, he will have to reconstruct the sustaining as well as the professional co-pattern. Let us suppose, for example, that he has excavated a city site without any evidence that the inhabitants cultivated the surrounding terrain. He should then search that terrain for village sites in which producers of food for the city dwellers might have lived. He may find the village sites some distance away from the city sites, in the vicinity of agricultural fields distributed along irrigation canals. Let us suppose further that he has encountered burials in the city sites but not in the village sites. He may conclude that the villagers buried their dead in the cities, but if this conclusion does not seem reasonable, he will have to seek elsewhere for the sustaining co-people's burials. He may find them in caves some distance away, in which case he will conclude that both the village sites and burial caves form parts of the sustaining co-pattern of the people under study.

Prehistorians who limit themselves to a supposedly professional co-pattern are running the risk of misidentifying the stage of development of the people under study. Some noncivilized peoples, such as the Magdalenians of Europe, have produced remains of as high quality, artistically speaking, as those of civilized people (Ucko and Rosenfeld, 1967). The only way to be sure whether or not such peoples were civilized is to determine whether or not they had sustaining co-patterns.

INTERPRETATION OF THE EVIDENCE. Having worked out a people's remnant activity pattern or co-patterns and obtained sufficient activity assemblages to illustrate each part of it, the prehistorian seeks to *infer* the original activity pattern or co-pattern from these evidences (R. H. Thompson, 1956). His first step is to convert his raw data into meaningful categories. He accomplishes this conversion by extrinsic classification and/or identification, first of his artifacts and then of his assemblages.

On the level of artifacts, he formulates types and modes consisting of technologically significant attributes, which provide him with information about toolmaking, the construction of residences, and so forth. He also formulates types and modes consisting of functionally significant attributes, in order to secure evidence about the activities in which the artifacts were used (Sec. 2.10).

On the level of activity assemblages, he formulates diagnostic complexes of the types and modes. First, he sets up tentative complexes, and then tests them by using them to classify his assemblages. If they do not work well, he revises them and reclassifies them, repeating this procedure until the complexes are satisfactory.

The procedure may be termed *activity classification,* since its aim is to set up complexes which will be indicative of particular activities. Once the complexes have been established, they may be used to identify additional assemblages belonging in the same class and indicative of the same activity.

Activity classification and identification are parallel to cultural classification and identification. Indeed, Figure 7, which illustrates the results of cultural classification, can also be used to illustrate the results of activity classification by substituting "activity assemblages" for "cultural assemblages" in the explanation of the bottom two circles and by replacing the names in the top two circles by "institution" on the left and "activity" on the right.

As this modification will illustrate, classes of activity assemblages are indicative not only of activities but also of the institutions that performed the activities. Only the activities concern us here; we shall consider the institutions later in connection with social structure (Secs. 5.13 and 5.16).

The prehistorian's next task is to fill out the knowledge that he has acquired about each activity by classifying and identifying the remains. In so doing, he makes use of analogies, or parallels drawn from his knowledge of other peoples' cultures (Ascher, 1961a). In effect, he uses these analogies to reconstruct perished materiel, activities, and norms from the surviving materiel.

There are two kinds of analogies, *general* and *specific* (Tax et al., 1953, pp. 229–230). General analogies are those based upon the comparative and experimental studies of cultural anthropologists, whereas specific analogies are obtained from ethnographic research on the descendants or successors of the people under study (cf. Secs. 1.4 and 1.5). Both kinds of analogies assume that archeological remains must have been produced and used in the same manner as similar specimens observed in an anthropological or ethnographic context. In the case of specific analogies, this assumption is supported by one's knowledge that the analogies occur in the same area as one's remains and hence may have been handed down from the prehistoric people who produced the remains.

The assumption suffers from two weaknesses. The first is that a remnant activity pattern and its activity assemblages may not be distinctive enough to provide clear evidence of activities and norms. For example, it is possible to infer the steps in chipping stone artifacts from the scars of manufacture, but in the case of ground-stone artifacts, the process cannot be inferred because the grinding has obliterated most traces of the previous steps in the procedure. The second is that there are often two or more alternative ways to account for one's evidence. For example, large pits dug into the ground could have been used as either houses, religious structures, or storage pits. In such a case, it is necessary to consider all possible uses and select those that are most likely to have produced the conditions encountered, in accordance with the principle of multiple working hypotheses (Sec. 1.5).

Each prehistorian must make his own judgment as to when a set of remains is distinctive enough to indicate the presence of a particular kind of perished materiel, activities, or norms and when there is sufficient evidence to justify making a choice between several alternative analogies. As we have seen (Sec. 5.2), some prehistorians are more conservative in these respects than others are. In any event, one should always publish one's evidence in full and discuss all alternative interpretations, so that the reader may have an opportunity to form his own judgment about the alternatives.

This problem of alternatives is where Soviet prehistorians tend to go astray. They infer perished materiel, behavior, and norms from the archeological evidence in terms of Marxian theory without considering alternative possibilities. The more scientific procedure would be to examine both non-Marxian and Marxian alternatives and to select those which best fit the facts.

Few Western archeologists have this bias, but some do skew their results by assuming that it is not necessary to look for parallels among contemporary peoples on a more advanced level of development than that of the peoples under study. On the contrary, the development of culture is cumulative, the customs of earlier peoples do tend to survive among more advanced peoples, and hence the prehistorian must search for parallels everywhere (Ucko and Rosenfeld, 1967, pp. 150–158).

But the prehistorian's task is not ended when he has selected the best possible analogy. He should then use his conclusions as a guide with which to search for new kinds of evidence not yet encountered in the sites of the people under study. In other words, the reconstructive process is not simply a matter of inferring perished materiel, activities, and norms from archeological evidence. It also includes the formulation of hypotheses as to the existence of materiel, activities, and norms for which no evidence has yet been found, followed by a search for evidence with which to prove or disprove one's hypotheses (Binford, 1967).

USE OF ETHNOGRAPHIC EVIDENCE. Thus far, we have been considering the use of archeological data to reconstruct and articulate cultural systems and have treated ethnographic data only as a source of analogies to be used in illuminating the indicative evidence provided by archeology. Some ethnologists (e.g., Gomme, 1908, pp. 167–169) have argued that ethnographic data can also be used as indicative evidence. They invoke the *age-area hypothesis,* which holds that the broader the distribution of a trait at the present time, the older it must be. If this hypothesis is correct, one should be able to set up accurate sequences of traits by placing those with the broadest distributions at the beginning of each sequence and those with the narrowest distributions at the end. Such ethnographically based sequences can then be correlated with archeologically established peoples in order to fill out one's knowledge of the peoples' cultures;

in this way, for instance, Forrest E. Clements (1932) has reconstructed the Upper Paleolithic method of diagnosing disease.

The age-area hypothesis has recently come under strong attack (e.g., by Wallis, 1945), and an attempt to test it by plotting the distributions of water mills and windmills in southern England during historic time has produced negative results, there being little regularity in the distribution of the traits that arose at about the same time (Hodgen, 1942). The age-area method should therefore be used only as a last resort, when archeologically based methods have failed to give adequate results.

PRESENTATION OF THE RESULTS. The foregoing research should enable the prehistorian to reconstruct and articulate a series of activities, norms, and materiel that, taken together, compose the culture of the people under study. He presents these categories in order of the activities, discussing each activity in terms of the norms that mediated it and in terms of the resultant kinds of specimens. This procedure marks him as a prehistorian rather than an archeologist, who would organize the specimens in the order of their materials (Steward and Setzler, 1938, p. 6).

11
Morphologies:
nature

INDIVIDUALS. Organisms are the key to the study of morphological systems, taking the place of behavior in the analysis of cultural systems. The human body is viewed as a series of parts, such as the brain, the skull, and various muscles, that fit together to form a structural whole. Since the reader has undoubtedly been exposed to this point of view through the study of biology, we need not go into it here.

REPRODUCTION. The behavior of reproduction includes sexual intercourse and the resultant birth of a child. The individuals who have intercourse contribute a mixture of their genes to the child, and the nature of this mixture determines the nature of the child's morphology. It is assumed that the reader has sufficient knowledge of genetics to understand this process.

NORMS. The reader is less likely to be aware of the effect of norms on the nature of children. Each morphological group has such norms, which mediate its members' selection of sexual partners. The norms include incest taboos, caste restrictions, marriage rules, and more subtle ideas about who is the best kind of mate, such as ideals of beauty and intelligence, all of which channel and limit an individual's choice of a mate and hence affect the nature of the genes that are passed on to the offspring.

The biologist need not concern himself with morphological norms because, as in the case of cultural norms, they do not occur among wild animals. Mating takes place randomly in nature, without a thought as to who will be a good or bad mate or the best parent for one's children. Man alone is capable of thinking in this manner.

On the other hand, domesticated animals and domesticated plants are affected by morphological norms. Consciously or unconsciously, man controls their breeding in accordance with his ideas about the best kinds of organisms to reproduce. There are, then, two sets of morphological norms, one for man himself and the other for the animals and plants he has domesticated.

12
Morphologies:
reconstruction

Prehistorians usually turn the task of reconstructing human organisms over to specialists in physical anthropology (Sec. 1.5), since highly technical knowledge, measurements, and terminology are involved. Such a specialist works with the assemblages of physical remains that have been used to distinguish species or races (Sec. 3.15). He identifies, describes, and measures the bones in the assemblages, in order to find out the range of variation in each species or race.

The specialist also articulates the bones by determining how they fit together in the form of skeletons and reconstructs the flesh, skin, and hair that once covered the skeletons. He does so by drawing analogies to modern races that are similar in their skeletal morphologies and by projecting characteristics of contemporary groups back to their prehistoric ancestors—a procedure that, unfortunately, is only feasible when dealing with late prehistory. Earlier races must be presumed to have differed too much from their modern descendants to be treated in this manner.

The bones in the assemblages are also studied for evidence of diseases or abnormalities, such as dental caries and rheumatism (e.g., Jarcho, 1966). The prehistorian also may find traces of curing practices, such as trepanation, that is, cutting of the skull to relieve pressure on the brain.

Similar procedures are followed in dealing with domesticated animals and plants, though the specialists consulted in these cases are likely to be biologists rather than physical anthropologists. The remnants of the organisms, as found archeologically, are used to reconstruct the original organisms and, if possible, their diseases and the remedies applied to them.

The behavior of reproduction is impossible to reconstruct from prehistoric remains, since it leaves no traces there, unless the people happen to have portrayed it in their art, as the Mochica people of Peru did (Bushnell, 1963, p. 82). Occasionally, however, the behavior can be projected back from history into prehistory.

Morphological norms are even more difficult to distinguish archeologically. One's only hope is to project the norms back from history into late prehistory.

Finally, the investigator must give thought to the possibility that certain races of man or domesticates may not have left any remains in the sites. He should attempt to reconstruct the missing morphologies. Again, these can only be projected back from the historic period or inferred indirectly from the nature of other remains. For example, in the Middle East, the presence of wheat is inferred from the occurrence in the remains of clay sickles and ovens for parching the grain (e.g., Chard, 1969b, p. 208).

13
Social structures:
institutions

The study of social structures, like the study of morphologies, focuses upon human beings, but it examines them as the personnel of institutions, not as individual organisms. An institution may be defined as a group of individuals organized for specific purposes. Its members are bound together by the ways in which they interact with one another, and their interaction is in turn mediated by social norms (Fig. 11). Institutions vary in size from small families to the United Nations.

But a society is also a group of individuals (Sec. 5.5). What is the difference between a society and an institution? Many authorities equate the two; for example, Beals and Hoijer (1953, pp. 206–210) apply the term "society" to a territorial organization such as a tribe or a nation, which would be an institution in our terminology. From our standpoint, this application is a misuse of the term "society." We are applying that term to all persons who share a common set of social norms and who consequently possess similar institutions (Sec. 3.4). A society defined in this way is rarely limited to a single nation; it includes the citizens of all nations that are organized according to the same set of norms. Moreover, the members of such a society are marked not only by the norms that affect their national governments, but also by those which affect all the other kinds of institutions listed in Table 6.

The fundamental difference between an institution and a society—or, indeed, any of the other kinds of ethnic groups in our dimension of form (Fig. 11)—is that an institution consists of persons who are in contact and who therefore are able to interact, if only by means of emissaries who travel long distances to establish contact, whereas a society normally includes some persons who do not interact. In other words, an institution is held together by the behavior of interaction, whereas a society, people, or other ethnic group is linked by norms, which can and do spread beyond the limits of interaction.

An institution should not be confused, either, with the buildings that house it or with the other artifacts that it uses. Thus, a university is an institution, composed of faculty, students, and administrative staff who interact among themselves. Each university has a campus, but the campus is not part of the university, considered as an institution. The campus consists of buildings and grounds, that is, cultural materiel, which for the most part have been produced by nonuniversity personnel carrying out cultural activities without interacting socially with the university personnel. Indeed, the campus may originally have been produced for the use of an entirely different institution. It is merely a part of the environment in which the university personnel interact—an environment that also includes the books in the university's libraries and the artifacts in its museums.

An institution is often organized for the purpose of carrying out a particular activity, but it should not be confused with that activity. For instance, a university is basically an educational institution, but it does not limit itself to the activity of education. It also undertakes scientific research, the production of works of art, and many of the other kinds of activities listed in Table 6, and it changes its activities from time to time. Thus, some American universities are now abandoning military training and research in response to the protests of faculty and students. Similarly, the American nation carries out a variety of activities, though it leaves more activities to private enterprises than the communist countries do. As these examples illustrate, an institution provides only the personnel and organization of an activity, not its content or its products, which are likely to be the same, regardless of the institution involved.

In Table 6, institutions are regarded as subsystems within an overall social system, in the same way that activities are subsystems within an overall cultural system. Like activities, institutions may be divided into several different categories, which we shall now consider in turn.

The first of these categories consists of *residential institutions,* so called because they are based upon the fact that man is a gregarious animal and tends to live in groups. Archeological traces of these groups are relatively easy to find because all except the most mobile peoples have left recoverable remains in their places of habitation. The residential institutions may be grouped into the following three-level hierarchy (see also Table 6):

1. *Communities.* The basic unit is the residential community, consisting of all individuals who live in continuous, face-to-face contact and who possess a single residential pattern. According to the archeological evidence (see, e.g., Chard, 1969b, pp. 88–91), the earliest communities consisted of bands of hunters and gatherers. Agricultural villages developed next, and towns and cities made their appearance toward the close of prehistory.

·2. *Divisions of communities.* Communities obviously break down into households, which can often be inferred archeologically from the buildings in which they lived. Groupings of households, such as wards or suburbs, can sometimes be distinguished by the clustering of their buildings or by enclosures.

3. *Groups of communities.* At the beginning of prehistory, human communities were probably independent, as is still the case among the other primates, but eventually they became organized into

larger, territorially based units. These units are practically impossible to distinguish on the basis of archeological evidence alone, but it is theorized that the first to develop was the tribe, consisting of all the bands and villages in a local district. The head of the paramount community commonly served as chief the tribe. As the number of constituent communities grew larger, the tribe developed into a state or nation, which was governed by a hierarchy of officials, often including a bureaucracy. From the evidence of oral and written history (see, e.g., Frankfort, n.d., pp. 57–58), we know that some early states were composed only of cities and their suburbs—the so-called city-states—some only of villages, and some of a combination of cities and villages.

The second major category is made up of *activity institutions,* which are organized to carry out specific cultural activities. We can trace their development during prehistoric time because archeological remains are products of the activities that they performed. They include the following (see also Table 6):

1. *Work groups.* The members of a community or another kind of residential institution may band together temporarily or permanently, and privately or publicly, in order to carry out cultural activities. Simple groups organized for this purpose are known by the name of the activity that they perform, such as hunting parties, pilgrimage groups, and science clubs, or else by the places in which they operate, for example, workshop groups. We find evidences of some of these groups at the beginning of prehistory (e.g., Howell, 1961).

2. *Sustaining and professional enterprises.* As human activities became more elaborate during the course of prehistory, new and more complex institutions had to be developed to handle them (e.g., Frankfort, n.d., pp. 111–113). We may call these new institutions "enterprises," and divide them into two kinds, based upon the contrasting co-cultures of civilized peoples: (1) sustaining enterprises, such as farms, estates, plantations, and ranches, and (2) professional enterprises, such as factories, markets, churches, and schools.

3. *Professional associations*. The participants in different enterprises who perform similar activities often unite themselves into trade unions, guilds, congresses for the exchange of knowledge, and other kinds of professional organizations. The American Anthropological Association, which is composed of experts on the subject matter of this book (Sec. 1.5), is a typical example.

A final category of institutions is based upon social relationships, rather than residential affiliation or the organization of activities. We shall call the institutions in this category *relational.* We do not know when they first developed, since the social relationships upon which they are based are not preserved in the archeological record, but they were all present by the close of prehistoric time. They may be summarized as follows (see also Table 6):

1. *Interaction groups*. Members of present-day communities or other residentially based institutions often band together to influence the other members of their own institutions or the members of related institutions. If their intentions are peaceful, they form parties, committees, or sociopolitical action groups, but if they believe that the only way to achieve their goals is by violence, they may set up subversive organizations, with which to combat posses, police, or other agencies for the enforcement of an institution's social norms. Some interaction groups are temporary, and others are permanent. Some are private, while others, notably the enforcement agencies, are maintained by communities or states.

2. *Descent groups*. These consist of individuals who are related through birth or marriage. Families are the basic units. Our own families are called nuclear, because they normally include only parents and children, but other societies have extended families, each containing additional relatives. In some societies, families are grouped into units known as "clans," "sibs," "phratries," or "moieties." Such units are based upon descent from a common ancestor in a manner that varies depending upon the unit.

3. *Rank groups*. The more complex societies possess hierarchies of age grades, classes, castes, and the like, based upon age, descent, inherited wealth, or some other criterion. Royalty, slaves, and the so-called working class are examples.

We have seen that many institutions contain officers and other personnel who occupy special statuses. We may define such a status as a position of authority, respect, or obligation within an institution. Each status carries with it a role, consisting of interactions that the person in that status is expected to perform on behalf of the institution. Conversely, the other members of the institution are often expected to react in specified ways to a person of status. These interactions hold the institution together; without them, the statuses would disappear, the personnel would break apart, and the institutions would disintegrate.

It is difficult to distinguish the behavior of interaction, which is social, from the behavior of activities, which is cultural, for the two are normally combined in the same behavioral sequences. Thus, there will be interaction among the members of a hunting party while it carries out the activity of obtaining food. Similarly, interaction between teacher and student is a normal concomitant of the activity of education, except insofar as the student learns cultural activities by himself or through experience.

The proportion of social to cultural behavior varies with the situation. Warfare and government are predominantly social, in that their aim is to solve problems of human interaction, but they also involve cultural techniques and therefore are included in the list of activities in Table 6. At the other extreme, the painting of a picture by an amateur artist is entirely cultural, unless done by a member of a work group organized for the purpose.

As a general rule, behavior that is directed toward other members of an institution and helps to maintain that institution may be considered social, whereas behavior that is directed toward nature and enables man to take advantage of it is cultural. Indeed, some socially oriented authors (e.g., Brace, 1967, p. 56) view culture as part of the environment in which institutional groups operate. This view is true of cultural materiel, which is fashioned from the environment, but not of cultural activities. Like social interaction, they take place within the environment.

In discussing cultural activities (Sec. 5.7), we noted that some are directed, not toward the natural environment, but toward supernatural qualities and persons believed to be a part of that environment. We also found that cultural activities may be directed toward other human beings regarded as part of one's environment, such as foreigners or members of a supposedly inferior race. Similarly, we must recognize that social behavior may be directed toward natural organisms that have been drawn into human institutions, such as pets and other domesticated animals.

15
Social structures:
norms

A biologist studying animal societies need concern himself only with the behavior of interaction and with the manner in which the interaction serves to maintain the society. The student of man must also take into consideration the norms that mediate interaction, that is, the society's ideas about what are the proper, normal, or customary ways of relating to other people.

Because nonhuman societies operate without the benefit of social norms, no such society extends beyond the boundary of a single residential institution. In other words, each animal society consists of a single community. It develops its own distinctive ways of interacting, which it perpetuates by habit and transmits to new members of the community by example. Its ways of interacting cannot spread from one society-institution to another in the manner of social norms because they are not conceptual.

Conversely, man models his behavior on the ideas we are calling norms or, if he is a rebel, acts contrary to the norms. Being ideas, the norms tend to spread from one community to another, and as a result each human society, unlike an animal society, consists of multiple communities that share common social norms (Sec. 5.13). Some human societies contain so many communities that it is impossible for all their personnel to interact, and the members of its communities are not all aware of one another.

Social norms, like cultural norms, may be said to express the nature of the systems and subsystems to which they belong. Each system and subsystem has its characteristic norms, and each is open to new norms, which may be developed within the system or borrowed from other systems.

16
Social structures:
reconstruction

As in the case of cultural reconstruction, the inference of social traits and their articulation into social structures is based upon the remnant settlement patterns. First, the prehistorian turns to the residential rather than the activity pattern and uses it to reconstruct and articulate the kinds of residential institutions present in the local society. He excavates dwelling sites and attempts to divide them into *residential components,* each occupied by a single community. Having done so, he is able to treat all the remains from each component as a separate *residential assemblage.*

A residential component should not be confused with a cultural component (Sec. 2.6). Chang (1967a, pp. 38–56) considers them the same, but this is true only if the cultural component is so small that it can be presumed to have been deposited by a single community. The two kinds of components must otherwise be distinguished. For example, in each cultural component at Olduvai Gorge, Tanzania, Leakey found a number of living floors, each of which is identifiable as a separate residential component (Isaac, 1969, pp. 8–11).

When one finds two residential components in the same cultural component, one is justified in concluding that the communities that occupied them belonged to the same cultural group, but not that they were organized alike and hence belonged to the same social group. To determine whether the two communities were organized alike, one must isolate each community's residential assemblages and infer from them the community's size, composition, and organization by drawing analogies to historic and contemporary communities.

Sedentary communities are the easiest to study in this fashion. When one recovers a residential assemblage that seems to have been deposited by a more or less permanent village, town, or city, one can assume that it constitutes practically all of that community's residential remains, and one is therefore justified in naming the community after the site from which the assemblage was obtained (e.g., Trigger, 1968a, pp. 20–23).

Distinguishing communities' assemblages is more difficult when one is studying the bands prevalent during early prehistory. One cannot assume that a single assemblage comprises all of a band's residential remains, because the band probably moved from one site to another. For example, the band may have spent the summer at one site and the winter at another. Only if one finds a summer and a winter site juxtaposed and clearly separated from other sites of the same kind is one justified in concluding that they constitute the remains of a single band. Such a band may more appropriately be named after the locality in which it occurs than after a site, since it is represented in several sites.

The assemblages of middle prehistoric villages that carried on shifting agriculture, moving periodically from one clearing in the forest to another, are equally difficult to distinguish, because it is necessary to correlate a series of dwelling sites some distance apart and to demonstrate that all were occupied by a single community. Nevertheless, these communities can be distinguished if one works at it carefully enough, as at the Bandkeramik site of Köln-Lindenthal in Germany (Piggott, 1955a, p. 52).

As the prehistorian approaches the dawn of history, he is able to project particular communities back into prehistory and to identify them archeologically. The city-state of Troy is a good example. Heinrich Schliemann was able to identify its site by following the clues given by the poet Homer. However, he obtained a succession of combined cultural and residential assemblages from that site. Since two were large enough to have been produced by city-states, Schliemann was faced with a choice between two assemblages in identifying the remains of Troy. Unfortunately, he selected the wrong one, as subsequent research has shown (Blegen, 1963, pp. 13–38).

After the prehistorian has isolated a community's residential assemblage(s), he must discover the way in which it was divided into households, wards, and so forth, and grouped into tribes, states, and so forth. In investigating the subdivisions of the community, he proceeds to examine its residential components, looking for loci that were occupied by single households, wards, or other parts of a residential community. Households can be identified by the buildings in which they lived, if these have survived, and groupings of households, by clusters of buildings or enclosures, if these existed. The identifications are made by drawing analogies to historic and contemporary occurrences of the different kinds of subgroups, as in the case of cultural reconstruction (Sec. 5.10).

It is similarly possible to infer tribes or states from clusters of residential components, if one has evidence that each clustering was due to social factors, as when one finds a flag, totem, or other symbol or else a government building. One should be wary of identifying a cluster of houses or villages as a social unit when there is reason to believe that it may be due to ecological or chronological factors, as in the case of the prehistoric village of Ipiutak, Alaska (Willey, 1966, pp. 437–439).

There has been considerable research on the size and density of residential institutions (Gabel, 1967, pp. 32–35), but the results have been crude and not very reliable. They are based upon the size of an institution's residental components, the volume of its refuse, the number of its houses and burials, and so forth.

When working with the second category of institutions, which is based upon activities rather than residence, the prehistorian turns from the residential to the activity pattern, focusing upon single activity loci and attempting to determine the nature of the social aggregate that operated in each one. Was it the community as a whole, a household, a specialist, a work group, or an enterprise such as a factory or farm? For example, the activity pattern one is studying may contain the remains of single communal workshops, workshops limited to the houses of specialists, workshops that were to be found in all the houses, or factories in place of workshops. Some prehistoric peoples, such as the Mochica of Peru (Bennett and Bird, 1964, pp. 131–133), portrayed activities in their art, and these portrayals may provide clues about the institutions involved. Also, specialists may be buried with the tools of their trade. In Iron Age Greek sites, it has been possible to distinguish several master painters of pottery by the quality and consistency of their products and by analogy to master potters named in the historic record (e.g., Beasley, 1911).

Relational institutions are the most difficult to distinguish archeologically. It is reasonable to conclude that the house ruins encountered in a village site were each occupied by a single family, unless they are unusually large, but this conclusion tells us nothing about the nature of the families. Nevertheless, it has been possible to draw certain inferences about families by interpreting architectural details or the contents of houses in terms of present-day family life. For instance, Longacre (1964) has shown that the northern and southern rooms of a prehistoric Pueblo dwelling in the American Southwest differed slightly in their pottery designs and that these same differences were also present in the graves and kivas (religious structures) associated with the two groups of rooms. Interpreting this evidence in the light of analogies among the modern Pueblo Indians, he postulates the existence of two local family groups, each organized according to rules of matrilocal residence.

Professional and ranked groups can be identified if they occupied special buildings, wore special insignia, or had other distinguishing artifacts that they deposited in their houses or graves. For instance, the members of an elite class are often buried in a different manner than the commoners. To distinguish such a rank group, therefore, one looks for more elaborate burials, with a greater wealth of grave objects than is normally found in the sites of a society. In the graves of the elite of the most complex societies, one may also find the bodies of servants or slaves who were killed to accompany a personage into the afterlife, as in the royal tombs at Ur (Childe, 1952, pp. 148–149), thus demonstrating the existence of another rank group.

Particular individuals who are mentioned in historic or ethnographic traditions can infrequently be correlated with prehistoric remains, as in the case of King Minos on the island of Crete, (Finley, 1970, pp. 10 and 40) and the kings of Benin in Nigeria (Conton, 1961, pp. 77–83). For the most part, however, the individuals of prehistory, like the institutions to which they belonged, must remain anonymous.

Once the prehistorian is sure that he knows the total range of institutions within the social structure being reconstructed, he may proceed to study the behavior and norms that bound each institution together (Fig. 11). Chang (1967a and 1967b) has termed this kind of study [social] articulation. According to him, it should have two aims: (1) reconstruction of the social interaction or relationships within the institution under study, which he calls its microstructure, and (2) reconstruction of the institution's external relationships, which he calls its macrostructure. (Caldwell, 1966, p. 338, prefers to call the second set of relationships an "interaction sphere.")

For example, an important part of a state's microstructure may be a belief in the divinity of kings; this belief was characteristic of the Egyptians and spread from them to the people of the Meroitic civilization in Negro Africa (Shinnie, 1967, pp. 29–61). Another example is the relationship between rural villages and ceremonial centers in the eastern United States (Jennings, 1968, pp. 216–217).

Drawing upon their knowledge of similar settlement patterns among historic peoples, prehistorians have concluded that the two were symbiotic, the rural villages supplying food and labor to the ceremonial centers in return for the supposed benefits to be derived from the religious ceremonies that were carried on in the centers.

Clues as to the macrostructure are provided by the occurrence in local settlements of artifacts made of foreign materials and decorated in a foreign style. The prehistorian identifies these as trade objects. By studying their distribution, he may be able to reconstruct a sub-system of trading relationships.

Alternatively, foreign objects such as these may have been brought into the local society as tribute or as the result of other kinds of social, political, or religious contacts. The prehistorian should consider all possible explanations and select the one that best fits the evidence, in accordance with the principle of multiple working hypotheses (Sec. 1.5).

In reconstructing behavior and norms, it is important to focus upon those artifacts that are most likely to yield social implications. (Binford, 1962, p. 219, calls these "socio-technic" and "ideo-technic" artifacts.) Highly decorated artifacts may be the most useful, since a society's social structure is often mirrored in its art (e.g., Fischer, 1961). It has even been suggested that personality traits can be inferred from the art (Wallace, 1950).

Finally, the prehistorian may want to attempt a reconstruction of the way in which a people's institutions functioned, by putting together its culture and its social structure. Insofar as possible, he will determine how the various cultural norms, activities, and materiel were distributed among the officials, other specialists, and ordinary personnel of each institution, and by so doing he will reconstruct the manner in which these individuals operated. His reconstruction may be presented to the reader either as a verbal or a graphic picture of the functioning of a people's social aggregates, as in the case of Breuil's scenes from the life of early man (Breuil, 1949).

17
Languages

We need not go into the nature of languages, for it is a subject that prehistorians cannot handle. The prehistorian's discipline is limited by definition to peoples that failed to produce adequate written

records, and so he cannot expect to obtain the data needed to reconstruct languages. (Indeed, many prehistorians are attracted to prehistory precisely because it does not require them to learn languages.)

   To be sure, it is sometimes possible for prehistorians to identify
languages without being able to analyze them, but only when dealing with the close of prehistory, when one begins to encounter
evidences of writing, and when, in addition, one may be able to
project historic languages back to prehistoric peoples. For instance,
linguists have succeeded in reconstructing the ancestral forms of
certain modern language groups, such as Indo-European, and have
worked out their approximate positions in space and time, in part
by use of the technique of glottochronology (Sec. 4.9). This chronology provides the prehistorian with an opportunity to correlate
each ancestral language with the people or peoples occupying the
same position in space and time (e.g., D. Taylor and Rouse, 1955).
Unfortunately, such correlations do not take us back further than a
few millenniums B.C. We know nothing about the languages spoken
by earlier peoples.

SUPPLEMENTAL READING

CHANG, K. C., *Rethinking Archaeology* (1967a).

CLARK, GRAHAME, *Archaeology and Society* (1960), pp. 169–250.

DEETZ, JAMES, *Invitation to Archaeology* (1967), pp. 67–134.

GABEL, CREIGHTON, *Analysis of Prehistoric Economic Patterns* (1967).

HOLE, FRANK, AND ROBERT F. HEIZER, *An Introduction to Prehistoric Archeology* (1969), pt. V.

KROEBER, A. L., AND CLYDE KLUCKHOHN, *Culture* (1963).

TAYLOR, WALTER W., *A Study of Archeology* (1967b).

6

CHANGES IN ETHNIC SYSTEMS

1
Dynamics and
explanation
After gaining as much knowledge as possible about the cultural, morphological, social, and linguistic systems under study, the prehistorian is prepared to answer the final question of his strategy: How and why did the groups acquire these systems? To answer this question, he must shift from a static to a dynamic point of view. Instead of focusing upon the systems per se, he must address himself to the changes from system to system or to the absence of change, as the case may be. Among students of contemporary ethnic groups, this shift in viewpoint is the difference between ethnography and ethnology (Sec. 1.4). We shall call the approach *dynamics* and *explanation*.

These two terms correspond to the "how'" and the "why" of the question. Dynamics is the study of the nature of changes—*how* they took place. Explanation is investigation of the reasons for the changes—*why* they did or did not happen.

The aim of dynamics is to distinguish *patterns of change,* that is, sequences of ethnic units that have developed one from another (Caldwell, 1958, pp. 1–2; Patterson, 1966). These patterns may be composed of cultural, morphological, social, or linguistic systems, or else they may consist of modes, types, or other components of the systems. Their development may be either progressive or regressive. The patterns upon which the technique of seriation is based are good examples (Sec. 4.7).

The aim of explanation is to determine what caused the patterns. The causes are usually expressed in the form of events or occurrences, which are called *processes of change* (e.g., Kroeber, 1963; Binford, 1965). For example, a change from one social structure to another may be ascribed to conquest of the local people by foreigners, who imposed their own social structure on the local people; and a change in a people's diet may be explained by postulating the extinction of certain animals that had previously been hunted.

2
Patterns of
change

The ethnologist is able to observe the patterns of change as they take place. The historian who works with archeological remains can learn about the patterns from documentary sources and need use archeological evidence only to supplement these sources. In the absence of both observations and documents, the prehistorian must reconstruct the patterns from archeological remains in accordance with the principle that all prehistoric interpretation has to be based primarily on the remains (Sec. 2.1).

His procedure is comparable to that used in reconstructing settlement patterns (Secs. 5.4 and 5.10). He looks for the archeological remnant of a pattern of change and reconstructs the pattern from this remnant, in much the same way that a settlement pattern is reconstructed from its remnant or an extinct animal from its fossil remains. The first step is to isolate units of change. Then the units are arranged in the order of their development one from another, so that they form a continuity. Finally, the investigator compares the units within each continuity in order to determine the nature of the changes from one unit to another (Barth, 1967, p. 665).

For example, the logical procedure in dealing with pottery is first to distinguish modes, which are the elemental units of ceramic change (Sec. 2.12). Then one arranges the modes in the order in which they have developed, for example, from the bottom to the top level of a site or from earlier to later deposits as determined by some other technique. Finally, one studies the changes that have taken place along the continuity thus established.

The most difficult part of this procedure is to establish the continuity between one's units of change. It is easy enough to do so when one is dealing with a continuous series of levels, one on top of another with no breaks between them, but when one encounters distinct layers or has to fit together materials from different sites, there is always the chance of a gap in one's sequence, or else one may be attempting to fit together materials belonging to two different sequences. It then becomes a matter of judgment how far one should attempt to extend a continuity.

The first three parts of the strategy of prehistory all contribute to the prehistorian's ability to establish a continuity. From the answers to the questions "Who?" and "What?" come the units of change and from the answer to "Where and when?" come the distributions through space and time that make it possible to link the units in the form of a continuity. The fact that the prehistorian relies upon the answers to the first three questions in answering the question "How and why?" is the reason for placing this question last in the strategy of prehistory.

Nevertheless, the prehistorian sometimes finds such strong prima facie evidences of continuity that it is better tactics for him to begin with the fourth question by studying the changes along the continuity before answering the first three questions (e.g., Sec. 4.7). The results obtained under such circumstances cannot be considered conclusive, however, until the first three questions have also been answered.

If the first three questions have been well answered, prehistorians will have little occasion to disagree about a continuity. Any differences of opinion can be resolved by weighing them against the evidence.

In judging the evidence, as well as in studying changes along continuities, the prehistorian is guided by his knowledge of theoretical models of change and of patterns of change that have been recorded in the literature of anthropology and related professions

(Fig. 6). Thus, he combines induction with analogy, as in reconstructing cultural systems (Sec. 5.10). He infers each pattern from its archeological remnant, utilizing both *models of change* and *parallels* among known changes.

3
Processes of
change

Like the models and parallels used in reconstructing patterns of change, processes of change are obtained from the literature of anthropology and related professions. The investigator searches the literature for the process or processes that best explain the pattern of change under study.

Unlike models and parallels of change, processes of change are not reconstructive devices. They do not help us to fill out the archeological record. Instead, they are postulates that have to be tested against the record, including those parts of it that have been reconstructed by the use of models and parallels of change. No process advanced to explain a change is ever "proved"; the most that can be claimed for it is that it provides a more plausible explanation than any alternative process.

To put this distinction another way, a process of change is a hypothesis, which may or may not be a valid explanation of the facts. It must be weighed against other hypotheses to determine which one best fits the pattern under study, in accordance with the principle of multiple working hypotheses (Sec. 1.5).

Unsophisticated prehistorians sometimes overlook this difference between a pattern and a process. Such a person, for example, may note striking similarities between two finds of pottery on opposite sides of the Pacific Ocean and jump to the conclusion that these similarities are due to a migration across the Pacific. He "proves" his hypothesis of migration by citing the similarities and demonstrating that they were approximately contemporaneous.

This procedure is not valid. One should work with dynamics as well as explanation, by first reconstructing the patterns of change on both sides of the ocean in order to determine how the similarities developed. Only after having reconstructed the patterns of change will one be in a position to weigh alternative processes of change, such as migration, convergence, or adaptation to a similar environment, and to determine which of these processes best fits the reconstructed patterns of change.

Since patterns of change are more fundamental, it is advisable to place more emphasis upon them in an introductory textbook such as this one. Moreover, the reconstruction of patterns of change from archeological evidence requires more systematic procedures than the application of anthropologically formulated processes of change to the evidence. For both these reasons, we shall devote proportionately more attention to the reconstruction of patterns of change, that is, to dynamics. The bulk of the chapter will be devoted to this subject, and explanation of the changes will be left until the end.

4
Systems versus
traits

The prehistorian works with two different kinds of units while reconstructing patterns of change. Some of his patterns are composed of ethnic systems and others of parts of systems. For example, he may reconstruct a series of cultures that have developed one from another, or he may work out a comparable pattern of change in cultural traits or trait complexes (Secs. 3.11 and 4.7). The same two options are open to him in studying morphological, social, and linguistic change. If he exercises both options in working with morphological change, he will be following standard biological procedure, which is to study changes in total systems—species and races—as well as in parts of the systems—the teeth, the brain, and so forth.

Some prehistorians (e.g., Ford, 1962) prefer to work only with individual traits or with trait complexes and to ignore the changes in total systems. This procedure is logically unsound, for it assumes that the systems are no more than the sums of their parts, when, in fact, each system is integrated in ways that cannot be discovered simply by studying its parts alone. The procedure can also be misleading, if the prehistorian uses only patterns of change in traits to resolve a problem also involving patterns of change in systems.

Theorizers about transoceanic migrations often make this mistake (e.g., Meggers, Evans, and Estrada, 1965, pp. 157–178). They assume that they need only ferret out transoceanic similarities in order to "prove" their theories, and they fail to realize that they must also take into consideration the ethnic systems to which the similarities belong. First, they should find out who produced the similarities on opposite sides of the ocean and should assure themselves that the number of peoples involved is not so great as to rule out the possibility of migration. Next, they should determine when and where the peoples lived, in order to establish that they were contemporaneous. Then, they should reconstruct each people's ethnic systems, in order to see whether the observed similarities extend into other aspects of the people's life. Finally, they should reconstruct the patterns of change in systems as well as in traits, insofar as the available data permit. Only when they have done so will they be able adequately to judge whether the observed similarities in traits are due to migration or to some other process of change.

Prehistorians have conceptualized changes in systems and traits in several different ways. Discussing archeological objects per se, Clarke (1968, p. 403) contrasts changes in classes of assemblages with changes in classes of artifacts. (He substitutes the term "type" for our word "class.") Focusing upon sites rather than objects, Willey and others (1956, pp. 7–8) contrast "site units" with "trait units." Both these pairs of terms are easily translated into the frame of reference of the present volume: assemblages come from sites (i.e., components), and both are indicative of cultures, while artifacts are indicative of traits (i.e., cultural norms).

In the present volume, we shall emphasize patterns of change in systems rather than in traits, as the heading of this chapter implies, because they are the more fundamental units and an introductory textbook has to concentrate on fundamentals. However, most of the following remarks are applicable to changes in traits and trait complexes as well as in systems. The reader is advised to consult Clarke (1968) for a more detailed account of patterns and processes of change in both kinds of units.

This emphasis does not mean that we shall ignore traits, for systems are composed of them. It only means that we shall view the traits as parts of the systems and shall abitrarily ignore the fact that many of them can also be studied profitably as independent entities.

Before turning to the systems, it may be well to clarify the meaning of the term *trait*. The term is being used to refer to any element of an ethnic system, including norms, behavior, and the products of behavior (Fig. 11). In the case of artifacts, it includes both extrinsic and intrinsic classes and types, the former because they refer to norms and activities and the latter because they refer to the nature of the artifacts. Not uncommonly, a prehistorian finds it necessary to do additional classification while studying cultural dynamics in order to bring out the patterns of attributes (extrinsic types) that best express the degree of development of a cultural system or its parts (Sec. 2.10).

5
Levels of evolution

We have seen that the prehistorian's study of changes in systems parallels the biologist's study of changes in species and races. It is only natural, therefore, that the prehistorian should use the models of change developed in biology in order to reconstruct the patterns of change in ethnic systems. To understand these models, we shall have to examine the biological theory of evolution.

Evolution may be defined as the overall development of the earth and of its occupants. In the words of Huxley (1955, p. 3), "evolution . . . is divisible into three very distinct sectors or phases, each with its own characteristic tempo of change, and its own type of products. The earliest and also the largest is the inorganic or cosmological sector; the much more restricted organic or biological sector arose at a later phase from the inorganic; and the still further restricted human or [superorganic] phase arose much later than the organic."

During the first of the three phases, evolution operated only on the inorganic level. The appearance of life ushered in the second phase, in which organic evolution was superimposed on the still existent inorganic evolution. The third phase began with the development of man and the consequent addition of superorganic evolution on top of the inorganic and organic levels. (See Sec. 3.3 for a discussion of the organic and superorganic levels.)

The three levels are portrayed by the wedges on the right face of our cube of knowledge (Fig. 1). The lowermost wedge, on the left side of the face, represents inorganic evolution. The second wedge, referring to wildlife, and the fourth wedge, referring to human morphology, are organic. The other three wedges, marked culture, social structure, and language respectively, are superorganic.

Organic evolution has to be divided between the wedges of wildlife and human morphology for the sake of consistency with the sections on the top face of the cube. The division is also justified theoretically by the fact that evolution of the human morphology is affected by a factor that does not operate in the case of wildlife. Among both wild organisms and human beings, genes evolve by means of mutation and natural selection, which permits only the best adapted mutants to survive (Alland, 1967). In the case of human beings, the mutant genes are affected not only by natural selection, but also by morphological norms, which regulate the breeding habits of man and hence the nature of the genes he passes down from generation to generation (Sec. 5.11).

In other words, man domesticated himself by forming ethnic groups and subjecting himself to the norms of the groups (Fig. 11). Subsequently, he succeeded in domesticating plants and other animals and, by so doing, subjected them to his morphological norms. Wildlife, on the contrary, remains untouched by norms of this kind.

To be sure, wild plants and animals are affected by human activities and hence by cultural norms, which mediate the activities. But cultural norms are simply a part of the environment—conditions to which all organisms, wild or domestic, must adapt in order to survive. By contrast, morphological norms mediate the breeding habits of man and the other domesticates, affecting the nature of their genes and, as a result, their morphological characteristics.

Here again, we may apply the distinction between dynamics (how) and explanation (why). Since genes serve as the primary mechanisms of organic change, they may be regarded as dynamic units. Morphological norms, on the contrary, are explanatory units, being one of a number of factors that can affect the nature of the genes. The process of natural selection and the modifications of nature by man must also be taken into consideration in explaining why a racial group has a particular set of genes and hence of morphological characteristics.

The reverse is true of superorganic change, whether in culture, social structure or language. Here, norms are the mechanisms of change, and the genes of the bearers of the norms serve only as one of the factors that may affect changes in the norms.

The role of norms in shaping the nature of cultures, social structures, and languages has already been discussed in Sections 5.5, 5.8, and 5.15. Genes enter into the picture only by providing the capabilities necessary to develop new norms and to learn those already in existence. Among the earliest forms of man, who had small-sized brains indicating limited ability to think, the cerebral genes must have been a restrictive factor, preventing the development and learning of more complex norms, but once man's brain had evolved to the point where it was fully capable of thought, genes lost this role, and cultural, social, and linguistic norms became truly superorganic, operating as independent systems and changing with little regard for the gene pools upon which they were based (Kroeber, 1963, pp. 61–62).

To be sure, certain individuals in any racial group may be expected to possess superior ability in activities such as art, music, sports, or abstract thinking, while other individuals will be inferior in one or more of these fields. But geniuses and incompetent individuals are present among all human groups and therefore cannot be held directly responsible for the nature of cultures, social structures, and languages.

Genes, then, play no part in the dynamics of superorganic change; instead, they may be a factor causing change. Men of genius have invented many cultural norms, as Thomas Edison did in the case of the electric light. But other factors also contributed to the success of that invention. The electric light could not have been produced until after development of the necessary technology and could not have been used until our social structure had developed to the point where it could organize the generation and distribution of electricity. Thus, invention by individuals of superior genetic ability will produce new cultural norms only when the results are adapted to a people's inorganic, organic, and superorganic conditions. This point is another example of the need to use the principle of multiple working hypotheses. It is not enough to cite a single explanatory process; one must consider all possible hypotheses and choose the combination of hypotheses that best explains the pattern of changes under study.

6
Role of norms
in superorganic
change

The central position of genes in the study of organic change is too well-known to require further discussion. The role of norms in the study of superorganic change needs to be further clarified, however, since it is frequently misunderstood.

The traits of cultural, social, and linguistic groups include not only norms, but also behavior and the products of behavior (Fig.

11). It is important to recognize that, of these three kinds of traits, only norms serve as units in the prehistorian's patterns of change. Each norm is an expression of similarities in behavior or in the products of behavior. For a norm to change, the members of the ethnic group must modify their behavior or alter their products. Hence, behavior and the products of behavior can be regarded as causes of changes in norms. They operate within the processes that produce changes in norms and therefore must be studied under the heading of explanation rather than dynamics.

For example, an individual may invent a new way of smelting iron. If this method catches on among the other members of his ethnic group, it will become a new norm, replacing the previous way of smelting iron or serving as an alternative to it. If it does not catch on, it may persist as an idiosyncrasy of its inventor, without ever becoming a norm of the group, or else it may be abandoned. Similarly, a potter may purchase a vessel from another ethnic group, may like the vessel, and may copy it. If the copy becomes popular and is reproduced by other potters, a new norm will have been added to the repertoire of the local potters.

Behavior and its products are not the only factors leading to the appearance of new norms. Any group of human beings is constantly changing in composition as its elder members die, new members are born into the group, and individuals immigrate or emigrate. Some of these changes in personnel will have no effect upon the norms of the group—for example, a baby simply learns the linguistic norms without modifying them—but other changes in the group's composition may contribute to changes in the norms, as when foreigners join the group in appreciable numbers and are able to impose many of their norms upon it.

But the list of explanatory factors does not end with the group, its behavior, and its products. The pressure of other ethnic groups, either through warfare or in other, more subtle ways, may lead to the alteration of the local group's norms. Changes in the environment may force the development of new norms, as when an extreme drought causes a people to abandon agriculture and to emphasize fishing. Finally, we must not forget that some norms are dependent on others, so that a change in one norm may produce a change in another, as when the abandonment of agriculture causes a people to give up their norms for processing cultivated plants.

Some authors have assumed that the process of natural selection operates on the superorganic as well as the organic level. This assumption, however, is a logical impossibility. The process of natural selection can only affect organisms, including the members of ethnic groups. We have just seen that the members of ethnic groups have only an indirect and intermittent effect upon their own norms. Hence, natural selection is twice-removed from the norms and can have had only a minimal effect upon them.

We all recognize that individuals can learn languages because we constantly see it happening among babies and in our schools. It is more difficult for us to realize that individuals can and do learn cultures and social structures in the same way. All three kinds of units have an existence of their own, apart from the individual organisms that learn them, as is implied by the term "superorganic."

If norms are things to be learned, then a person's norms cannot be used as a measure of his potential ability, as is sometimes assumed. So-called primitive people are not primitive in their organic makeup, but only in their superorganic qualities, that is, in their cultures, social structures, or languages. If a member of a primitive group is brought into a more advanced group as a small child, he should be able to learn the more advanced culture, social structure, and language as easily as the local children.

Persons who judge the intelligence of individuals by the complexity of their cultures, social structures, and languages fail to recognize that these units are not, like genes, encased in the bodies of individuals. Genes can only pass from the body of one individual to that of another by means of sexual intercourse and the resultant birth of a new individual. Cultural, social, and linguistic norms, on the other hand, can pass from one individual to another without any contact at all, as when a student learns from a book how to produce an art object. Indeed, whole cultures, social structures, or languages have sometimes been handed down from one group of people to another without contact, as when classical civilization was abandoned at the beginning of the Middle Ages, only to be reconstructed in a modified form during the Renaissance, after having been preserved in the meantime on artifacts, by means of documents, and in the minds of a few scholars (e.g., Sec. 4.3).

It has been impossible to store and retrieve genes in this fashion, though geneticists are now working on techniques for doing so. Until they succeed, human genes will continue to be subject to natural selection, which means that only the best adapted mutations will survive. By contrast, cultural, social, and linguistic norms accumulate with the passage of time. Their number has increased exponentially during the course of prehistory and history, each new norm serving as the basis for development of an ever larger number of additional norms. As a result, the specialist in norms is faced with such a complex situation that he must arbitrarily divide the norms into four systems, cultural, morphological, social, and linguistic, whereas the specialist in genes can handle all of them within a single, morphological system (Sec. 5.5).

7
*Models of macro-
and microevolution*

Let us now return to the subject of evolution, discussed in Section 6.5. There, the word "evolution" was applied to the overall development of the earth and its occupants. Not all studies of overall development are evolutionary, however. There are two alternative ways of proceeding: (1) by examining the changes that have led to modern conditions, or (2) by putting past developments in their proper chronological order, culminating in modern conditions. Only the first alternative can be considered evolutionary, for the term means unfolding or growth, that is, changes rather than sequences of events. Evolution, then, must be defined as the changes that have taken place in the earth and its occupants since their inception. It does not include mere sequences of events, even when they cover the entire evolutionary span.

Biologists apply the term "macroevolution" to changes that take place on the level of species or above and the term "microevolution" to changes that take place on the level of races, that is, within species (Goldschmidt, 1940). Macroevolution has to be approached via the side face of our cube of knowledge (Fig. 1) and microevolution via the front face, for the following reasons.

The model of *macroevolution* takes the form of a phylogeny, consisting of a series of vertical and branching lines extending from species to species like the trunk and branches of a tree (e.g., Hulse, 1963, fig. 47). The vertical dimension of this model represents the time that has elapsed since the beginning of the phylogeny and the horizontal dimension represents the degree to which the constituent species have diverged since the origin of the phylogeny. Hence, phylogenies are an expression of change through the dimensions of time and form. This places them on the side face of our cube of knowledge (Fig. 13*a, right*). If we were to transfer them from the side to the front face of the cube, they would appear there only as sequences of occurrences (Fig. 13*a, left*).

Species evolve in a phylogenetic manner because, by definition, each is a closed system. The members of each species can only breed among themselves, and as a result the genes of other species are unable to enter the system. The genes of the original species are passed down from generation to generation among the members of that species, becoming more and more modified with the passage of time until there are so many changes from the morphology of the original species that a new species is born. Alternatively, the members of the original species may become separated geographically into two groups, each of which develops somewhat differently and eventually produces a new species. Every species, then, changes by giving birth to a new species, much as a tree trunk sends out branches. This kind of change produces the phylogenetic model, in which each species passes its genes on to descendant species via ever diverging lines.

By contrast, the model of *microevolution,* that is, of overall change in races, takes the form of a trellis, the lines of which extend in every direction from one race to another (Hulse, 1963, fig. 48). The vertical dimension of this model again represents time, but the horizontal dimension is a measure of space rather than form. It expresses the geographic position of the races, not the degree to which their morphologies have diverged from a common ancestor. Hence, the trellis model belongs on the front face of the cube, bounded by the dimensions of space and time (Fig. 13*b, left*). If we were to transfer it from the front to the side face of the cube, it would appear there with less clarity as a reticulate pattern, contained within the phylogenetic line that connects two species (Fig. 13*b, right*).

The evolution of races is better shown on the front than on the side face of the cube because races are open systems. Except in the presence of a barrier of some kind, the members of a race are able not only to breed among themselves, but also to interbreed with

FIGURE 13. *Models of organic change:* (a), left, *an evolutionary sequence;* (a), right, *macroevolution via the phylogenetic model;* (b), left, *microevolution via the trellis model;* (b), right, *microevolution via the reticulate model.* S_{1-4} = *species.* G_{1-3} = *grades.* R_{1-4} = *races.* [*Grades, traditions, and stages have been omitted from* (b) *in order to simplify it. For grades, see* (a), *and for traditions and stages, see Fig. 14.*]

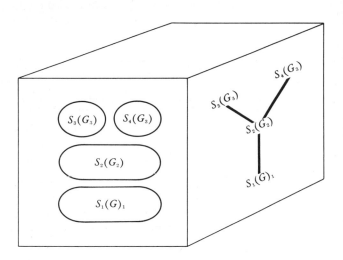

(a)

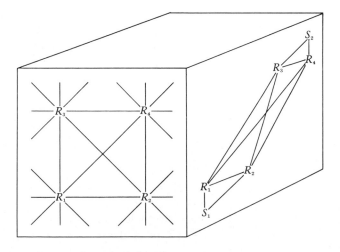

(b)

the members of adjacent races. As a result, the changes in their morphologies take place through both time and space. There is change through time when members of a race breed with one another and pass their own genes on to their descendants, as species do. There is change through space when members of one race enter the territory of members of another race, interbreed, and impart a mixture of the genes of the two races to their descendants, as happened when Cortez conquered Mexico.

The lines of the trellis model indicate that genes can pass in any direction across the front face of our cube of knowledge: vertically via the dimension of time when only breeding takes place, horizontally via the dimension of space when only interbreeding takes place, diagonally across both dimensions when breeding and interbreeding are combined. All three of these routes are normally operative, except in the presence of a physical barrier, such as a mountain range, or of deterrent norms, such as the current prejudice against miscegenation between whites and blacks in the United States. Such factors may also cause some routes to be used more than others (Sec. 6.8).

It makes no difference whether races are human or nonhuman, or wild or domesticated. In all cases they evolve in a trellis model on the front rather than the side face of our cube of knowledge, contrary to species, which evolve in a phylogenetic model on the side face of the cube.

Turning from organic to superorganic change, we find the same microevolutionary situation as among races. Cultures, social structures, and languages are likewise open systems, and so they, too, change in a trellis model on the front face of the cube, that is, in the dimensions of time and space (Fig. 14, *left*). Cultural, social, and linguistic norms may not only be passed down from generation to generation through time, but also may spread from settlement to settlement through space. If the spread is slow, the norms will pass through time as well as space, not reaching the peripheries of their distribution until considerable time has elapsed. The norms will proceed from one cultural, social, or linguistic system to another, with appropriate modifications to fit each new system, until they reach a system with which they are incompatible or are stopped by some other kind of barrier, such as a mountain range.

If we transfer our model of superorganic change from the front to the side face of the cube, it takes the form of a series of occur-rences (Fig. 14, *right*). This form results because we will have eliminated the dimension of space, which is all-important in the development of open systems.

Because species are closed systems and racial, cultural, social, and linguistic groups are open systems, the specialists tend to approach the evolution of the two kinds of groups with contrary assumptions. The physical anthropologist who studies the macroevolution of species looks for divergence; that is, he expects each species to give birth to several new species or, failing that, to a single new species, as when a tree puts forth branches. The prehistorian who studies the microevolution of races, peoples, societies, and speech communi-ties expects instead to encounter convergence, that is, the spread of genes or cultural norms from one group to another, causing the groups to become more alike. Nevertheless, the student of ethnic change must take care not to underestimate the effect of barriers against the spread of genes and norms. The fact that there are so

FIGURE   14. *Model of cultural change:* C_{1-9} = *cultures.* S_{1-3} = *stages. Thick lines* = *traditions. The front face of the cube shows the trellis model of evolution. The side face shows instead an evolutionary chronology. (This figure can be con-verted into a model of morphological, social, or linguistic change by substituting morphologies, social structures, or languages for cultures.)*

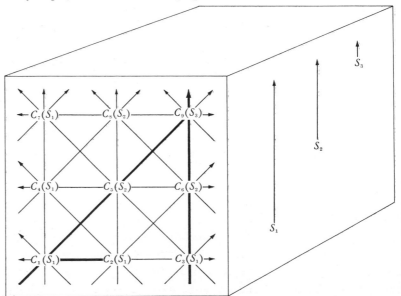

many different ethnic groups and subgroups in today's world is proof that genes and norms are unable to pass freely from one ethnic system to another.

8
Lines and
traditions

The phylogenetic and trellis models just discussed are applicable to overall change or evolution. In studying increments of change within these overall models, the physical anthropologist or prehistorian, as the case may be, must use less inclusive concepts, referring to parts of the models. These will now be discussed.

Physical anthropologists refer to the stems and branches of a phylogeny as *lines*. A line may be defined as a pattern of change that has resulted in the development of several successive species. Lines may diverge, as we have seen, but cannot converge because species are, by definition, closed systems. Hence, lines have to be delineated on the side face of our cube of knowledge (Fig. 13*a*, *right*).

When one wishes to study the history of a line, one must shift from the side to the front face of the cube, in order to plot the distribution of the line in space as well as time. This face provides a record of the occurrences of the line, but not of change, and therefore is not evolutionary. The evolution of the line can only be seen on the side face of the cube.

The prehistorian's counterpart of a line is a *tradition* (Rouse, 1964a, pp. 458–460). We anticipated this concept when considering the complementary concept of series in Section 3.11. As indicated there, a series consists of a number of peoples who share a considerable proportion of their diagnostics, while a tradition consists of the diagnostics that are shared by the peoples in a series and cause them to be distinguished as a unit.

In Section 3.11, we viewed series and traditions as systematic units, but they also have implications of change to which we must now address our attention. From this point of view, a tradition may be defined as a pattern of changes and no changes that extends from culture to culture. Each tradition consists of several norms that have passed from one culture to another and may or may not have been modified as they spread. In Section 3.11, we focused on the norms that remained unchanged because they are taxonomically more significant; now we shall be concerned with the entire pattern of norms (cf. Caldwell, 1966, p. 3). In Section 3.11 we also limited ourselves to the traditions that are used to define series. Now we must take into consideration, in addition, the traditions that extend from the peoples of one series to the peoples of another series. Finally, in Section 3.11 we limited our attention to cultural traditions; now we must study morphological, social, and linguistic traditions as well, in order to fill out our answer to the question "How and why?"

Morphological traditions are organic and consist of genes rather than norms. In this respect, they resemble lines of organic development. Each differs from a line, however, in that it normally includes only a part of the genes in the morphological systems that it has affected, for those systems are open and can therefore incorporate genes belonging to various traditions. By contrast, a line includes *all* of the genes in its constituent systems, for its systems are closed to influences from other lines.

Cultural, social, and linguistic traditions are superorganic; each is a complex of norms rather than genes. Again, each tradition incorporates only a fraction of the norms present in the cultural, social, or linguistic systems that have been affected by it, for these systems are open to influences from other traditions as well.

Traditions have to be diagrammed on the front face of our cube of knowledge, in the dimensions of space and time, rather than on the side face, in the dimensions of form and time. This requirement means using a chronological chart, as in answering the question "Where and when?" However, the chart must be marked in a different manner. We are no longer concerned with ethnic groups, but with their systems of genes or norms, for each group is distinguished by its system, and any change in the group must therefore result from a change in its system (Sec. 6.6). We may mark the position of each system by a symbol placed in the center of its distribution, which is the point where it presumably appeared in its most typical form (Sec. 3.6). Then we may draw lines from each symbol to all adjacent symbols, thereby producing the trellis model (Fig. 14, *left*).

The lines of the trellis model mark the potential routes along which genes or norms may have passed from one system to another. When one examines these routes, one finds that genes or norms have passed more frequently along some routes than along others, as is indicated by the heavy lines in Figure 14, *left*. It is these strong continuities, together with the accompanying changes in genes or norms, that are conceptualized as traditions.

In the case of morphological traditions, genes are transmitted from one race to its successor by means of breeding and from one race to a neighboring race by means of interbreeding. A prevalence of breeding produces vertical traditions; a prevalence of inter-breeding, horizontal traditions; and a combination of the two, oblique traditions (Sec. 6.7). The transmission of genes along the route of each tradition is accompanied by mutation and by selection of those mutations that are adapted to the existing morphological system and to its environment. In addition, there is preselection of genes by the morphological norms that regulate breeding and inter-breeding (Sec. 6.5).

In the case of cultural, social, or linguistic traditions, the transmission takes place conceptually rather than biologically. Within any local series of peoples, societies, or speech communities, each generation inculcates its norms in the subsequent generation by education and by other, less formal kinds of training; and the norms are similarly diffused to neighboring peoples, societies, or speech communities by proselytizing, advertising, and other more subtle methods of persuasion. A prevalence of ingroup training produces vertical traditions; a prevalence of diffusion to other groups, horizontal traditions; and a combination of the two, oblique traditions.

At first thought, it might seem that vertical traditions, in which the distinctive persistences and changes are distributed through time from one generation to another within a local series of groups, ought to be more common than horizontal traditions, which extend through space from one local group to another, for innovations should be more compatible with the local series of systems in which they were developed than with other systems to which they might spread. However, the ethnic systems in adjacent areas tend to be so much alike that it is almost as easy for an innovation to diffuse from one system to another as to persist from one system to its successor. Moreover, it is not common for members of an ethnic group to migrate from one area to another and to impose their own traditions on the occupants of the second area, as Europeans did when they conquered the New World. Conversely, a revolution may take place within a local group, causing it to abandon its old system, to develop a new one, and in the process to give up many of its previous traditions. For instance, the Russian people used to conform to the West European tradition of capitalism, but as a result of the Soviet revolution, they have developed a new economic tradition—communism—that they are now attempting to extend to the rest of the world in competition with the capitalist tradition. Their aim is to make of communism a horizontal tradition replacing capitalism, which is a vertical tradition.

It is worth noting that, while the Soviet revolution caused a change from the economic tradition of capitalism to that of communism, it did not produce a corresponding change in the political tradition of absolutism, which continues to prevail among the Soviet people. Horizontal and vertical traditions often coexist in this manner.

In Section 1.5, we saw that an ethnic group cannot be transferred from the front or top face of our cube to the side face, since this transfer would destroy it. The members of the group would be coalesced into mankind as a whole, and the traits of the group would similarly be coalesced into the morphology, culture, social structure, or language of the entire human species (*Homo sapiens*). Since traditions consist of relationships among ethnic systems, they, too, would disappear if the attempt were made to transfer them from the front to the side face of the cube.

Traditions, which thus are limited to the front face of the cube, are obviously not comparable to lines, which can only be shown on the side face of the cube. Traditions are units of space and time, whereas lines are units of form and time. Nevertheless, those traditions that have been established by cultural classification and link together the peoples of a series are easily confused with lines, since lines, too, are formed by means of classification and link species together. Both traditions and lines are useful in systematics, but that is the end of their similarity. When one plots the distribution of systematic traditions on a chronological chart, one finds that they do not link together all the local cultures. Some cultures always appear on the charts as isolated units, not connected by systematic traditions with any other cultures, apparently because they obtained their norms from so many different sources that it is impossible to distinguish particular sources. Other cultures are linked to previous cultures by convergent traditions, which show that each culture has developed from several previous cultures. Every species, on the contrary, must develop from but one other species via a straight or divergent line.

Prehistorians and ethnologists have been slow to recognize the differences between traditions and lines. The early authors assumed that man had passed through a single line of cultural development culminating in Western civilization. This assumption was their justification for attempting to apply the sequence of ages they had developed for western Europe to the rest of the world (Sec. 4.3). The approach they used has been called *unilinear*. It has fallen out of favor in recent years, since the weight of the evidence indicates that cultures, social structures, and languages have developed differently in various parts of the world.

Retreating from the unilinear approach, some contemporary authors have argued that there have been different lines of development in the Middle East and Europe, the Far East, and the New World, for example. They call their approach *multilinear* (e.g., Steward, 1955).

If our models of macro- and microevolution (Figs. 13 and 14) are correct, all kinds of linear approaches to the study of modern man are invalid. For the last 15,000 years, at least, all mankind has belonged to a single species, *Homo sapiens* (e.g., Dobzhansky, 1966, p. 189). Taken as a whole, the human species constitutes a closed system; it cannot exchange genes with other species nor can it exchange cultural, social, and linguistic norms with them, since they have none. We can, therefore, trace lines from the human species to other species. But when we move within the human species in order to study ethnic groups, we shift from a closed system to open systems, which cannot be studied linearly. We must study them in terms of the concept of tradition rather than that of line.

Each cultural, morphological, social, and linguistic group tends to be marked by a number of different traditions, derived from different sources. It does not obtain all of its traits from a single ancestor, as in the case of a line of genera and species. To think that it does is to confuse microevolution with macroevolution.

9
Grades and stages

Returning to the evolution of the human species, let us now consider the concept of grade. We have seen that the species within a phylogeny evolve along lines that diverge from a common ancestor. The species belonging to such lines are limited in the extent to which they can diverge by the fact that they all have a common genetic background and, being closed systems, are not subject to the intrusion of foreign genes. As a result, the species develop in a homologous manner, especially if they all remain adapted to the same kind of environment. Physical anthropologists express this condition by saying that all species that develop homologically belong to the same grade (Coon, 1962, pp. 305–306).

A *grade* may be defined as the level of development that has been attained by species evolving along divergent lines. If the species have evolved at the same rate, those which belong to the same grade will be contemporaneous, as in Figure 13*a, right*. However, the species in one line may evolve more slowly, in which case it will attain a particular grade at a later time than the species in other lines; or it may cease to evolve and become stable, in which case the line will remain permanently at a lower grade.

Grades are normally plotted on the side face of our cube of knowledge, as illustrated in Figure 13*a, right,* but they can also be studied on the front face of the cube by noting where and when the species of each grade occurred. The latter approach is not very meaningful, however, for it only chronicles the distribution of the grade. The changes from one grade to another have to be studied on the side face of the cube because they take place within closed systems.

Prehistorians have a counterpart of the physical anthropologist's grade, which they call a *stage* (Rouse, 1964a, pp. 461–464). We anticipated this concept, though without naming it, in our consideration of the technique of dating known as seriation (Sec. 4.7). As noted there, one way of putting the assemblages of a local area into their proper chronological order is to seriate them in terms of their patterns of development. Such a pattern of development constitutes a tradition, and the segments into which it is divided are stages. By definition, each stage in the tradition must have developed out of the one that preceded it, and hence they have a sequential relationship, which the person doing the seriation reconstructs and uses to arrange his assemblages in their proper order. The order can be one of either progression or regression, and the investigator must use other methods of dating to decide between the two in any particular instance.

Prehistorians currently use the term "stage" in several different ways, and we must settle on one of these if we are to be systematic in our approach to prehistory. It seems appropriate to follow the usage that is most consistent with the biological concept of grade. Just as a grade is a division that cuts across the lines of a phylogeny, indicating the species that are homologous, so a stage may be regarded as a division that cuts across several traditions within a trellis pattern of change. A grade expresses the level of development attained by species belonging to divergent lines. Similarly, a stage may be defined as the level of development reached in several different traditions.

It is easy to understand why traditions that have a common background of genes or norms tend to pass through the same stages. As in the case of lines, the fact that they share the same background causes them to develop in a homologous fashion, especially if they have not been affected by intrusions of foreign genes or norms. But traditions with different backgrounds can also develop through the same stages, for one of the following reasons:

1. Morphologies, cultures, social structures, and languages are open systems, each of which can, and often does, incorporate the key developments of another system. When this happens, the receiving system passes from its own stage of development to that of the other system. The spread of civilization from Mesopotamia to the rest of the Western World is a good example.

Organic stages are able to spread in this manner through interbreeding and the consequent transmission of genes; and superorganic stages, through the diffusion of norms from one tradition to another. These kinds of transfer are both so common that students of change tend to think of them first when they encounter two ethnic systems that have reached the same stage of development.

2. Stages are also to be found among traditions that are so remote from one another in space or time or both as to eliminate the pos-

sibility of any connection between them, as in the case of the rise of civilizations in the Old and New Worlds (Adams, 1966). Such instances are explained by the principle of limited possibilities, which states that, given the nature of ethnic traits, there are only a limited number of ways in which man can develop (Herskovits, 1964, p. 157). He cannot help but hit more than once upon the same alternative within the small range open to him.

For example, there are relatively few ways to bury a human body. When, therefore, the same burial custom turns up in different parts of the world, the correspondence is not necessarily the result of diffusion. Two peoples may have independently made the same choice from among the limited number of possibilities (Ucko, 1969).

In Section 4.3, we found it necessary to distinguish between ages and stages. An age, it will be recalled, is an arbitrary division of space and time, that is, of the front face of our cube of knowledge or of a sectional chronology abstracted from it. A stage is not a division of a chronology but of traditions. Ages follow one another simply because they are so situated on a chronology; stages do so because they have developed one from another within converging, diverging, or parallel traditions. Hence, ages record occurrences, whereas stages are an expression of change.

Each system of ages may be established by arbitrarily selecting a number of key innovations, or time-markers, and plotting the time of the first appearance of each innovation on a chronological chart in order to subdivide that chart into periods of relative time. Each age will then be marked by the innovation with which it began and the innovation with which it ended.

Sequences of stages, on the contrary, are established by dividing traditions into segments. Each stage consequently consist of a complex of genes or norms that has developed from a previous complex, and it is defined by listing the changes from the preceding complex. A stage is thus marked by a number of innovations, occurring in the context of its traditions, whereas an age may be marked by single traits, occurring out of context.

Once stages have been established, however, they may be used to define ages in place of the procedure described above. For instance, it is a common practice to define the Neolithic age in the Western

World as the time when the peoples of that region had achieved the stage of intensive agriculture (Sec. 4.10). This procedure is valid so long as, within any one region, the age is defined only in terms of that stage, or in terms of that stage plus another trait, with which it is associated throughout the region. In this respect, stages are comparable to traditions. Certain stages may be arbitrarily selected for systematic use in answering the question "Where and when?" just as certain traditions may be arbitrarily selected for systematic use in answering the question "Who?" But like the remainder of the traditions, the remainder of the stages must be taken into consideration in answering the substantive question "How and why?"

Stages need not be limited to cultural traditions. Brace (1967) has formulated a set of morphological stages for the early part of prehistory in the Old World, although he does not apply those stages to specific traditions of morphological development.

Summarizing the discussion to this point, we may say that stages tend to extend across a relatively large number of traditions, whereas grades do not tend to cut across a large number of lines. Moreover, stages can extend across otherwise unrelated traditions, whereas grades are limited to those lines that have diverged from a common ancestor (cf. Figs. 14, *left* and 13a, *right*). As a result, stages tend to overshadow the traditions to which they refer, whereas grades are merely subdivisions of lines and therefore secondary to them.

Stages may even be extended beyond traditions to independent ethnic systems, which cannot be assigned to traditions (Fig. 14, *left*). This usage, however, is a secondary application of the concept of stages. Since stages are units of change, they must originally be defined in situations of change, that is, among traditions, before being applied to independent systems.

The actual extent of a stage depends upon how tightly it has been defined. The proper procedure is to begin by defining stages within one or more local traditions. One's tendency in defining these stages will be to incorporate a relatively large number of changes in the definition of each stage and thus limit the stage to the few traditions under study. As one proceeds to examine the changes in traditions in other areas, one will set up parallel sets of stages, each likewise defined by a relatively large number of innovations. Such units may be called *specific stages,* since they are the product of detailed study of particular traditions and are limited in applicability to those traditions.

Once one has established a number of sets of specific stages, it becomes possible to compare them, abstract their similarities, and use these regularities to set up a sequence of more general stages. If this procedure is continued throughout the world, as advocated by Steward (1955), one will end up with a single set of stages that is generally applicable. We may refer to such a set of stages as *generalized stages*.

In making the transition from specific to generalized stages, it is important to work with as many traditions and in as many parts of the world as possible. The contents of specific stages vary greatly from tradition to tradition, especially among those traditions that lack a common background. Only by taking into consideration all variations in the specific stages can the investigator be assured of discovering valid regularities, which can then be conceptualized as generalized stages.

Specific stages have to be demarcated on the front face of the cube, because they refer to particular traditions occurring in limited parts of the world. Generalized stages, on the other hand, belong on the side face of the cube, because they are the product of comparative research and express regularities of form that have not been affected by the factor of space. They denote the accumulation of generalized forms through time, which is symbolized by the expanding wedges on the side face of our cube (Fig. 1).

Only specific stages are an expression of change and hence of evolution. Generalized stages provide instead a record of occurrences, as is indicated by the vertical lines in Figure 14, *right*. These lines cannot be said to portray change because they are unconnected, and change takes place along continuities (Sec. 6.1). Nevertheless, it is possible to convert generalized stages into a record of change, and hence of evolution, by transferring them from the side to the front face of the cube and applying them to specific traditions, as is illustrated in Figure 14, *left*.

10
Centers and
climaxes

So far, we have discussed only those qualities of ethnic change that have counterparts in the evolution of species. Now we come to qualities peculiar to cultural, social, and linguistic groups, that is, to superorganic as opposed to organic change. The first is the development of *centers* or nuclear areas, the inhabitants of which are more advanced than those in the peripheries (e.g., Caldwell, 1958, pp. v–vi).

We have already seen how the principle of centers operates within ethnic groups (Sec. 3.6). The central members of each group tend to be typical and the peripheral members, transitional, because they are open to influences from neighboring groups (Fig. 8). When we compare groups from the same point of view, we find that the central groups also tend to be more advanced than peripheral groups. In contemporary terminology, the central groups are "developed" and the peripheral groups "underdeveloped."

In dealing with contemporary underdeveloped peoples, we tend to assume that they can all be brought up to the highest level of development achieved by mankind. When we look back into the past, however, we find that this uniformity has never been accomplished, either in history or prehistory. Except possibly at the very beginning of human development, some ethnic groups have always been more advanced than others, just as some human individuals are always more successful than others. The more advanced ethnic groups may be said to have constituted centers, which influenced the surrounding, less advanced groups, in the same way that the present-day North American and European centers influence the rest of the world.

There are a number of theoretical reasons for the existence of centers. One is that certain environments are more favorable for cultural advance than others. Another is that norms consist of ideas, which are cumulative, so that each new idea may stimulate several additional innovations. Finally, cultural, social, or linguistic groups in a central position are able to absorb new ideas from all the surrounding regions, whereas peripheral groups are exposed to only a portion of the innovations.

Once an area has become a center, the people living there tend to export their innovations to the surrounding, less advanced peoples. This exportation results in the formation of oblique traditions, which spread out from the central areas slowly enough that there is a considerable lapse of time before they reach the peripheries. Alternatively, the peripheral peoples may reject the influences from the centers and retain their own, relatively backward traditions. The Japanese are an example of the first alternative; originally an offspring of the Chinese center of cultural development, their culture has been strongly influenced by the Western centers and is now producing a center of its own. The Australian aborigines exemplify the second alternative; during prehistoric time they resisted the opportunity to acquire Indonesian civilization, and they now spurn Western civilization.

Because the inhabitants of a center are such innovators, they tend to manifest vertical traditions of longer and shorter duration. This tendency causes them to look at change from the inside out, an attitude that is known as *ethnocentrism*. The Chinese are a good example. As a center of development, they have experienced a long, unbroken tradition, and this tradition has led them to view their country as the center of the world. They regard the surrounding peoples as peripheral "barbarians."

Ethnocentrism is not limited to the peoples that live in centers, however. The reason some peripheral peoples retain their own underdeveloped traditions, rejecting innovations from the centers, is that they, too, look at the world from the inside out and hence fail to see the value of the innovations.

Since most prehistorians live in centers, such as Europe and the United States, it is only natural for them to be influenced by their own experiences to attach more significance to centers than to peripheral regions. We may call this tendency *centrism*. It is an improvement over ethnocentrism, but it, too, gives a distorted picture of the nature of ethnic changes. For example, prehistorians have until recently paid much more attention to the centers of development in Mesopotamia and Greece than to the intervening periphery in Anatolia, on the assumption that all important events took place in the centers. Now that they have come to work in Anatolia, they find it the key to many Mesopotamian and Greek developments (Mellaart, 1965).

Centers are not permanent. They tend to shift from one area to another, so that an area that is peripheral today may become a center tomorrow. Thus, western Europe was a peripheral region for nearly 10,000 years before a center came into existence there during the Renaissance. While still a periphery, it developed a number of local traditions that have strongly influenced the present central development. The centrists would have us overlook the earlier, more backward traditions, but we must study them if we are to understand present conditions in the West European center.

The concept of center is sometimes confused with that of line, this confusion being a common error of the multilinear evolutionists (Sec. 6.8). They assume that each major center consists of a single line of development. On the contrary, each center is actually composed of several different traditions and also of a number of independent cultures, social structures, and languages, which cannot be assigned to any tradition. In other words, a center is a spatial concept, not an expression of continuity.

The gradation through space from more advanced ethnic groups in a center to less advanced groups on its peripheries has a counterpart in the dimension of time. The earlier groups in the center tend to be "underdeveloped" and to lead up to a *climax,* which is followed by a decline. Thus, they conform to a cyclical model, which has sometimes been compared to the youth, maturity, and old age of an organism (e.g., Kroeber, 1944). This comparison is apt when one is dealing with only a single tradition, as in the case of Early, Middle, and Late Minoan in the Aegean area (G. Clark, 1969, pp. 135–137). It is inappropriate, however, when one takes into consideration all the traditions and independent cultures, social structures, and languages in a center, for example, the Helladic as well as the Minoan tradition in the Aegean area.

The fact is that superorganic patterns of change rarely conform entirely to the theoretical models of regular gradation to and from centers in space and climaxes in time. There are too many disturbing factors such as geographic barriers, migrations, and the tendency of ethnic groups to reject incompatible norms. Nevertheless, centers and climaxes do occur throughout prehistory and must be taken into consideration.

We have now covered the principal models used by physical anthropologists and prehistorians to reconstruct patterns of change, and a review is in order. We have seen that physical anthropologists specialize in the changes from prehuman species to the human species (*Homo sapiens*). They begin by delineating lines and then distinguish grades along related lines. Both lines and grades have to be demarcated on the side face of our cube of knowledge, in the dimensions of form and time, because they are composed of closed systems of genes.

Prehistorians specialize in the changes from one ethnic group to another within the human species. They begin by delineating traditions and then distinguish stages within the traditions. Both traditions and stages have to be demarcated on the front face of the cube, in the dimensions of space and time, because they are composed of open systems of genes, in the case of organic change, or of norms, in the case of superorganic change. However, the specific stages can be generalized by studying them comparatively from tradition to tradition.

Prehistorians also attempt to distinguish centers and peripheries. Centers are places of higher superorganic development, where innovations tend to originate and whence they spread to the peripheries. The peripheral peoples may or may not accept the innovations, depending upon the degree of their ethnocentrism. Within each center, there is often a rise to a climax and then a decline.

The actual patterns of change are never completely regular, and therefore it would be a mistake to assume that they necessarily follow the models we have been discussing. The prehistorian should start with archeological data and derive patterns of change from them, instead of slavishly imposing his theoretical models on the data.

11
Development of dynamic research

To judge by conditions among contemporary nonliterate peoples, early man is not likely to have had much knowledge of, or interest in, change. He probably assumed that his own ethnic traits were changeless, instead of regarding change as a normal part of his life, as we do. This assumption, however, need not have prevented him from theorizing about the origin of his own traits. He may well have explained his organic traits by postulating descent from, or creation by, gods or other supernatural beings, as many contemporary peoples do. He may also have theorized that his own superorganic traits were created by the gods or else invented by a "culture hero." In other words, he probably overlooked patterns of change, the answer to the first part of the question "How and why?" And he probably answered the second part by postulating the processes of birth, creation, and invention.

The Sumerians and Egyptians, who were the first peoples to leave historical records, had a similar attitude toward change (Frankfort et al., 1949, pp. 59–70 and 165–174). The Chinese and classical thinkers added a belief in the Stone-Bronze-Iron sequence (Sec. 4.3), but they considered this sequence to be a record of events rather than an expression of change. To them, each unit in the sequence was an age rather than a stage. Thus, Lucretius discussed a surprising number of the innovations that have taken place during the course of human existence but failed to fit them together within a pattern, or tradition, that would be divisible into stages (Phillips, 1964, p. 176). He could hardly have dealt with change anyway, since he thought of the three-stage system as being generally applicable. This point of view puts the system on the side of our cube, where it is impossible to study changes in ethnic norms, as we have seen (Sec. 6.8). In other words, the Chinese and classical scholars continued to overlook the subquestion "how?" and answered the subquestion "why?" by postulating the process of creation or invention.

The medieval scholars obtained their answers to the two subquestions by reading the Bible. There, they were informed that the world and everything in it had been created by God in its present form. This information eliminated the need to answer "how?" and provided an acceptable answer to "why?" To be sure, the medieval scholars did distinguish two ages, antediluvian and diluvian (Sec. 4.3), but they considered them to be alike in all essential characteristics. Indeed, it was Noah's great achievement that he was able to carry the antediluvian conditions through the disaster of the flood without change. The medieval scholars also overlooked the changes that had taken place between Biblical time and the Middle Ages. In effect, they assumed a pattern of no change as their answer to the subquestion "how?"

The rediscovery of classical learning during the Renaissance did nothing to break down this assumption, since the classical scholars had also overlooked change. To find out how Western thinkers eventually became aware of change, we must turn to a different subject, natural history. Both scholars and laymen developed an intense interest in this subject during the eighteenth century and began to distinguish varieties of wild plants and animals. As more and more of these became known, there developed a welter of overlapping classifications and confusing terminologies. The Swedish naturalist C. Linnaeus proposed a binomial classification to correct this situation. It was generally accepted and has remained the standard biological approach to taxonomy to this day. Each kind of plant and animal is assigned to a genus and species and is given a pair of names, the first referring to its genus, or grouping of similar categories, and the second to its species, that is, its own particular category. Linnaeus brought man into the system as the genus *Homo* and the species *sapiens* (Buettner-Janusch, 1966, pp. 33–40).

The Linnaean classification was originally intended to be purely descriptive. The fact that two species were assigned to the same genus did not mean that one had developed out of the other but merely that the two looked alike. Each species was regarded as a separate, stationary state, like the units of the Stone-Bronze-Iron-Age classification. Linnaeus and his followers did not study the pattern of change from one species to another; instead, they accounted separately for each species by invoking the Biblical theory of creation (Dobzhansky, 1966, p. 162).

Nevertheless, the Linnaean classification ultimately led to the first successful studies of change by Charles Darwin and the other nineteenth-century discoverers of organic evolution. These writers conceived of the phylogenetic model of change, though they did not yet have the paleontological evidence needed to apply it in detail, and devised the theory of natural selection in order to explain why change is phylogenetic. Recognizing that species are not stationary states, as the Linnaeans had thought, the Darwinians concluded that each species continually gives birth to new forms, which struggle for survival until the one that is best adapted to local conditions prevails. There was strong opposition from religious thinkers, who could not bring themselves to abandon the Biblical belief in the pattern of no change and the process of creation, but eventually the theory of change through organic evolution won out (Eiseley, 1958, pp. 117–204).

The Darwinians have been proved right about the phylogenetic model of change by the paleontological discoveries of the late nineteenth and twentieth centuries. When these finds are plotted in the dimensions of form and time, they assume a phylogenetic configuration, as the Darwinians had foreseen. For example, a number of the precursors of the apes and man are now known, and they fit nicely into the proper pattern (Pilbeam, 1970, pp. 76–85).

Many fossil bones of man himself have also been discovered during the past century. It was originally assumed that these finds, too, would fit the phylogenetic model. However, as more and more finds have been plotted in the dimensions of form and time, it has become increasingly clear that they do not fit the assumed model. Recently, certain physical anthropologists have thought to plot the finds in space and time instead and have found that they do conform to the trellis model (e.g., Hulse, 1963, fig. 48).

This conformity to the trellis model has several consequences, which have not yet been fully realized. The first is that all human forms (except for the very earliest, where the record is unclear) must have been able to interbreed, for otherwise, some, at least, would fit into the phylogenetic rather than the trellis model. Second, all forms (with the same exception) must belong to the human species (*Homo sapiens*), since by definition a species includes all forms that are capable of interbreeding. Finally, it follows that all except the earliest part of human evolution must be studied in terms of races and approached via the front face of the cube. The approach via the side face has to be abandoned, except as a means of denoting the sequence of morphological traits through time (cf. Fig. 13*b, left* and *right*).

The practice of grouping all except the very earliest forms of man within the human species (*Homo sapiens*) has already been pioneered by Buettner-Janusch (1966) and Brace (1967). However, neither of these authors has followed out the implications of his innovation by plotting the distributions of the subdivisions of the human species in space and time, rather than form and time.

From research on organic change, let us now turn to the study of superorganic change. This research has developed along three lines:

GENERAL APPROACH. A number of nineteenth-century anthropologists were inspired by the theories of organic evolution to postulate *general sequences* of cultural, social, and even linguistic innovations. They arranged these innovations in the order of increasing complexity, culminating in the norms of the Victorian period in which they lived (e.g., Tylor, 1960).

Lucretius and the other classical scholars had used this approach. The Victorians possessed two advantages over them. First, they were able to check the presumed order of many innovations against the archeological evidence that was accumulating at the time, and, second, they could include infinitely more details because of the ethnographic knowledge available to them.

Like the classical theorists before them, the Victorians were unable to study superorganic change, and hence evolution, because they had chosen to approach our cube of knowledge via its side face, in the dimensions of form and time, and this approach prevented them from assuming the roles of prehistorian and ethnologist, through which they could have dealt with change and evolution (Sec. 6.7).

The general approach went into eclipse during the first part of the twentieth century. In Europe, anthropologists came to realize that they could not use it to study change—they called it "history"—and decided to concentrate instead on the contemporary scene. Most became "functionalists" and studied the significance of cultural, social, and linguistic norms to the peoples who possessed them, or else "structuralists," who studied the formal relationships among the norms (e.g., Beattie, 1964, pp. 49–64). In America, a major effort was instead made to trace the distribution of norms at the time of first contact between Europeans and the natives, in an attempt to reconstruct the prehistory of the natives, but eventually this effort, too, gave way to functional and structural studies as it became apparent that prehistory could better be approached by the study of archeological data (e.g., Hoebel, 1958, pp. 516–518). In both Europe and America, therefore, the trend has been away from the formulation of a general sequence of superorganic norms to research on the function and structure of the norms.

Nevertheless, interest in the general sequence of norms has been kept alive in the United States by Leslie A. White (1959) and his students, who claim to be evolutionists despite the fact that their sequences of cultural and social advances do not involve change. Sahlins (in Sahlins and Service, 1960, pp. 12–44) does recognize this fact but argues that change can nevertheless be studied in form and time, that is, on the side face of our cube, by shifting from "general cultural evolution" to "specific cultural evolution." Unfortunately, his argument is based upon a false analogy between the origin of species, which is macroevolutionary and therefore conforms to the phylogenetic model (Fig. 13), and the origin of cultures, which is microevolutionary and therefore conforms to the trellis model (Fig. 14). This false analogy leads him to the erroneous conclusion that specific cultural evolution takes the form of a "phylogenetic development" (p. 24).

Notwithstanding these flaws, White and his followers have made significant progress beyond previous studies of the sequence of cultural and social advances, notably by demonstrating that certain cultural and social norms are necessary prerequisites to the development of more advanced norms. They have not, however, studied the changes from more primitive to more advanced norms—this study would have to be done on the front rather than the side face of our cube—nor have they studied changes in systems of norms.

LINEAR APPROACHES. Nineteenth-century European prehistorians were stimulated by the work of their biological colleagues to try a different approach to superorganic evolution. Just as the biologists had converted the Linnaean taxonomy into a phylogenetic pattern of change and had explained this pattern by developing the theory of natural selection, so the prehistorians proceeded to convert their extant classification, the three-age system, into a pattern of change, and developed an explanation for the pattern. The conversion was accomplished by reformulating the Stone, Bronze, and Iron Ages into stages, representing levels within a line of development rather than divisions of relative time (e.g., Childe, 1944). The explanation was accomplished by postulating a theory of progress. It was assumed that, since man is a thinking animal, he must constantly be devising ways to improve himself, and that these have enabled him to progress onward and upward through the Stone, Bronze, and Iron Ages to the heights achieved during the Victorian era (Rouse, 1964a, pp. 462–463).

This approach had the advantage over the general approach that it operated via the front rather than the side face of the cube, in the dimensions of space and time rather than form and time (Fig. 14), and therefore was concerned with specific changes that could be empirically observed, rather than with chronological sequences of traits (Fig. 9c). Nevertheless, it was doomed to failure for three reasons:

1. It assumed the existence of a single line of development, proceeding through the same three ages everywhere in the world, for which reason it is called *unilinear*. In effect, the nineteenth-century prehistorians failed to recognize that they should have substi-

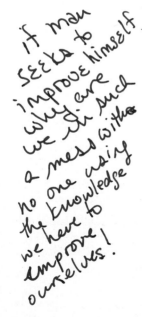

[handwritten margin note, left] if man seeks to improve himself why are we in such a mess with no one using the knowledge we have to improve ourselves!

[handwritten margin note, right] There are such things as regression.

tuted the concept of tradition for the Darwinian concept of line
and marked off their stages on the traditions, as grades are marked
off on lines. This oversight was understandable, since stages play so
much more important a role in cultural change than traditions do
(Sec. 6.9), but nevertheless it was a mistake. It caused the prehistorians to view cultural change in terms of their own West European traditions, without recognizing that different kinds of change
have taken place in other parts of the world.

2. Whereas the Linnaean classification had provided the Darwinians with a valid series of units that they could fit together to
form a pattern of change, the Stone, Bronze, and Iron "stages"
were not suitable for this purpose. They consisted of individual
traits, as in the general approach, when in fact they should have
been conceived of as structurally organized systems of traits, each
possessed by a different ethnic group. Unfortunately, the kind of
classification that would produce ethnic groups had not yet been
devised.

3. The criteria used to define the Stone, Bronze, and Iron stages
covered only a small part of the dimension of form. These criteria
were limited to toolmaking and did not include any other cultural
activities or any aspects of morphology, social structure, or language.
As we have seen (Secs. 6.8 and 6.9), all traditions and stages have
this weakness, in that each applies only to a small part of the dimension of form. By itself, none of them gives an overall picture of
change.

In an unsuccessful attempt to correct the third problem, several
nineteenth-century ethnologists redefined the Stone-Bronze-Iron sequence in terms of more fundamental activities. Thus, Lewis H.
Morgan postulated the following stages: Lower, Middle, and Upper
Savagery; Lower, Middle, and Upper Barbarism; and Civilization
(Daniel, 1950, pp. 186–187). These were based primarily upon criteria not preserved in the archeological record.

The weaknesses in the Stone-Bronze-Iron-stage system gradually
became apparent to European prehistorians, and by the end of
World War I they had largely abandoned it as an expression of
superorganic evolution, though they retained it as a system of ages

and expanded it by dividing the Stone Age into the Paleolithic, Mesolithic, and Neolithic (Sec. 4.3). There were, however, two notable exceptions: V. Gordon Childe in western Europe and the Soviet prehistorians in the East. Childe made a valiant, though ultimately unsuccessful, attempt to improve the utility of the system as an expression of evolution by redefining the Paleolithic, Mesolithic, Neolithic, Bronze, and Iron stages primarily in terms of the means of production. In this attempt he was influenced by Marxian theories of evolution (Sec. 4.3). Since Marx himself had been strongly influenced by Morgan's previous reformulation of the three-stage system in ethnographic terms, the system now took a full turn back into prehistory in a revised form. Thus, Childe redefined the Neolithic stage in terms of agriculture (Morgan's Barbarism) and the Bronze stage in terms of urbanism (Morgan's Civilization).

Childe also introduced into his stage theory the concept of ethnic units or cultures, which he had pioneered (Sec. 3.5). He assigned his cultures to their proper stages but unfortunately did not think to organize the cultures by traditions before doing so. This omission did not matter so much in Mesopotamia, where he first worked out his new stage definitions, since there was only a single tradition to be taken into consideration in Mesopotamia. When he turned to Egypt, however, his failure to take traditions into consideration caused him to overlook significant differences between the cultural and social changes that had taken place in the two regions. For example, urbanism, which he had used as his criterion for the Bronze stage in Mesopotamia, does not occur in the corresponding stage of the Egyptian tradition. Nevertheless, Childe assumed its presence because of his belief that civilization had developed in the same way in the two regions. Late in his life, Childe came to realize that there were, indeed, marked differences in the cultural changes that had taken place in various parts of the Western World (Childe, 1963), but he did not conceptualize these differences by establishing traditions.

The Soviet prehistorians have adhered more strictly to the Marxian approach. They use the Paleolithic-Mesolithic-Neolithic-Bronze-Iron-Age sequence and continue to define it technologically, so that, for them, the Neolithic is marked by ground-stone tools instead of agriculture, by which it is marked for Childe. Nevertheless, they treat the ages as stages, in the terminology being used here. To each stage they assign its proper means of subsistence, kinds of social organization, languages, and so forth, in accordance with Marx's theories concerning the sequence of elements of culture, social structure, and language.

In order to elaborate the stages in this manner they have had to perpetuate the unilinear fallacy by assuming that all peoples throughout the world belong to the same cultural, social, and linguistic tradition and hence must pass through the same stages—much as each tree in a forest grows in a similar fashion—unless prevented from doing so by factors in their environment or by conservatism. This conception of change is obviously false—it does not fit either the phylogenetic model of organic change or the trellis model of cultural, morphological, social, and linguistic change—and hence the Soviet approach has not met with favor except among communist prehistorians. Indeed, current events within the communist countries are proving their prehistorians wrong, for separate local traditions are springing up despite the Soviet attempts to force the satellite countries to develop in the same way as Russia.

In the New World, early attempts to apply the Paleolithic-Mesolithic-Neolithic-Bronze-Iron system failed because it obviously conflicts with the local archeology. The failure was explained by assuming that man had entered the New World too recently to have passed through the Old World stages since his entry. Recent excavations, on the contrary, have revealed a series of local developments that extend back in time as far as the Upper Paleolithic age in Europe. The existence of these developments and of comparable, but different, developments in other parts of the world, such as Asia and Africa, has led Julian Steward (1955) to postulate a *multilinear* theory of cultural evolution, in opposition to the general theory of White and his followers and the unilinear theory espoused by Soviet prehistorians. Steward assumes that each of the world's cultural centers has developed linearly and in a parallel fashion, so that it is necessary to set up a separate sequence of stages for each center.

Steward's multilinear approach has not been widely adopted by prehistorians except in the New World. There, Willey and Phillips (1962) have established a separate sequence of stages for the New

World, based upon the developments in the Mesoamerican cultural center. These are known as Lithic, Archaic, Formative, Classic, and post-Classic.

The Willey-Phillips sequence was originally well received but has fallen out of favor as prehistorians have discovered that it clashes with our knowledge of the development of local traditions in the New World. It has become clear that the Willey-Phillips stages do not fit all the New World traditions, to say nothing of the cultures that cannot be assigned to traditions, and as a result, Willey himself has emphasized traditions rather than stages in his latest synthesis of New World prehistory (Willey, 1966). Linear systems of stages have therefore fallen into disrepute in both the Old and New Worlds, except among communist prehistorians.

TRELLIS APPROACH. The foregoing account of the vicissitudes of the linear approaches may be viewed as a struggle by prehistorians to rid themselves of a false analogy between the Darwinian theory of macroevolution and the reality of microevolution. In other words, prehistorians have organized their stages in terms of the lines in the phylogenetic model, when in fact they should have been organizing them in terms of the traditions in the trellis model.

In distinguishing traditions, one has to keep in mind that they may conform to any part of the trellis model. As we have seen, Soviet prehistorians recognize only the vertical members of the trellis and as a result view cultural change as a unilinear development proceeding in the same way throughout the world. Some Western prehistorians, on the contrary, have recognized only the horizontal members of the trellis by viewing change as the result of a succession of long-scale migrations (for a discussion of these theories, see Daniel, 1964, pp. 82–101). Instead of making a priori assumptions such as these, one should rely upon archeological evidence to indicate the part of the trellis to which each tradition belongs.

One should also bear in mind that many of the cultures, social structures, and languages in the trellis cannot be assigned to traditions, at least in the present state of our knowledge. It is necessary to take these systems, too, into consideration if one's survey of ethnic change is to be comprehensive and unbiased.

12
Processes of change:
modification of
existing systems

To this point, we have been primarily concerned with dynamics, that is, with reconstruction of patterns of change. Let us now turn to explanation, that is, to postulation of the processes that produced the reconstructed patterns. Since the reader is presumably familiar with the processes of organic change, such as mutation, gene flow, and natural selection, we shall omit them from the present discussion and concentrate on the processes of superorganic change, without, however, going into detail, for superorganic processes are more properly the subject of a book on cultural, physical, social, or linguistic anthropology (Sec. 2.2). More extended discussions of processes can be found in Kroeber (1963) and Clarke (1968).

While the following processes will be discussed separately, it should not be assumed that they operate that way. Any change is effected by various factors or "contingencies" (Skinner, 1969). In explaining each change, the prehistorian must consider the total range of processes and try to determine which processes are most likely to have caused that particular change, in accordance with the principle of multiple working hypotheses.

The processes may be divided into three groups, based upon the magnitude of the changes they produce: (1) modification of existing ethnic systems, (2) development of new systems, and (3) major improvement in human life. We shall begin with the processes causing modifications in systems.

ECOLOGICAL PROCESSES. The environment acts as a limiting factor, particularly in areas of extreme heat, cold, moisture, or dryness. Under such circumstances, an ethnic system must adjust to local conditions. This process is known as *ecological adaptation*.

On the positive side, each microenvironment offers certain potential resources, which may or may not be utilized by the local people (Coe and Flannery, 1964; Flannery, 1968). The process of discovering and taking advantage of these resources may be termed *exploitation.*

ORGANIC PROCESSES. When man began to differentiate from his precursors, the extent of his superorganic development was limited by the state of his organic development. For example, he could not plan toolmaking procedures until his brain had reached a certain size and complexity. He was therefore subject to a process of *morphological adaptation,* paralleling ecological adaptation. This process ceased to operate after man had become fully human, that is, after the middle of the Pleistocene epoch (e.g., Pilbeam, 1970, pp. 180–194).

Men of genius, who are endowed with greater genetic capacities than the other members of their respective races, have the potentiality of exerting a positive effect upon the development of cultural, social, and linguistic systems, but this effect cannot be studied archeologically. It is virtually impossible, too, to determine the role of physiological and personality traits in the development of prehistoric ethnic systems, a process which may be called *psychological adaptation.*

Migration of a people from one area to another is likely to produce changes by bringing a foreign ethnic system into contact with the local system and causing them to exchange genes, if the systems are organic, or norms, if the systems are superorganic. The foreign system may also have to adapt to different ecological conditions in the new area.

SUPERORGANIC PROCESSES. Prehistorians are accustomed to refer to the creation of new norms as "invention" (Harrison, 1930). This term is a poor one, since most norms develop accidentally and gain acceptance, not because they are promoted by an inventor, but because someone happens to notice that they fit a certain need. *Innovation* is therefore more appropriate and will be used here (Barnett, 1957).

Few innovations are unique, for there are only a limited number of ways of meeting the needs of human existence. Peoples in different parts of the world have not infrequently hit upon the same ones quite independently. Such a parallel development is known as *convergence* (e.g., Bordes, 1968, pp. 228–234, 1969, p. 8).

Similarities between adjacent areas are normally due, not to convergence, but to the spread of norms or traditions from person to person. This spread of norms or traditions is known as *diffusion.* It results from an exchange of ideas through trade, intermarriage, or any other kind of contact. Diffusion is sometimes confused with migration but is better kept separate, since it is a superorganic process, whereas migration is organic (Harrison, 1954).

Diffusion can take place from one individual to another within a community, from one community to another within a single ethnic group, or from one ethnic group to another. The quality of a norm changes little, if at all, as it passes from individual to individual and from community to community within the same ethnic group. What does change is its frequency; that is, it increases or decreases in popularity. Frequency changes are the basis for a common technique of seriating types of pottery, described in Section 4.7 (see also Deetz, 1967, pp. 26–33).

When a norm is adopted by a new ethnic group, it tends to change in nature as well as in frequency. It has to be modified to fit the new group's cultural, social, or linguistic system, as when foreign words are adapted to the phonetics of a local language. If a people adopts many of another's cultural norms, the first people is said to have become acculturated. In extreme cases, *acculturation* results in the capture of one people by another—usually the capture of a less advanced cultural group by a more advanced one. The members of the two groups merge into a single group, which retains the more advanced of the two cultures.

sometimes →

questionable as to which is advanced — who's criterion.

13
Processes of
change:
ethnogenesis

Since ethnic traits are integrated into morphological, cultural, social, and linguistic systems, one might expect that prehistorians would have devoted much attention to the factors that caused one system to change into another. In fact, American dictionaries do not even contain a word for the origin of ethnic systems. Russian and Japanese anthropologists, however, are accustomed to refer to the process as *ethnogenesis* (e.g., Taryo, 1966).

Ethnogenesis may be defined as the process whereby a series of genes or norms comes together to form a new system, whether this system be a morphology, culture, social structure, or language. In some cases, the new system appears full-blown in the archeological record, without any recognizable antecedents, while in other cases we may recognize a change from one system to another. If there are no antecedents, we may say that the new morphology, culture, social structure, or language has arisen as the result of a *synthesis* of genes or norms from various sources. If there is evidence of a change from one system to another, we may call the process a *transformation* (Clarke, 1968, p. 262); and if two systems have merged, we may call the process a *fusion*.

Prehistorians have spent much time and energy in searching for the origin of morphologies, cultures, social structures, or languages that have no recognizable antecedents. This problem is a false one, arising from the misconception that ethnic systems are closed and can therefore only develop one from another in a linear or furcate manner. As we have seen (Sec. 6.7), the systems are open and can incorporate genes or norms from various sources. If the number of sources is great and their effect is even, we will not be able to say that the new system developed out of any previous system. We will only be able to investigate the source of the genes or norms that combined to form the new system and to say that the system is the result of a synthesis of these traits that took place at such and such a point in time and space. If, on the other hand, the new system is linked by genes or norms, or by traditions (complexes of genes or norms), with one or more antecedent systems, we may say that a transformation or fusion has taken place.

Innovation is often confused with ethnogenesis, but the two are easily distinguished. Innovation refers to the origin of individual norms and traditions within single ethnic systems. It therefore operates on the level of classes of artifacts—the units discussed in Chapter 2. Ethnogenesis, on the contrary, refers to the origin of new systems. Thus it operates on the level of classes of assemblages—the units discussed in Chapter 3.

14 Processes of change: revolution

Variations within ethnic systems and changes from one system to another tend to have a cumulative effect. Such incremental changes build up gradually until they reach a point at which they make possible a new level of complexity, either in a single ethnic system, such as a culture, or in accompanying systems, such as a morphology and a social structure. When this point is reached, we may say that there has been a *revolution,* that is, a radical change in the life of the participating people (e.g., Childe, 1950).

A revolution, then, is divided into two parts: a long, slow, developmental stage, which builds up to a threshold, and a period of radical change after the threshold has been crossed. The first part may be termed "incipient"; the second is the truly revolutionary part of the process. It is important to note that a revolution cannot take place without a long, incipient period of development.

15
Attitudes toward
change

Thus far, we have assumed that ethnic systems are open, so that all innovations compatible with a system will be incorporated into it, whether as the result of invention or of diffusion. But we must also take into consideration the attitudes toward ethnic change of the people who possess the system.

At the present time, perhaps the most extreme attitude against change is manifested on the other side of the iron curtain, where communist society strives to maintain a closed social structure and justifies this action by "scientific" analogy to evolutionary changes among genera and species of animals, conveniently ignoring the fact that evolution within the human species, as within any other species, normally operates in terms of open rather than closed systems. On our side of the iron curtain, Western society is more of an open system, but our conservatives also oppose social change.

It is a curious fact that, despite the opposition to social change on both sides of the iron curtain, communists and Westerners actively promote cultural change, especially in the field of technology. Both tend to be socially conservative, in the sense that each strives to maintain its present social structure, but culturally progressive. A neutral observer from Mars would doubtless wonder why it is that the two societies see relatively little need to improve their social structures and yet strive so hard to improve their common civilization.

The same observer would also consider it odd that the citizens of the United States tend to regard the Caucasoid and Mongoloid morphologies as closed systems and have kept them closed by their prejudice against miscegenation, whereas the two systems are considerably more open in Latin America. As a result of this attitude, less morphological change has taken place in the United States than in many parts of Latin America, especially Brazil and Cuba.

As for linguistic change, some contemporary speech communities, notably the French, deplore foreign influences upon their languages and have consciously attempted to make them closed systems. The French feel much the same about the purity of their language as white and black racists in the United States feel about the purity of their morphologies. By contrast, few Americans are concerned about the purity of the English language.

Attitudes like these must have been in operation throughout prehistoric time. The archeological record shows that the rates of change in cultural, morphological, social, and linguistic systems have varied greatly from area to area and from period to period. Much of this variation is doubtless a result of the processes of change discussed in the previous sections, but differing attitudes toward change may also have been a factor. Unfortunately, such attitudes cannot be detected archeologically and as a result are rarely taken into account by prehistorians.

16
Reductionism

The processes of change noted in the foregoing sections may be viewed as a series of layers. The topmost consists of purely normative and conceptual processes, such as innovation and diffusion, to which the term superorganic is applicable. Peeling off this layer, one finds a second layer containing migration and other kinds of movements of human beings from place to place. Next comes a dual layer, composed on the one hand of ecological factors and on the other hand of psychological factors. The ecological factors operate mainly on cultural systems, since these are oriented toward the environment (Sec. 5.7), while the psychological factors have more of an effect on social systems, which are oriented toward human beings (Sec. 5.13).

Peeling off the ecological-psychological layer, one comes to physiological factors, that is, to the capabilities of the human organism. Beneath this layer are still others, composed of factors inherent in matter rather than life. If we were to follow up these factors, we would ultimately come to atomic particles, upon which the entire world and its contents are based.

As has been implied in the previous sections, the prehistorian in search of explanations is best able to operate on the topmost layer, in terms of superorganic processes, for his data are primarily of that kind. The second layer is more difficult to handle, although a total break in either a cultural or a morphological system may be regarded as evidence of a migration. On the third layer, it is possible to do more with ecological than with psychological explanations. Little can be accomplished below the third layer except when dealing with early man, where primitive morphological traits may be presumed to be limiting factors. The prehistorian's inability to handle many factors below the second or third level is another reason why he achieves less success in studying explanations—the "why" of the fourth question—than in studying dynamics—the "how" of that question.

These considerations do not excuse the investigator from attempting to peel off as many layers as possible. Too many prehistorians are content to operate only on the top level of norms. Binford (1965, pp. 203–210) has overreacted to this deficiency by rejecting the normative approach. Norms have their place, however, if only on the superorganic level.

SUPPLEMENTAL READING

CHILDE, V. GORDON, *Man Makes Himself* (1951).

CHILDE, V. GORDON, *Social Evolution* (1963).

CLARKE, DAVID L., *Analytical Archaeology* (1968).

DANIEL, GLYN, *The Idea of Prehistory* (1964).

HERSKOVITS, MELVILLE J., *Cultural Dynamics* (1964).

HOLE, FRANK, AND ROBERT F. HEIZER, *An Introduction to Prehistoric Archeology* (1969), pt. VI.

KROEBER, A. L., *Anthropology: Culture Patterns and Processes* (1963).

SAHLINS, MARSHALL D., AND ELMAN R. SERVICE, eds., *Evolution and Culture* (1960).

TYLOR, SIR EDWARD B., *Anthropology* (1960).

7

CONCLUSION

1
Summary of
prehistorical
methods We have characterized prehistory as a historical discipline, because it approaches the study of man primarily by way of the dimensions of space and time (Fig. 1). But it is also scientific, for it is developing a systematic set of concepts with which to study the dimension of form. It shares most of these concepts with the rest of anthropology.

Prehistorians work mainly with archeological data, which they obtain by recovering and processing human remains. Their basic unit of study is a cultural assemblage, consisting of the remains deposited at a site by a single people. While the unworked parts of assemblages are classified as natural objects, the artifacts are grouped into classes on the basis of their culturally significant attributes. The set of attributes diagnostic of each class of artifacts is known as its "type" (Fig. 4). Important features of the artifacts are also classified separately in order to form modes, or kinds of features.

Since classification is an arbitrary procedure and can be done in a variety of ways, one must always be careful to use the kind of classification that is best suited to one's objectives. In recognition of this principle, prehistorians have distinguished three major kinds of types and modes: intrinsic, extrinsic, and cognitive. Intrinsic types and modes are designed to express the inherent nature of the artifacts; extrinsic types and modes, to extract information from the artifacts about the people who made and used them; and cognitive types and modes, to approximate the ideas the people themselves had about their artifacts.

Types and modes are used in combination with secondary kinds of evidence to answer four major questions (Fig. 6): (1) Who produced the archeological remains under study? (2) Where and when did the producers live? (3) What were they like? (4) How and why did they become that way? The first two of these questions are systematic. By answering them the prehistorian arbitrarily distinguishes and organizes his units of study. The last two questions are substantive. By answering them, the prehistorian learns about the cultural, morphological, social, and linguistic systems possessed by the ethnic groups and about the changes that have taken place in those systems, that is, about human evolution. The procedures for answering the four questions are as follows:

1. *Who?* Selecting typical cultural assemblages, the prehistorian groups them into classes, each characterized by a diagnostic complex of types, modes, and other cultural norms (Fig. 7). Each class is assumed to be the product of a single cultural group or people, which is named after a typical site or a diagnostic trait. If the people is civilized, it can be divided into a sustaining co-people, who produced food, and a professional co-people, who specialized in other, less essential activities. Peoples or co-peoples may be divided into subpeoples or, if they share a diagnostic cultural tradition, may be said to belong to the same series of peoples. When feasible, prehistorians also classify morphological assemblages, using biological procedures to distinguish races and species parallel to peoples and series.

2. *Where and when?* The peoples and series are plotted on a chronology, which is a map with its vertical dimension converted from space to time (as on the front face of the cube in Figure 1). The investigator first works out a number of local sequences of peoples, basing them insofar as possible upon stratigraphic columns of refuse, and then synchronizes the sequences by studying the peoples' cultural relationships. The synchronization enables him to draw up a chronology, in which his peoples are arranged horizontally through space and vertically in absolute time (Fig. 10). He uses radiocarbon dates to assign calendrical values to each people's position in the chronology. In addition, he may plot the times of first appearance of major innovations on the chronology, in order to delimit units of relative time such as the Bronze Age (Fig. 10). Morphological, social, or linguistic groups may also be inserted in the chronology if they can be correlated with peoples already there.

3. *What?* This question must be answered primarily in terms of peoples, since most of the evidence is cultural. The prehistorian reconstructs as much as possible of each people's cultural system and learns all that he can about its social, morphological, and linguistic systems, as follows:

a. *Cultural system (culture)*. First he reconstructs the people's activity pattern, that is, its activities and the manner in which they were distributed over the landscape (Fig. 11). He isolates loci in which the different activities were performed, recovers assemblages from these loci, makes inferences from the assemblages concerning the activities that produced them, and plots the distribution of the activities. Then he is able to determine the extent to which the people exploited its natural resources by studying the relationship of its reconstructed pattern to the local microenvironments and by examining the content of each activity assemblage. From the two, he also infers the total range of the people's activities, including not only those which furnish the means of subsistence, but also those which are more purely intellectual, such as art and religion (Table 6). He then articulates the various activities in order to reconstruct the people's cultural system. He also uses the activity assemblages to fill out his knowledge of the people's cultural norms and materiel.

b. Social system(s). Since peoples and societies (culturally versus socially defined groups) do not always coincide, the prehistorian must consider the possibility that the people he is studying may have possessed more than one social system or structure (Fig. 11). First he reconstructs each society's residential pattern, that is, the nature of its households, communities, and other residential institutions and the manner in which they were distributed over the landscape. He recovers representative residential (as opposed to cultural or activity) assemblages, infers the composition of the institution that deposited each assemblage, and plots the distribution of the institutions. Then he returns to his activity assemblages and attempts to determine who deposited each one; was it a residential institution, such as a household, or another kind of institution organized especially for the purpose, such as a work group or temple community (Table 6)? He should not limit himself to residential or activity institutions but should also study relational institutions, based upon criteria of age, wealth, or descent, though he will be able to learn little about them in the absence of closely related ethnographic or ethnohistorical evidence. Ideally, he should also reconstruct the way in which each institution was organized and the norms that affected its organization, but these, too, are usually beyond the range of his evidence.

c. Morphological and linguistic systems. If sufficient remains of the people per se have been recovered, the prehistorian may proceed to study its morphological system(s), which again may be either singular or plural depending upon whether or not the cultural group (people) was limited to a single morphological group (race or species of man). Working separately with each morphological group, he attempts to reconstruct the organic structure, appearance, and capabilities of its members, as well as their reproductive behavior and the norms that affected that behavior, insofar as these can be determined from archeological evidence (Fig. 11). There are never enough data to make a comparable study of a people's linguistic system(s)—its language(s)—except in the presence of historical records.

4. *How and why?* Finally, the prehistorian reconstructs patterns of change in the cultural, social, morphological, and linguistic sys-

tems of the peoples under study and postulates processes of change to explain the patterns. He employs very different procedures in dealing with patterns and processes:

a. Patterns.   In reconstructing patterns of change, he makes use of biological models of evolution. He is able to arrange the earliest human morphologies in phylogenetic lines of development because these morphologies are closed systems, belonging to separate genera and species, the members of which were unable to interbreed and hence to exchange genes (Fig. 13). In dealing with our own species (*Homo sapiens*), on the contrary, he must employ the trellis model of change, since the members of our species have always been able to interbreed and to exchange genes. The trellis model also applies to changes in cultural, social, and linguistic systems, for these changes take place in terms of norms, which spread even more easily than genes (Fig. 14). As a result, our ethnic systems cannot be arranged lineally, but must be fitted into traditions and stages. Prehistorians who advocate a linear arrangement are confusing macroevolution, which takes place in terms of closed systems, with microevolution, which takes place in terms of open systems.

Another frequent source of confusion is between organic change, which takes place in terms of genes, and superorganic change, which takes place in terms of norms. Organic changes in open systems need only be studied in terms of traditions and stages, but superorganic changes must also be studied in terms of centers and climaxes. These develop because of the tendency of norms to accumulate rather than alternate, as genes do. Certain peoples or societies accumulate larger numbers of cultural or social norms than others and as a result are able to synthesize more complex cultural or social systems, which then become examples for adjacent peoples or societies to follow.

b. Processes.   The processes of change that prehistorians cite in order to explain the patterns of change they have reconstructed are hypothetical; they must be postulated rather than reconstructed. They range from purely superorganic processes, such as innovation and diffusion, through organic processes, such as migration and intermarriage, to ecological, psychological, and physiological factors. The prehistorian obtains his most reliable results when working with processes that take place on

the superorganic level, because most of his data are superorganic.

2
Relevance of
prehistorical
research

In this volume, we have assumed that prehistory is a pure science,
like historical geology, rather than an applied science, like economic
geology, and that its aim is to recover the truth, not to resolve current problems. It is hoped that the reader will have acquired herein
the conceptual tools he needs in order to understand the nature and
development of mankind, but he will not have learned how to improve the world in which he lives.

Many of today's students reject the distinction between pure
and applied science and are skeptical of the ability of pure scientists
to arrive at the truth. They cite instances in which supposedly pure
scientists have distorted the truth, either for their own benefit or
on behalf of some "establishment" or power group. Such instances
do occur, though more commonly in the social than in the natural
sciences. Indeed, a number of them have been cited in the present
volume. (Readers interested in learning more about them are advised to consult the last chapter in G. Clark, 1960, and the Transla-
tor's Foreword in Mongait, 1961.)

The skeptics who cite these distortions are expecting too much
of science. They overlook the difference between scientists' ideals
and their realization of the ideals, or, in the terminology of this
book, between norms and the behavior mediated by the norms. Our
world is not perfect and never will be, but this fact is no reason for
us to abandon the search for perfection. We can and should aim
for the truth and come as close to it as possible even though, like
infinity, it is not completely attainable. The Christian concept of sin
is a recognition that we will never attain perfection so far as
morality is concerned, but this recognition does not eliminate the
need for morality. Similarly, scientists must seek the truth even
though they cannot expect to be completely successful in doing so.

From this point of view, scientific methods, such as the ones
discussed here, may be regarded as devices with which to overcome
the factors that tend to distort the truth, insofar as it is possible to
overcome them. The methods presented here are designed to check
the prehistorian's thinking at every stage in his research and to
determine whether or not his conclusions have been affected by personal or ethnic bias.

It is easier to avoid bias in the hard sciences, such as physics and chemistry, because those disciplines are concerned with matter, which is so far removed in the evolutionary scale from ourselves that it can be treated objectively. The problem becomes increasingly difficult among life scientists as they move up the evolutionary scale toward ourselves. Life scientists must constantly guard against the danger of reading human traits into the lesser animals; they call this projection *anthropomorphism*.

The scientists who study human beings are faced with an even more difficult problem (Skinner, 1965, pp. 11–12). It is inevitable that each person views his fellow human beings in terms of his own limited knowledge and experience and his own limiting values and prejudices. In the previous pages, we have referred to this kind of approach as "ethnocentrism." To be successful in his search for truth, the scientist who studies man must overcome his natural tendency toward ethnocentrism.

The discipline of modern history provides a good example of the ethnocentric approach. Contemporary American historians are divided into two opposing groups, the members of the historical "establishment," who view current events in terms of the beliefs, values, and prejudices of the older generation, and the so-called revisionists, who reinterpret the events in terms of the attitudes of the younger generation. Because these two groups differ so sharply, we tend to think that their conflict is unique. In fact, only the intensity of the conflict is unique. We live in a time of unusually rapid change, and so we are more conscious of the differences between the generations than in the past. Such differences have always existed, however, and each generation of historians has modified and reinterpreted the research of previous generations in terms of its own outlook.

This interpretation is a necessary and useful activity. We would be unable to assimilate the changes in culture, morphology, social structure, and language that are now taking place if historical research and teaching were to be abandoned. But the research is applied rather than pure science. Historians reinterpret past events in terms of the values and prejudices of their own ethnic groups and subgroups and hence are unable to approximate the truth about past peoples and events.

The conflict between capitalist and communist historians provides another example. Each are apologists for their own kind of social structure and perform a useful social function in helping to maintain it, if not in urging its imposition upon others. By that very fact, however, capitalist and communist historians are applied rather than pure scientists, with an ethnocentric rather than an objective point of view.

For a third and final example, let us look at history of art. The specialists in this field also operate in terms of the values and the prejudices of their own groups, though in this case the values are cultural rather than social. They are avowedly humanists, limiting themselves to works that they consider to be esthetically significant and imparting that significance to the layman. There is no reason, however, why art cannot also be studied from the standpoint of truth rather than beauty; prehistorians study it in this manner, working as scientists rather than humanists.

The point of view taken in this volume, as in all pure-scientific studies of man, is that different kinds of ethnic groups have existed since the beginning of mankind and will continue to exist until our species disappears from the earth. The scientist's task is to study these groups and their systems objectively, as the biologist studies nonhuman species and the physicist studies the qualities of matter, instead of viewing the systems ethnocentrically, in the manner of historians, applied social scientists, and historians of art.

The pure scientist has the further task of making known the facts about different ethnic groups, so that the layman may have a better basis for understanding and appreciating the groups. This task is particularly important in a nation such as the United States, whose wealth, power, and success have led its citizens to believe that their way of life is the best and to try to impose it upon other, "less fortunate" ethnic groups. Prehistory and history are full of examples of successful peoples, societies, and speech communities who took this point of view and, partially because of it, declined and disappeared. Just as no animal species has ever been able to impose itself upon all other animal species, because organic evolution does not work that way, so no social, cultural, or linguistic group has ever been able to impose its own system upon the rest of mankind, because superorganic evolution does not work that way either. Ethnic systems are too tenacious.

Prehistory occupies a key position in the development of a pure-scientific approach to the study of ethnic groups and their systems because it is concerned with the earliest human beings. One can more easily be objective about the first human beings, because they are so remote and so different from ourselves. In studying them, moreover, one can more easily develop the proper conceptual tools, for two reasons. Early man is so much like the lesser animals that biological concepts are more readily applied to him, and his ethnic systems are so simple as to facilitate the development of new concepts to be used in studying uniquely human traits. For all these reasons, prehistory may be expected to play a leading role in the pure-scientific study of man.

This book is, in effect, a progress report on prehistorians' efforts to develop a pure-scientific approach. It is presented as a contribution to the continuing effort of all pure scientists to perfect conceptual tools with which to approximate the truth about the earth and its inhabitants.

Is the effort worth it? Why not restrict ourselves to studies within the frames of reference of our own ethnic groups and subgroups, as historians do, instead of rising above the groups and viewing mankind as a whole? We must develop an objective, pure-scientific approach because there are so many different ethnic groups—not to mention subgroups—in today's world and because all are potential sources of conflict. We shall never be able to achieve lasting peace, security, and prosperity until we are able, by the use of concepts like those presented in the present volume, to recognize the existence of other groups and subgroups, to understand and respect their ways of life, and to mutually adjust to them. Upon our ability to do so rests the future of the world.

BIBLIOGRAPHY

ADAMS, ROBERT MCC., 1966. *The Evolution of Urban Society: Early Mesopotamia and Prehispanic Mexico*. Aldine Publishing Company, Chicago.

AITKEN, M. J., 1961. *Physics and Archeology*. Interscience Publishers, Ltd., London.

ALBRIGHT, W. F., 1960. *The Archaeology of Palestine*. Pelican Books, Penguin Books, Ltd., Harmondsworth.

ALLAND, ALEXANDER, 1967. *Evolution and Human Behavior*. American Museum Science Books, The Natural History Press, Garden City, N.Y.

ANONYMOUS, 1952. *Notes and Queries on Anthropology*. 6th ed. Royal Anthropological Institute, London.

ANTHROPOLOGICAL SOCIETY OF WASHINGTON, 1968. *Anthropological Archeology in the Americas*. Washington, D.C.

ARKELL, A. J., AND PETER J. UCKO, 1965. Review of Predynastic Development in the Nile Valley. *Current Anthropology*, vol. 6, no. 2, pp. 145–166. Chicago.

ARNOLD, DEAN E., 1971. Ethnomineralogy of Ticul, Yucatan Potters: Etics and Emics. *American Antiquity*, vol. 36, no. 1, pp. 20–40. Washington, D.C.

ASCHER, ROBERT, 1961a. Analogy in Archaeological Interpretation. *Southwestern Journal of Anthopology*, vol. 17, no. 4, pp. 317–325. Albuquerque.

Ascher, Robert, 1961b. Experimental Archaeology. *American Anthropologist,* vol. 63, no. 4, pp. 793–816. Menasha, Wis.

Ascher, Robert, 1968. Teaching Archaeology in the University. *Archaeology,* vol. 21, no. 4, pp. 282–287. New York.

Ascher, Robert, and Marcia Ascher, 1965. Recognizing the Emergence of Man. *Science,* vol. 147, no. 3655, pp. 243–250. Washington, D.C.

Avebury, the rt. hon. lord, 1900. *Pre-historic Times, as Illustrated by Ancient Remains and the Manners and Customs of Modern Savages.* 6th ed. rev. Williams & Norgate, Ltd., London.

Bandi, Hans-Georg, 1969. *Eskimo Prehistory.* Studies of Northern Peoples, no. 2. University of Alaska Press, College.

Barnett, Homer G., 1957. *Innovation: The Basis of Cultural Change.* McGraw-Hill Paperbacks, McGraw-Hill Book Company, New York.

Barth, Fredrik, 1967. On the Study of Social Change. *American Anthropologist,* vol. 69, no. 6, pp. 661–669. Menasha, Wis.

Barth, Fredrik, ed., 1969. *Ethnic Groups and Boundaries: The Social Organizations of Culture Differences.* Universitetsforlaget, Bergen-Oslo.

Beals, Ralph L., and Harry Hoijer, 1953. *An Introduction to Anthropology.* The Macmillan Company, New York.

Beasley, J. D., 1911. The Master of the Berlin Amphora. *The Journal of Hellenic Studies,* vol. 31, pp. 276–295. London.

Beattie, John, 1964. *Other Cultures: Aims, Methods and Achievements in Social Anthropology.* The Free Press, New York.

Benedict, Ruth, 1959. *Patterns of Culture.* Sentry Editions, Houghton Mifflin Company, Boston.

Bennett, Wendell C., 1948. The Peruvian Co-tradition. In *A Reappraisal of Peruvian Archaeology,* assembled by Wendell C. Bennett. Memoirs of the Society for American Archaeology, no. 4, pp. 1–7. Menasha, Wis.

Bennett, Wendell C., and Junius Bird, 1964. *Andean Culture History.* American Museum Science Books, The Natural History Press, Garden City, N.Y.

Biek, Leo, 1963. *Archaeology and the Microscope: The Scientific Examination of Archaeological Evidence.* Lutterworth Press, London.

Binford, Lewis, 1962. Archaeology as Anthropology. *American Antiquity,* vol. 28, no. 2, pp. 217–225. Salt Lake City.

Binford, Lewis R., 1964. A Consideration of Archaeological Research Design. *American Antiquity,* vol. 29, no. 4, pp. 425–441. Salt Lake City.

Binford, Lewis R., 1965. Archaeological Systematics and the Study of Cultural Process. *American Antiquity,* vol. 31, no. 2, pp. 203–210. Salt Lake City.

Binford, Lewis R., 1967. Smudge Pots and Hide Smoking: The Use of Analogy in Archaeological Reasoning. *American Antiquity,* vol. 32, no. 1, pp. 1–12. Salt Lake City.

Binford, Sally R. and Lewis R., eds., 1968. *New Perspectives in Archeology.* Aldine Publishing Company, Chicago.

Blegen, Carl W., 1963. *Troy and the Trojans.* Ancient Peoples and Places, vol. 32. Thames & Hudson, Ltd., London.

Bloomfield, Leonard, 1933. *Language.* Holt, Rinehart and Winston, Inc., New York.

Bordes, François, 1961. *Typologie du paléolithique ancien et moyen.* Publications de l'Institut de Préhistoire de l'Université de Bordeaux, Mémoire no. 1. Bordeaux.

Bordes, François, 1968. *The Old Stone Age.* Translated from the French by J. E. Anderson. World University Library, McGraw-Hill Book Company, New York.

Bordes, François, 1969. Reflections on Typology and Techniques in the Paleolithic. *Arctic Anthropology,* vol. 6, no. 1, pp. 1–29. Madison, Wis.

BRACE, C. LORING, 1967. *The Stages of Human Evolution*. Foundations of Modern Anthropology. Prentice-Hall, Inc., Englewood Cliffs, N.J.

BRAIDWOOD, ROBERT J., 1952. *The Near East and the Foundations for Civilization: An Essay in Appraisal of the General Evidence*. Condon Lectures, Oregon State System of Higher Education, Eugene.

BREUIL, HENRI, 1949. *Beyond the Bounds of History: Scenes from the Old Stone Age*. P. R. Gawthorn, Ltd., London.

BREW, JOHN OTIS, 1946. The Use and Abuse of Taxonomy. In his *Archaeology of Alkali Ridge, Southeastern Utah*. Papers of the Peabody Museum of American Archaeology and Ethnology, Harvard University, vol. 21, pp. 44–66. Cambridge, Mass.

BRØNSTED, JOHANNES, 1954. Norsemen in North America before Columbus. *Annual Report of the Smithsonian Institution for 1953,* pp. 367–405. Washington, D.C.

BROTHWELL, DON AND ERIC HIGGS, eds. 1969. *Science in Archaeology: A Survey of Progress and Research*. Revised and enlarged edition. Thames & Hudson, Ltd., London.

BRUNER, JEROME, 1960. *The Process of Education*. Harvard University Press, Cambridge, Mass.

BUETTNER-JANUSCH, JOHN, 1966. *Origins of Man: Physical Anthropology*. John Wiley & Sons, Inc., New York.

BUNZEL, RUTH L., 1929. *The Pueblo Potter*. Columbia University Press, New York.

BURKITT, MILES C., 1963. *The Old Stone Age*. 4th ed. Atheneum Paperbacks, Atheneum Publishers, New York.

BUSHNELL, G. H. S., 1963. *Peru*. Praeger Paperbacks, Frederick A. Praeger, Inc., New York.

BUTZER, KARL W., 1966. *Environment and Archeology: An Introduction to Pleistocene Geography*. Aldine Publishing Company, Chicago.

CALDWELL, JOSEPH R., 1958. *Trend and Tradition in the Prehistory of the Eastern United States*. Memoirs of the American Anthropological Association, no. 88. Menasha, Wis.

CALDWELL, JOSEPH R., 1966. The New American Archaeology. In *New Roads to Yesterday: Essays in Archaeology*, edited by Joseph R. Caldwell, pp. 333–347. Basic Books, Inc., Publishers, New York.

CAMDEN, WILLIAM, 1586. *Britannia*. 1st ed. London(?).

CARPENTER, RHYS, 1963. Archaeology. In *Art and Archaeology*, by James S. Ackerman and Rhys Carpenter, pp. 1–222. Prentice-Hall, Inc., Englewood Cliffs, N.J.

CHAMBERLIN, T. C., 1965. The Method of Multiple Working Hypotheses. *Science*, vol. 148, no. 3671, pp. 754–759. Washington, D.C.

CHANG, K. C., 1967a. *Rethinking Archaeology*. Studies in Anthropology. Random House, Inc., New York.

CHANG, K. C., 1967b. Towards a Science of Prehistoric Society. In *Settlement Archaeology,* edited by K. C. Chang, pp. 1–9. National Press Books, Palo Alto, Calif.

CHANG, KWANG-CHIH, 1968. *The Archaeology of Ancient China*. Rev. ed. Yale University Press, New Haven, Conn.

CHARD, CHESTER S., 1969a. Archeology in the Soviet Union. *Science,* vol. 163, no. 3869, pp. 774–779. Washington, D.C.

CHARD, CHESTER S., 1969b. *Man in Prehistory*. McGraw-Hill Book Company, New York.

CHIERA, EDWARD, 1938. *They Wrote on Clay: The Babylonian Tablets Speak Today*. The University of Chicago Press, Chicago.

CHILDE, V. GORDON, 1929. *The Danube in Prehistory*. Clarendon Press, Oxford.

CHILDE, V. GORDON, 1944. Archaeological Ages as Technological Stages. *Journal of the Royal Anthropological Institute,* vol. 74, pp. 1–19. London.

CHILDE, V. GORDON, 1946a. *Scotland before the Scots, Being the Rhind Lectures for 1944*. Methuen & Co., Ltd., Lodon.

CHILDE, V. GORDON, 1946b. *What Happened in History*. Pelican Books, Penguin Books, Ltd., Harmondsworth.

CHILDE, V. GORDON, 1950. The Urban Revolution. *Town Planning Review,* vol. 21, pp. 3–17. London.

CHILDE, V. GORDON, 1951. *Man Makes Himself.* Mentor Books, New American Library, Inc., New York.

CHILDE, V. GORDON, 1952. *New Light on the Most Ancient East.* Routledge & Kegan Paul, Ltd., London.

CHILDE, V. GORDON, 1956. *Piecing Together the Past: The Interpretation of Archaeological Data.* Routledge & Kegan Paul, Ltd., London.

CHILDE, V. GORDON, 1958a. *The Prehistory of European Society.* Pelican Books, Penguin Books, Ltd., Harmondsworth.

CHILDE, V. GORDON, 1958b. Retrospect. *Antiquity,* vol. 32, no. 126, pp. 69–74. Newbury.

CHILDE, V. GORDON, 1963. *Social Evolution.* Meridian Books, The World Publishing Company, Cleveland.

CHILDE, V. GORDON, 1964. *The Dawn of European Civilization.* 6th ed. Vintage Books, Inc., Random House, Inc., New York.

CHORLEY, RICHARD J., AND PETER HAGGETT, eds., 1967. *Models in Geography.* Methuen & Co. Ltd., London.

CLARK, GRAHAME, 1951. Folk Culture and the Study of European Prehistory. In *Aspects of Archaeology in Great Britain and Beyond: Essays Presented to O. G. S. Crawford,* edited by W. F. Grimes, pp. 49–65. H. W. Edwards, London.

CLARKE, GRAHAME, 1952. *Prehistoric Europe: The Economic Basis.* Methuen & Co., Ltd., London.

CLARK, GRAHAME, 1954. *Excavations at Star Carr, an Early Mesolithic Site at Seamer, near Scarborough, Yorkshire.* Cambridge University Press, London.

CLARK, GRAHAME, 1960. *Archaeology and Society.* University Paperbacks, Barnes & Noble, Inc., New York.

CLARK, GRAHAME, 1967. *The Stone Age Hunters.* McGraw-Hill Paperbacks, McGraw-Hill Book Company, New York.

CLARK, GRAHAME, 1969. *World Prehistory—a New Outline.* Cambridge University Press, London.

CLARK, GRAHAME, 1970. *Aspects of Prehistory.* University of California Press, Berkeley.

CLARK, J. D., G. H. COLE, G. L. ISAAC, AND M. R. KLEINDIENST, 1966. Precision and Definition in African Archaeology: Implications for Archaeology of the Recommendations of the 29th Wenner-Gren Symposium, "Systematic Investigation of the African Tertiary and Quaternary," 1965. *South African Archaeological Bulletin,* vol. 21, no. 83, pp. 114–121. Capetown.

CLARK, J. D., AND G. L. ISAAC, eds., 1968. *Pan-African Congress on Prehistory and the Study of the Quaternary.* Commission on Nomenclature Bulletin no. 1. Berkeley, Calif.

CLARKE, DAVID L., 1968. *Analytical Archaeology.* Methuen & Co., Ltd., London.

CLEMENTS, FORREST E., 1932. *Primitive Concepts of Disease.* University of California Publications in American Archaeology and Ethnology, vol. 32, no. 2. Berkeley.

COE, MICHAEL D., AND KENT V. FLANNERY, 1964. Microenvironments and Mesoamerican Prehistory. *Science,* vol. 143, no. 3607, pp. 650–654. Washington, D.C.

COLTON, HAROLD SELLERS, AND LYNDON LANE HARGRAVE, 1937. *Handbook of Northern Arizona Pottery Wares.* Museum of Northern Arizona Bulletin no. 11. Flagstaff.

CONKLIN, HAROLD C., 1964. Ethnogeneological Method. In *Explorations in Cultural Anthropology: Essays in Honor of George Peter Murdock,* edited by Ward H. Goodenough, pp. 25–55. McGraw-Hill Book Company, New York.

CONTON, W. F., 1961. *West Africa in History,* vol. 1, *Before the Europeans.* George Allen & Unwin, Ltd., London.

COON, CARLETON S., 1962. *The Origin of Races.* Alfred A. Knopf, Inc., New York.

CORNWALL, I. W., 1956. *Bones for the Archaeologist.* Phoenix House, Ltd., London.

CORNWALL, I. W., 1958. *Soils for the Archaeologist.* The Macmillan Company, New York.

COTTRELL, LEONARD, ed., 1971. *The Concise Encyclopaedia of Archaeology.* 2d ed. Hawthorne Books, Inc., New York.

CRAWFORD, O. G. S., 1953. *Archaeology in the Field.* Phoenix House, Ltd., London.

DANIEL, GLYN E., 1943. *The Three Ages: An Essay in Archaeological Method*. Cambridge University Press, London.

DANIEL, GLYN E., 1950. *A Hundred Years of Archaeology*. Gerald Duckworth & Co., Ltd., London.

DANIEL, GLYN, 1964. *The Idea of Prehistory*. Pelican Books, Penguin Books, Ltd., Harmondsworth.

DANIEL, GLYN, 1967. *The Origins and Growth of Archaeology*. Pelican Books, Penguin Books, Ltd., Harmondsworth.

DEETZ, JAMES, 1967. *Invitation to Archaeology*. American Museum Science Books, The Natural History Press, Garden City, N.Y.

DEEVEY, EDWARD S., RICHARD FOSTER FLINT, AND IRVING ROUSE, 1967. Radiocarbon Measurements: Comprehensive Index, 1950–1965. *American Journal of Science*, New Haven, Conn.

DIMBLEBY, G. W., 1965. Overton Downs Experimental Earthwork. *Antiquity*, vol. 39, no. 154, pp. 134–136. Cambridge.

DIMBLEBY, G. W., 1967. *Plants and Archaeology*. John Baker (Publishers) Ltd., London.

DOBZHANSKY, THEODOSIUS, 1966. *Mankind Evolving, the Evolution of the Human Species*. Yale Paperbounds, Yale University Press, New Haven, Conn.

DRIVER, HAROLD E., 1965. Survey of Numerical Classification in Anthropology. In *The Use of Computers in Anthropology*, edited by Dell Hymes. Studies in General Anthropology, vol. 2, pp. 301–344. Mouton and Co., The Hague.

DUMAS, FREDERIC, 1962. *Deep-water Archaeology*. Translated from the French by Honor Frost. Routledge & Kegan Paul, Ltd., London.

EHRICH, ROBERT W., ed., 1965. *Chronologies in Old World Archaeology*. The University of Chicago Press, Chicago.

EIMERL, SAREL, IRVEN DEVORE, AND OTHERS, 1965. *The Primates*. Time-Life Books, New York.

EISELEY, LOREN C., 1958. *Darwin's Century: Evolution and the Men Who Discovered It*. Anchor Books, Doubleday & Company, Inc., Garden City, N.Y.

ELLESMERE, EARL OF, ed., 1848. *Guide to Northern Archaeology by the Royal Society of Northern Antiquaries of Copenhagen*. James Bain, Haymarket, London.

EMORY, KENNETH P., W. J. BONK, AND Y. SINOTO, 1959. *Hawaiian Archaeology: Fishhooks*. Bishop Museum Special Publications, no. 47. Honolulu.

FAGAN, BRIAN, 1970. *Introductory Readings in Archaeology*. Little, Brown Paperbacks, Little, Brown and Company, Boston.

FAIRBANKS, CHARLES H., 1942. The Taxonomic Position of Stallings Island, Georgia. *American Antiquity*, vol. 7, no. 3, pp. 223–231. Menasha, Wis.

FINLEY, M. I., 1970. *Early Greece: The Bronze and Archaic Ages*. W. W. Norton & Company, Inc., New York.

FIRTH, RAYMOND, 1956. *Elements of Social Organization*. 2d ed. C. A. Watts & Co., Ltd., London.

FISCHER, J. L., 1961. Art Styles as Cultural Cognitive Maps. *American Anthropologist*, vol. 63, no. 1, pp. 79–93. Menasha, Wis.

FLANNERY, KENT V., 1967. Cultural History vs. Cultural Process: A Debate in American Archaeology. *Scientific American*, vol. 217, no. 2, pp. 119–122. New York.

FLANNERY, KENT V., 1968. Archeological Systems Theory and Early Mesoamerica. In *Anthropological Archeology in the Americas,* edited by Betty J. Meggers, pp. 67–87. The Anthropological Society of Washington, Washington, D.C.

FLINT, RICHARD FOSTER, 1957. *Glacial and Pleistocene Geology*. John Wiley & Sons, Inc., New York.

FLINT, RICHARD F., 1971. *Glacial and Quaternary Geology*. John Wiley & Sons, Inc., New York.

FORD, JAMES A., 1962. *A Quantitative Method for Deriving Cultural Chronology*. Pan American Union Technical Manual no. 1. Washington, D.C.

FORDE, C. DARYLL, 1951. The Integration of Anthropological Studies. *Journal of the Royal Anthropological Institute,* vol. 78, nos. 1–2, pp. 1–10. London.

FRANKFORT, HENRI, n.d. *The Birth of Civilization in the Near East.* Anchor Books, Doubleday & Company, Inc., Garden City, N.Y.

FRANKFORT, HENRI, MRS. H. A. FRANKFORT, JOHN A. WILSON, AND THORKILD JACOBSEN, 1949. *Before Philosophy.* Pelican Books, Penguin Books, Ltd., Harmondsworth.

FRIEDRICH, PAUL, 1970. *Proto-Indo-European Trees: The Arboreal System of a Prehistoric People.* The University of Chicago Press, Chicago.

GABEL, CREIGHTON, 1967. *Analysis of Prehistoric Economic Patterns.* Studies in Anthropological Method, edited by George and Louise Spindler. Holt, Rinehart and Winston, Inc., New York.

GARDIN, J. C., 1965. A Typology of Computer Uses in Anthropology. In *The Use of Computers in Anthropology,* edited by Dell Hymes, pp. 103–180. Mouton and Co., London.

GARN, STANLEY M., 1965. *Human Races.* 2d ed. Charles C. Thomas, Publisher, Springfield, Ill.

GETNER, W., AND H. J. LIPPOTT, 1965. The Potassium-Argon Dating of Upper Tertiary and Pleistocene Deposits. In *Science in Archaeology,* edited by Don Brothwell and Eric Higgs, pp. 72–84. Basic Books, Inc., Publishers, New York.

GLOB, P. V., 1969. *The Bog People: Iron Age Man Preserved.* Translated from the Danish by Rupert Bruce-Mitford. Cornell University Press, Ithaca, N.Y.

GOGGIN, JOHN M., 1968. *Spanish Majolica in the New World: Types of the Sixteenth to Eighteenth Centuries.* Yale University Publications in Anthropology, no. 72. New Haven, Conn.

GOLDSCHMIDT, R., 1940. *The Material Basis of Evolution.* Yale University Press, New Haven, Conn.

GOMME, GEORGE L., 1908. *Folklore as a Historical Science.* London.

GOODWIN, A. J. H., 1953. *Method in Prehistory: An Introduction to the Discipline of Prehistoric Archaeology with Special Reference to South African Conditions.* 2d ed. The South African Archaeological Society Handbook Series no. 1. Claremont, Capetown.

GREENBERG, JOSEPH H., 1968. *Anthropological Linguistics: An Introduction.* Studies in Anthropology. Random House, Inc., New York.

GRIFFIN, JAMES B., 1952. Culture Periods in the Eastern United States. In *Archeology of the Eastern United States,* edited by James B. Griffin, pp. 352–364. The University of Chicago Press, Chicago.

HARDEN, D. B., ed., 1957–. *Medieval Archaeology: Journal of the Society for Medieval Archaeology,* vols. 1–. London.

HARRINGTON, M. R., 1924. *An Ancient Village Site of the Shinnecock Indians.* Anthropological Papers of the American Museum of Natural History, vol. 22, pt. 5. New York.

HARRISON, H. S., 1930. Opportunities and Factors of Invention. *American Anthropologist,* vol. 32, no. 1, pp. 106–125. Menasha, Wis.

HARRISON, H. S., 1954. Discovery, Invention, and Diffusion. In *A History of Technology,* edited by Charles Singer, E. J. Holmyard, and A. R. Hall, pp. 58–84. Oxford University Press, London.

HEIZER, ROBERT F., ed., 1962. *Man's Discovery of His Past: Literary Landmarks in Archaeology.* Spectrum Books, Prentice-Hall, Inc., Englewood Cliffs, N.J.

HEIZER, ROBERT F., AND RICHARD A. BROOKS, 1965. Lewisville—Ancient Campsite or Wood Rat Houses? *Southwestern Journal of Anthropology,* vol. 21, no. 2, pp. 155–165. Albuquerque.

HEIZER, ROBERT F., AND JOHN A. GRAHAM, 1967. *A Guide to Field Methods in Archaeology: Approaches to the Anthropology of the Dead.* National Press Books, Palo Alto, Calif.

HERSKOVITS, MELVILLE J., 1964. *Cultural Dynamics.* Abridged from his *Cultural Anthropology.* Alfred A. Knopf, Inc., New York.

HOCKETT, CHARLES F., AND ROBERT ASCHER, 1964. The Human Revolution. *American Scientist,* vol. 52, pp. 70–92. New Haven, Conn.

HODGEN, MARGARET T., 1942. Geographical Distribution as a Criterion of Age. *American Anthropologist,* vol. 44, no. 3, pp. 345–368. Menasha, Wis.

HODGES, HENRY, 1964. *Artifacts: An Introduction to Early Materials and Technology.* John Baker (Publishers) Ltd., London.

HODSON, F. R., 1962. Some Pottery from Eastbourne, the 'Marnians' and the Pre-Roman Iron Age in Southern England. *Proceedings of the Prehistoric Society for 1962,* new series, vol. 28, no. 7, pp. 140–155. Cambridge.

HOEBEL, E. ADAMSON, 1958. *Man in the Primitive World: An Introduction to Anthropology.* 2d ed. McGraw-Hill Book Company, New York.

HOLE, FRANK, AND ROBERT F. HEIZER, 1969. *An Introduction to Prehistoric Archeology.* 2d ed. Holt, Rinehart and Winston, Inc., New York.

HOMANS, GEORGE C., 1950. *The Human Group.* Harcourt, Brace and Company, Inc., New York.

HOWELL, F. CLARK, 1961. Isimila: A Paleolithic Site in Africa. *Scientific American,* vol. 205, no. 4, pp. 119–129. New York.

HOWELL, F. CLARK, 1962. Potassium-Argon Dating at Olduvai Gorge. *Current Anthropology,* vol. 3, no. 3, pp. 306–308, Chicago.

HUDSON, KENNETH, 1963. *Industrial Archaeology.* John Baker (Publishers) Ltd., London.

HUDSON, KENNETH, 1964–. *The Journal of Industrial Archaeology,* vols. 1–. Sidcup, Kent.

HULSE, FREDERICK S., 1963. *The Human Species: An Introduction to Physical Anthropology.* Random House, Inc., New York.

HUME, IVOR NOËL, 1969. *Historical Archaeology.* Alfred A. Knopf, Inc., New York.

HUXLEY, JULIAN S., 1955. Evolution, Cultural and Biological. In *Yearbook of Anthropology—1955,* edited by William L. Thomas, Jr., pp. 3–25. Wenner-Gren Foundation for Anthropological Research, Inc., New York.

ISAAC, GLYNN LL., 1969. Studies of Early Culture in East Africa. *World Archaeology,* vol. 1, no. 1, pp. 1–28. London.

JARCHO, SAUL, ed., 1966. *Human Palaeopathology: Proceedings of a Symposium on Human Palaeopathology Held in Washington, D.C., January 14, 1965 under the Auspices of the Subcommittee on Geographic Pathology, National Academy of Sciences-Natural Research Council.* Yale University Press, New Haven, Conn.

JENNINGS, JESSE D., 1968. *Prehistory of North America.* McGraw-Hill Book Company, New York.

JEWELL, P. A., AND G. W. DIMBLEBY, eds., 1966. The Experimental Earthwork on Overton Down, Wiltshire, England: The First Four Years. *Proceedings of the Prehistoric Society for 1966,* vol. 32, pp. 313–342. Cambridge.

KENYON, KATHLEEN M., 1961. *Beginning in Archaeology.* Rev. ed., with sections on American archeology by Saul S. and Gladys D. Weinberg. Praeger Paperbacks, Frederick A. Praeger, Inc., New York.

KIDDER, A. V., 1962. *An Introduction to the Study of Southwestern Archaeology with a Preliminary Account of the Excavations at Pecos.* Yale Paperbounds, Yale University Press, New Haven, Conn.

KLINDT-JENSEN, OLE, 1957. *Denmark before the Vikings.* Ancient Peoples and Places, vol. 4. Thames & Hudson, Ltd., London.

KLUCKHOHN, CLYDE, 1962. The Position of Bc51. In *Culture and Behavior: The Collected Essays of Clyde Kluckhohn,* edited by Richard Kluckhohn, pp. 74–87. Free Press Paperbacks, The Free Press, New York.

KLUCKHOHN, CLYDE, 1965. *Mirror for Man: A Survey of Human Behavior and Social Attitudes.* Premier Books, Fawcett World Library, New York.

KOSSINNA, GUSTAV, 1920. *Die Herkunft der Germanen; zur Methode die Siedlungsarchäologie.* 2 Aflage, Neudruck der Ausgabe von 1911. Mannus-Bibliothek, no. 6. Verlag von Curt Kabitzsch, Leipzig.

KRAMER, SAMUEL NOAH, 1959. *History Begins at Sumer.* Anchor Books, Doubleday & Company, Inc., Garden City, N.Y.

KRIEGER, ALEX D., 1944. The Typological Concept. *American Antiquity,* vol. 9, no. 3, pp. 271–288. Menasha, Wis.

KROEBER, A. L., 1940. Statistical Classification. *American Antiquity,* vol. 6, no. 1, pp. 29–44. Menasha, Wis.

KROEBER, A. L., 1944. *Configurations of Culture Growth.* University of California Press, Berkeley.

KROEBER, A. L., 1948. *Anthropology.* Harcourt, Brace and Company, Inc., New York.

KROEBER, A. L., 1962. *A Roster of Civilizations and Culture.* Viking Fund Publications in Anthropology, no. 33. New York.

KROEBER, A. L., 1963. *Anthropology: Culture Patterns and Processes.* Harbinger Books, Harcourt, Brace & World, Inc., New York.

KROEBER, A. L., AND CLYDE KLUCKHOHN, 1963. *Culture.* Vintage Books, Inc., Random House, Inc., New York.

KUBLER, GEORGE, 1962. *The Shape of Time: Remarks on the History of Things.* Yale Paperbounds, Yale University Press, New Haven, Conn.

LEAKEY, L. S. B., 1936. *Stone Age Africa: An Outline of the Prehistory of Africa.* Oxford University Press, London.

LEROI-GOURHAN, ANDRÉ, 1957. *Prehistoric Man.* Translated from the French by Wade Baskin. Philosophical Library, Inc., New York.

LEROI-GOURHAN, ANDRÉ, 1968. Evolution of Paleolithic Art. *Scientific American,* vol. 218, no. 2, pp. 58–73. New York.

LÉVI-STRAUSS, CLAUDE, 1963. *Structural Anthropology.* Translated from the French by Claire Jacobson and Brooke Grundfest Schoepf. Basic Books, Inc., Publishers, New York.

LIBBY, WILLARD F., 1955. *Radiocarbon Dating.* 2d ed. The University of Chicago Press, Chicago.

LINTON, RALPH, 1936. *The Study of Man: An Introduction.* D. Appleton-Century Company, Inc., New York.

LONGACRE, W. A., 1964. Archeology as Anthropology: A Case Study. *Science,* vol. 144, no. 3625, pp. 1454–1455. Washington, D.C.

LORENZ, KONRAD, 1966. *On Aggression.* Harcourt, Brace & World, Inc., New York.

MACCURDY, GEORGE GRANT, 1926. *Human Origins: A Manual of Prehistory.* 2 vols. D. Appleton & Company, Inc., New York.

MCKERN, WILLIAM C., 1939. The Midwestern Taxonomic Method as an Aid to Archaeological Study. *American Antiquity,* vol. 4, no. 4, pp. 301–313. Menasha, Wis.

MCKERN, WILLIAM C., 1940. Application of the Midwestern Taxonomic Method. Bulletin of the Archaeological Society of Delaware, vol. 3, pp. 18–21. Wilmington.

MACNEISH, R. S., 1962. *Second Annual Report of the Tehuacán Archaeological-Botanical Project.* R. S. Peabody Foundation, Andover, Mass.

MARTIN, PAUL S., 1939. *Modified Basket Maker Sites, Ackman-Lowry Area, Southwestern Colorado.* Anthropological Series, Field Museum of Natural History, vol. 23, no. 3. Chicago.

MARUYAMA, M., 1963. The Second Cybernetics: Deviation Amplifying Mutual Causal Processes. *American Scientist,* vol. 51, no. 2, pp. 164–179. New Haven.

MEAD, MARGARET, 1964. *Anthropology: A Human Science, Selected Papers, 1939–1960.* Insight Books, D. Van Nostrand Company, Inc., Princeton, N.J.

MEGGERS, BETTY J., CLIFFORD EVANS, AND EMILIO ESTRADA, 1965. *Early Formative Period of Coastal Peru: The Valdivia and Machalilla Phases.* Smithsonian Contributions to Anthropology, vol. 1, Washington, D.C.

MELLAART, JAMES, 1965. *Earliest Civilizations of the Near East.* McGraw-Hill Paperbacks, McGraw-Hill Book Company, New York.

MENGHIN, OSWALD, 1931. *Weltgeschichte der Steinzeit.* Anton Schroll and Co., Wien.

MICHAEL, HENRY N., AND ELIZABETH K. RALPH, 1971. *Dating Techniques for the Archaeologist.* The M.I.T. Press, Cambridge, Mass.

MICHELS, JOSEPH W., 1967. Archeology and Dating by Hydration of Obsidian. *Science,* vol. 158, no. 3798, pp. 211–214. Washington, D.C.

MOERMAN, MICHAEL, 1965. Ethnic Identification in a Complex Civilization: Who Are the Lue? *American Anthropologist,* vol. 67, no. 5, pp. 1215–1230. Menasha, Wis.

MONGAIT, A. L., 1961. *Archaeology in the U.S.S.R.* Pelican Books, Penguin Books, Inc., Harmondsworth.

MOVIUS, HALLAM L., 1942. *The Irish Stone Age: Its Chronology, Development and Relationships.* Cambridge University Press, London.

MURDOCK, GEORGE PETER, 1949. *Social Structure.* The Macmillan Company, New York.

MURDOCK, GEORGE P., et al., 1950. *Outline of Cultural Materials.* 3d rev. ed. Behavior Science Outlines, vol. 1. Human Relations Area Files, Inc., New Haven.

NARROLL, RAOUL, 1964. On Ethnic Unit Classification. *Current Anthropology,* vol. 5, no. 4, pp. 283–312. Chicago.

OAKLEY, KENNETH P., 1963. Analytical Methods of Dating Bones. In *Science in Archaeology: A Comprehensive Survey of Progress and Research,* edited by Don Brothwell and Eric Higgs, pp. 24–34. Basic Books, Inc., Publishers, New York.

OLIVER, DOUGLAS, 1964. *Invitation to Anthropology: A Guide to Basic Concepts.* American Museum Science Books, The Natural History Press, Garden City, N.Y.

OLSEN, STANLEY J., 1961. A Basic Annotated Bibliography to Facilitate the Identification of Vertebrate Remains from Archeological Sites. Bulletin of the Texas Archeological Society, vol. 30, pp. 217–222. Austin.

OLSON, ALAN P., 1962. A History of the Phase Concept in the Southwest. *American Antiquity,* vol. 27, no. 4, pp. 457–472. Salt Lake City.

ONIONS, C. T., ed., 1956. *The Shorter Oxford English Dictionary on Historical Principles.* 3d ed. Clarenden Press, Oxford.

PARSONS, ELSIE CLEWS, 1940. Relations between Ethnology and Archaeology in the Southwest. *American Antiquity,* vol. 5, no. 3, pp. 214–220. Menasha, Wis.

PATTERSON, THOMAS C., 1966. *Pattern and Process in the Early Intermediate Period Pottery of the Central Coast of Peru.* University of California Publications in Anthropology, vol. 3. Berkeley.

PENNIMAN, T. K., 1965. *A Hundred Years of Anthropology.* 3d ed., rev. Gerald Duckworth & Co., Ltd., London.

PETRIE, W. M. FLINDERS, 1899. Sequences in Prehistoric Remains. *The Journal of the Royal Anthropological Institute of Great Britain and Ireland,* vol. 29, nos. 3 and 4, pp. 295–301. London.

PETRIE, W. M. FLINDERS, 1904. *Methods and Aims in Archaeology.* Macmillan & Co., Ltd., London.

PETSCHE, JEROME E., 1968. *Bibliography of Salvage Archeology in the United States.* Smithsonian Institution, River Basin Surveys, Publications in Salvage Archeology, no. 10. Lincoln, Nebraska.

PHILLIPS, E. D., 1964. The Greek Vision of Prehistory. *Antiquity,* vol. 38, no. 151, pp. 171–178. Cambridge.

PIGGOTT, STUART, 1965a. *Ancient Europe from the Beginnings of Agriculture to Classical Antiquity.* Aldine Publishing Company, Chicago.

PIGGOTT, STUART, 1965b. *Approach to Archaeology.* McGraw-Hill Paperbacks, McGraw-Hill Book Company, New York.

PILBEAM, DAVID, 1970. *The Evolution of Man.* Funk & Wagnalls, a division of Reader's Digest Books, Inc., New York.

PLATT, COLIN, 1969. Medieval Archaeology in England. *Pinhorns Handbooks,* no. 5. Shalfleet Manor, Isle of Wight.

PORADA, EDITH, 1965. The Relative Chronology of Mesopotamia. Part I. Seals and Trade (6000–1600 B.C.). In *Chronologies in Old World Archaeology,* edited by Robert W. Ehrich, pp. 133–200. The University of Chicago Press, Chicago.

PYDDOKE, EDWARD, ed., 1963. *The Scientist and Archaeology.* Phoenix House, Ltd., London.

RAPPORT, SAMUEL, AND HELEN WRIGHT, eds., 1964. *Archaeology.* The New York University Library of Science, New York.

RÉAU, LOUIS, 1953. *Dictionnaire polyglotte des termes d'art et d'archéologie.* Presses Universitaires de France, Paris.

RITCHIE, WILLIAM A., 1969. *The Archaeology of New York State.* Rev. ed. The Natural History Press, Garden City, N.Y.

Rosenfeld, Andrée, 1965. *The Inorganic Raw Materials of Antiquity*. Frederick A. Praeger, Inc., New York.

Rouse, Irving, 1941. *Culture of the Ft. Liberté Region, Haiti*. Yale University Publications in Anthropology, no. 24. New Haven, Conn.

Rouse, Irving, 1952. *Porto Rican Prehistory*. New York Academy of Sciences, Scientific Survey of Porto Rico and the Virgin Islands, vol. 18, nos. 3–4, pp. 307–578. New York.

Rouse, Irving, 1960. The Classification of Artifacts in Archaeology. *American Antiquity*, vol. 25, no. 3, pp. 313–323. Salt Lake City.

Rouse, Irving, 1962. Southwestern Archaeology Today. In *An Introduction to the Study of Southwestern Archaeology*, by A. V. Kidder, pp. 1–53. Yale Paperbounds, Yale University Press, New Haven, Conn.

Rouse, Irving, 1964a. Archaeological Approaches to Cultural Evolution. In *Explorations in Cultural Anthropology*, edited by Ward H. Goodenough, pp. 455–468. McGraw-Hill Book Company, New York.

Rouse, Irving, 1964b. Prehistory of the West Indies. *Science*, vol. 144, no. 3618, pp. 499–513. Washington, D.C.

Rouse, Irving, 1965a. Caribbean Ceramics: A Study in Method and in Theory. In *Ceramics and Man*, edited by Frederick R. Matson. Viking Fund Publications in Anthropology, no. 41, pp. 88–103. New York.

Rouse, Irving, 1965b. The Place of 'Peoples' in Prehistoric Research. *Journal of the Royal Anthropological Institute*, vol. 95, pt. 1, pp. 1–15. London.

Rouse, Irving, 1967. Seriation in Archaeology. In *American Historical Anthropology: Essays in Honor of Leslie Spier*, edited by Carroll L. Riley and Walter W. Taylor, pp. 153–195. Southern Illinois University Press, Carbondale.

Rouse, Irving, 1968. Prehistory, Typology, and the Study of Society. In *Settlement Archaeology*, edited by K. C. Chang, pp. 10–30. National Press Books, Palo Alto, Calif.

Rouse, Irving, 1969. The Education of a President. In *Annual Report 1968 and Directory*. Bulletin of the American Anthropological Association, vol. 2, no. 1, pp. 1–11. Washington, D.C.

Rouse, Irving, 1970. Classification for What? *Norwegian Archaeological Review*, vol. 3, pp. 4–12. Oslo.

Rouse, Irving, 1971. Settlement Patterns in Archaeology. In *Man, Settlement and Urbanism*, edited by Peter Ucko, Ruth Tringham, and Geoffrey Dimbleby. Gerald Duckworth & Co., Ltd., London.

Rouse, Irving, ms. Classification in American Archaeology. Manuscript to be published in *Theory and Methodology in Archaeological Interpretation*, edited by Robert W. Ehrich. Publishing arrangements have not yet been made.

Rouse, Irving, and José M. Cruxent, 1963. *Venezuelan Archaeology*. Yale University Press, Caribbean Series, no. 6. New Haven, Conn.

Rowe, John H., 1961a. Archaeology as a Career. *Archaeology*, vol. 14, no. 2, pp. 45–56. New York.

Rowe, John Howland, 1961b. Stratigraphy and Seriation. *American Antiquity*, vol. 26, no. 3, pp. 324–330. Salt Lake City.

Sahlins, Marshall D., 1960. The Origin of Society. *Scientific American*, vol. 203, no. 3, pp. 76–87. New York.

Sahlins, Marshall D., and Elman R. Service, eds. 1960. *Evolution of Culture*. The University of Michigan Press, Ann Arbor.

Sapir, Edward, 1939. *Language: An Introduction to the Study of Speech*. Harcourt, Brace and Company, Inc., New York.

Sapir, Edward, 1951. Time Perspective in Aboriginal American Culture, a Study in Method. Reprinted in *Selected Writings of Edward Sapir*, edited by David Mandelbaum, pp. 389–462. University of California Press, Berkeley.

SCHMIDT, R. R., 1936. *The Dawn of the Human Mind: A Study of Palaeolithic Man*. Translated by R. A. S. MacAlister. Sidgwick & Jackson, Ltd., London.

SEARS, WILLIAM H., 1961. The Study of Social and Religious Systems in North American Archaeology. *Current Anthropology*, vol. 2, no. 3, pp. 223–246. Chicago.

SHEPARD, ANNA O., 1957. *Ceramics for the Archaeologist*. Carnegie Institution of Washington Publication no. 609. Washington, D.C.

SHETRONE, HENRY CLYDE, 1941. *The Mound-builders*. D. Appleton-Century Company, Inc., New York.

SHINNIE, P. L., 1967. *Meroe, a Civilization of the Sudan*. Ancient Peoples and Places, vol. 55. Thames & Hudson, Ltd., London.

SKINNER, B. F., 1965. *Science and Human Behavior*. The Free Press, New York.

SKINNER, B. F., 1969. *Contingencies of Reinforcement: A Theoretical Analysis*. Appleton Century Crofts, New York.

SMITH, HARLAN I., 1899. *The Ethnological Arrangement of Archaeological Materials*. Museum Association of the United Kingdom, Report for 1898, Sheffield Meeting. London.

SMITH, HARLAN I., 1910. *The Prehistoric Ethnology of a Kentucky Site*. Anthropological Papers of the American Museum of Natural History, vol. 6, pt. 2. New York.

SMITH, M. G., 1965. *The Plural Society in the British West Indies*. University of California Press, Berkeley.

SOKAL, R. R., AND P. H. A. SNEATH, 1963. *Principles of Numerical Taxonomy*. W. H. Freeman & Company, London.

SOLLAS, W. J., 1924. *Ancient Hunters and Their Modern Representatives*. 3d ed., rev. The Macmillan Company, New York.

SPAULDING, A. C., 1953. Statistical Techniques for the Discovery of Artifact Types. *American Antiquity*, vol. 18, no. 4, pp. 305–313. Salt Lake City.

SPAULDING, ALBERT C., 1960a. The Dimensions of Archaeology. In *Essays in the Science of Culture in Honor of Leslie A. White*, edited by Gertrude E. Dole and Robert L. Carneiro, pp. 437–456. Thomas Y. Crowell Company, New York.

SPAULDING, ALBERT C., 1960b. Statistical Description and Comparison of Artifact Assemblages. In *The Application of Quantitative Methods in Archaeology*, edited by Robert F. Heizer and Sherburne F. Cook. Viking Fund Publications in Anthropology, no. 28, pp. 60–83. Chicago.

SPRAGUE, RODERICK, 1968. A Suggested Terminology and Classification for Burial Description. *American Antiquity*, vol. 33, no. 4, pp. 479–485. Salt Lake City.

STEWARD, JULIAN H., 1942. The Direct Historical Approach to Archaeology. *American Antiquity*, vol. 7, no. 4, pp. 337–343. Menasha, Wis.

STEWARD, JULIAN H., 1950. *Area Research: Theory and Practice*. Social Science Research Council Bulletin no. 63. New York.

STEWARD, JULIAN H., 1954. Types of Types. *American Anthropologist*, vol. 56, no. 1, pp. 54–57. Menasha, Wis.

STEWARD, JULIAN H., 1955. *Theory of Culture Change: The Methodology of Multilinear Evolution*. The University of Illinois Press, Urbana.

STEWARD, JULIAN, AND FRANK M. SETZLER, 1938. Function and Configuration in Archaeology. *American Antiquity*, vol. 4, no. 1, pp. 4–10. Menasha, Wis.

STEWART, JAMES, 1958. *Archaeological Guide and Glossary*. Titus Wilson & Son, Ltd., Kendal.

STOKES, MARVEN A., AND TERAH L. SMILEY, 1968. *An Introduction to Tree-ring Dating*. The University of Chicago Press, Chicago.

STUIVER, MINZE, AND HANS E. SUESS, 1966. On the Relationship between Radiocarbon Dates and True Sample Ages. *Radiocarbon*, vol. 8, pp. 534–540. New Haven, Conn.

SWADESH, MORRIS, 1952. Lexico-statistic Dating of Prehistoric Ethnic Contacts, with Special Reference to North American Indians and Eskimos. *Proceedings of the American Philosophical Society,* vol. 96, no. 4, pp. 452–463. Philadelphia.

SWADESH, MORRIS, 1960. Tras la huella lingüística de la prehistoria. *Supplementos del Seminario de Problemas Científicos y Filosóficos,* segunda series, no. 26. Mexico City.

TARYO, OBAYASHI, 1966. The Present Situation of Research on the Ethnogenesis of the Japanese. *The Japanese Journal of Ethnology,* vol. 30, no. 4, pp. 269–273. Tokyo.

TAX, SOL, LOREN C. EISELEY, IRVING ROUSE, AND CARL F. VOEGELIN, 1953. *An Appraisal of Anthropology Today.* The University of Chicago Press, Chicago.

TAYLOR, DOUGLAS, AND IRVING ROUSE, 1955. Linguistic and Archeological Time Depth in the West Indies. *International Journal of American Linguistics,* vol. 21, no. 2, pp. 105–115. Baltimore.

TAYLOR, WALTER W., ed., 1957. *The Identification of Non-artifactual Archaeological Materials.* National Academy of Sciences-National Research Council Publication no. 565. Washington, D.C.

TAYLOR, WALTER W., 1967a. The Sharing Criterion and the Concept of Culture. In *American Historical Anthropology: Essays in Honor of Leslie Spier,* edited by Carroll L. Riley and Walter W. Taylor, pp. 221–230. Southern Illinois University Press, Carbondale.

TAYLOR, WALTER W., 1967b. *A Study of Archeology.* Arcturus Books, Southern Illinois University Press, Carbondale.

THOMAS, DAVID H., MS. The Use and Abuse of Numerical Taxonomy in Archaeology. Manuscript of an article submitted for publication.

THOMPSON, M. W., 1965. Marxianism and Culture. *Antiquity,* vol. 39, no. 154, pp. 108–116. Cambridge.

THOMPSON, RAYMOND H., 1956. The Subjective Element in Archaeological Inference. *Southwestern Journal of Anthropology,* vol. 12, no. 3, pp. 327–332. Albuquerque.

TRENT, CHRISTOPHER, 1959. *Terms Used in Archaeology: A Short Dictionary.* Philosophical Library, Inc., New York.

TRIGGER, BRUCE G., 1967. Settlement Archaeology: Its Goals and Promise. *American Antiquity,* vol. 32, no. 2, pp. 149–160. Salt Lake City.

TRIGGER, BRUCE G., 1968a. *Beyond History: The Methods of Prehistory.* Studies in Anthropological Method, edited by George and Louise Spindler. Holt, Rinehart and Winston, Inc., New York.

TRIGGER, BRUCE G., 1968b. The Determinants of Settlement Patterns. In *Settlement Archaeology,* edited by Kwang-chih Chang, pp. 53–78. National Press Books, Palo Alto.

TUGBY, DONALD J., 1965. Archaeological Objectives and Statistical Methods: A Frontier in Archaeology. *American Antiquity,* vol. 31, no. 1, pp. 1–16. Salt Lake City.

TYLOR, SIR EDWARD B., 1960. *Anthropology.* Ann Arbor Paperbacks, The University of Michigan Press, Ann Arbor.

UCKO, PETER J., 1969. Ethnography and Archaeological Interpretation of Funerary Remains. *World Archaeology,* vol. 1, no. 2, pp. 262–280. London.

UCKO, PETER J., AND ANDRÉE ROSENFELD, 1967. *Paleolithic Cave Art.* World University Library, McGraw-Hill Book Company, New York.

UCKO, PETER, RUTH TRINGHAM, AND GEOFFREY DIMBLEBY, eds., 1971. *Man, Settlement and Urbanism.* Gerald Duckworth & Co. Ltd., London.

VANSINA, JAN, 1965. *Oral Tradition: A Study in Historical Methodology.* Translated from the French by H. M. Wright. Aldine Publishing Company, Chicago.

VOGT, EVON Z., 1956. An Appraisal of "Prehistoric Settlement Patterns in the New World." In *Prehistoric Settlement Patterns in the New World,* edited by Gordon R. Willey. Viking Fund Publications in Anthropology, no. 23, pp. 173–82. New York.

WACE, A. J. B., 1962. The Greeks and Romans as Archaeologists. In *Man's Discovery of His Past: Literary Landmarks in Archaeology,* edited by Robert F. Heizer. Spectrum Books, Prentice-Hall, Inc., Englewood Cliffs, N.J.

WAINWRIGHT, F. T., 1962. *Archaeology and Place-names and History, an Essay on Problems of Co-ordination*. Routledge & Kegan Paul, Ltd., London.

WALLACE, ANTHONY F. C., 1950. A Possible Technique for Recognizing Psychological Characteristics of the Ancient Maya from an Analysis of Their Art. *The American Image*, vol. 7, no. 3, pp. 239–258, n.p.

WALLIS, WILSON D., 1945. Inference of Relative Age of Cultural Traits from Magnitude of Distribution. *Southwestern Journal of Anthropology*, vol. 1, no. 1, pp. 142–159. Albuquerque.

WASHBURN, SHERWOOD L., 1963. The Study of Race. *American Anthropologist*, vol. 65, no. 3, pp. 521–531. Menasha, Wis.

WEAVER, KENNETH F., 1967. Magnetic Clues Help Date the Past. *National Geographic*, vol. 131, no. 5, pp. 696–701. Washington, D.C.

Webster's New International Dictionary, 3d ed.

WELLS, CALVIN W., 1964. *Bones, Bodies and Disease: Evidence of Disease and Abnormality in Early Man*. Ancient Peoples and Places, vol. 37. Thames & Hudson, Ltd., London.

WHEELER, SIR MORTIMER, 1956. *Archaeology from the Earth*. Pelican Books, Penguin Books, Ltd., Harmondsworth.

WHEELER-VOEGELIN, ERMINIE, ed., 1954–. *Ethnohistory*, vol. 1–. Indiana University Press, Bloomington.

WHITE, LESLIE A., 1959. *The Evolution of Culture: The Development of Civilization to the Fall of Rome*. McGraw-Hill Book Company, New York.

WHITE, LESLIE A., n.d. *On the Use of Tools by the Primates*. The Bobbs-Merrill Reprint Series in the Social Sciences, The Bobbs-Merrill Company, Inc., Indianapolis.

WILLEY, GORDON R., 1953. *Prehistoric Settlement Patterns in Virú Valley, Peru*. Bureau of American Ethnology Bulletin no. 155. Washington, D.C.

WILLEY, GORDON R., 1956. *Prehistoric Settlement Patterns in the New World*. Viking Fund Publications in Anthropology, no. 23. New York.

WILLEY, GORDON R., 1966. *An Introduction to American Archaeology*, vol. 1, *North and Middle America*. Prentice-Hall, Inc., Englewood Cliffs, N.J.

WILLEY, GORDON R., CHARLES C. DIPESO, WILLIAM A. RITCHIE, IRVING ROUSE, JOHN H. ROWE, AND DONALD W. LATHRAP, 1956. An Archaeological Classification of Culture Contact Situations. In *Seminars in Anthropology: 1955*, edited by Robert Wauchope. Memoirs of the Society for American Archaeology, no. 11, pp. 1–30. Salt Lake City.

WILLEY, GORDON R., AND PHILIP PHILLIPS, 1962. *Method and Theory in American Archaeology*. Phoenix Paperbacks, The University of Chicago Press, Chicago.

WILMSEN, EDWIN, 1970. Review of *Man in Prehistory* by Chester S. Chard. *American Anthropologist*, vol. 72, no. 3, pp. 689–691. Menasha, Wis.

WISSLER, CLARK, 1923. *Man and Culture*. Thomas Y. Crowell Company, New York.

WOOLLEY, C. LEONARD, 1965. *Ur of the Chaldees: A Record of Seven Years of Excavation*. The Norton Library, W. W. Norton & Company, Inc., New York.

GLOSSARY AND INDEX

ACCULTURATION 232 (*see also* FUSION)
> The process whereby one people adopts cultural norms from another people. If and when this process is carried to completion, the first people becomes assimilated to the second people.

ACCUMULATION 166, 217, 241
> The tendency of cultural norms to develop additively, whereas genes tend to be alternatives.

ACTIVITIES

Intellectual 161–164, 239
> Activities that are limited to mankind and are made possible by man's ability to think conceptually.

Sustaining 160–162, 239
> Activities that mankind shares with the lesser animals.

ACTIVITY 44, 68, 80, 82–83, 94–95, 119, 138, 146–147, 150–152, 154–157, 159–164, 166, 168–176, 179–181, 183, 187, 189, 197–199, 226, 238–239
> A subsystem of behavior that fulfills a particular need, as for food.

ACTIVITY ASSEMBLAGE 44–45, 58, 82, 105, 118, 142, 152, 169, 171, 173, 174, 239–240
> The remains obtained from an activity locus.

ACTIVITY ASSEMBLAGES

Class of 173
> All activity assemblages that share a diagnostic complex and hence are indicative of a single activity.

ACTIVITY ASSEMBLAGES (*continued*)

Classification of See CLASSIFICATION, Activity

Identification of See IDENTIFICATION, Activity

ACTIVITY CO-PATTERN 82
The activity pattern of a sustaining or professional co-people. It does not include the total range of a people's activities.

Professional 170, 172, 188–189
The activity co-pattern of a professional co-people.

Sustaining 170, 172, 188–189
The activity co-pattern of a sustaining co-people.

ACTIVITY INSTITUTION See INSTITUTION, Activity

ACTIVITY LOCUS 152, 169, 171–172, 187, 239
A division of a cultural component containing the remains of a minimum number of activities.

ACTIVITY PATTERN 82, 239
The manner in which a people's activities are distributed over the landscape.

Concentrated 82, 169, 171–172
A remnant pattern in which the activity loci are concentrated in relatively permanent residential sites.

Dispersed 82, 169–171
A remnant pattern in which the activity loci are widely distributed, either because the people were mobile or because they performed many activities away from their residences.

Original 151–153, 171–173
The full activity pattern, as observed by an ethnographer or recorded in a people's writing.

Remnant 152–153, 159, 168–169, 184, 187
The traces of an activity pattern that survive archeologically. They include a series of activity loci and assemblages, distributed among a people's sites and over the landscape.

ADAPTATION

Ecological 158–159, 192, 194, 212, 228, 230–231, 235
Adjustment of an ethnic system to the conditions of its environment.

Morphological 230–231
Adjustment of an ethnic system to the capabilities of the human organism.

Psychological 231, 235
Adjustment of an ethnic system to the personality traits of its possessors.

AGE 105–116, 118, 136–138, 144, 211, 214–215, 220–222, 225–228, 239
A section of a chronology that is demarcated by the first appearance of innovations such as bronze (at the beginning of the Bronze Age) and iron (at its end).

ANALOGY   146–147, 174–175, 186, 194, 224, 234 (*see also* CHANGE, Analogous)
> An ethnographic or ethnohistorical parallel used in inferring ethnic traits from archeological evidence. Synonyms: parallel, substantive model.

Anthropological   See ANALOGY, General

Ethnographic   See ANALOGY, Specific

General   145, 174
> An analogy to an unrelated ethnographic or ethnohistorical group. Synonym: anthropological analogy.

Specific   145, 174
> An analogy to an ethnographic or ethnohistorical group related to the prehistoric group under study. Synonyms: ethnographic analogy, ethnographic model.

ANALYTIC DISCIPLINES   *See* DISCIPLINES, Analytic

ANALYTIC STRATEGY   *See* STRATEGY, Analytic

ANTHROPOLOGICAL MODEL   *See* MODEL, Anthropological

ANTHROPOLOGY   16–25, 62–65, 145, 153, 193–195, 224, 237
> A group of disciplines that study man, doing so primarily from the point of view of pure, rather than applied, science. It includes the analytic disciplines of archeology and ethnography, the synthetic disciplines of prehistory and ethnohistory, and the comparative disciplines of cultural, physical, social, and linguistic anthropology.

Archeological   65
> The use of archeological evidence to solve problems of cultural, physical, social, or linguistic anthropology. Synonyms: anthropological archeology, comparative archeology, experimental archeology, processual archeology, scientific archeology.

Biological   See ANTHROPOLOGY, Physical

Cultural   16–25, 28, 61–62, 69, 147, 174, 230
> The discipline that studies the nature and development of cultural traits from a topical and comparative point of view.

Ecological   22
> Topical and comparative study of mankind's adaptation to its environment.

Economic   22
> Topical and comparative study of mankind's economic activities and relationships.

Educational   16
> Topical and comparative study of education; application of the results of this study in our own educational system.

Linguistic   16–25, 28, 61–62, 147, 230
> The discipline that studies the nature and development of linguistic traits from a topical and comparative point of view.

ANTHROPOLOGY (*continued*)

Medical 16
>   Topical and comparative study of medical practices; application of the results of this study in our own society.

Physical 16–25, 28, 61–62, 90, 120, 147, 177–178, 206–207, 212, 219, 230
>   The discipline that studies the nature and development of human biological traits from a topical and comparative point of view. Synonym: biological anthropology.

Political 22
>   Topical and comparative study of political activities and relationships.

Psychological 22
>   Topical and comparative study of the psychological traits of mankind.

Religious 22
>   Topical and comparative study of religious practices and beliefs.

Social 16–25, 28, 61–62, 69, 145, 147, 230
>   The discipline that studies the nature and development of human social traits from a topical and comparative point of view.

ANTHROPOMORPHISM 243
>   The fallacy of imputing human traits to the lesser animals.

ANTIQUITY *See* ARTIFACT

APPLIED SCIENCE *See* SCIENCE, Applied

ARCHEOGRAPHY *See* ARCHEOLOGY

ARCHEOLOGY 6–11, 12–15, 16–18, 20–25, 26–60, 61–65, 71, 83, 89, 96, 107, 109, 112–114, 118, 120, 141–147, 149–151, 153, 157–158, 167–169, 172, 175–176, 180–181, 186, 192, 194–195, 212, 220, 223–224, 226, 228–229, 231–234, 237
>   Study of the nature of human and cultural remains, excluding written records. Synonyms: analytic archeology, archeography.

Analytic *See* ARCHEOLOGY

Anthropological *See* ANTHROPOLOGY, Archeological

Comparative *See* ANTHROPOLOGY, Archeological

Experimental *See* ANTHROPOLOGY, Archeological

Historical 6–11 (*see also* HISTORY, Archeological)
>   Analysis of historic remains.

Industrial 11
>   Analysis of the remains of the industrial revolution.

Medieval 11
>   Analysis of the remains of the Middle Ages.

ARCHEOLOGY (*continued*)

Prehistoric 11 (*see also* PREHISTORY)
Analysis of prehistoric remains.

Processual See ANTHROPOLOGY, Archeological

Salvage 11, 15, 32
Recovery and preservation of archeological remains that are in danger of being destroyed.

Scientific See ANTHROPOLOGY, Archeological

Settlement 148–151
Study of remnant settlement patterns.

Synthetic See PREHISTORY

Underwater 11
Analysis of the remains found in rivers, lakes, and seas.

ARCHEOMAGNETISM 135
Dating a fired-clay object by correlating its direction of magnetism with the direction to a dated position of the magnetic pole. Synonym: magnetic dating.

AREA

Cultural See REGION

Local 76–77, 84, 95, 108, 112–114, 117–118, 120–122, 126–127, 129–130, 141, 143, 212, 218
A division of a region small enough to be culturally homogeneous.

ARTICULATION 45, 145–148
Fitting together ethnic traits in order to reconstruct the systems to which they belonged.

Cultural 140–141, 146, 148–149, 151, 166, 184, 239
Articulation of cultural traits in order to reconstruct a culture.

Linguistic 146
Articulation of linguistic traits in order to reconstruct a language.

Morphological 140, 142, 146, 176
Articulation of morphological traits in order to reconstruct a morphology.

Social 146, 149, 184–185, 188
Articulation of social traits in order to reconstruct a social structure.

ARTIFACT 13, 29–31, 40–41, 48–57, 59, 66, 68, 70–74, 83, 109, 119, 125–130, 143, 147–150, 155, 167–168, 173–174, 179, 188–189, 196, 197, 238 (*see also* EQUIPMENT, Worked)
A structure, tool, etc., modified in accordance with the norms of a culture. Wild animals cannot make artifacts, for they lack cultural norms, but they can and do make tools and other equipment. Synonym: antiquity.

ARTIFACTS

Class of 45–49, 78, 83, 87, 96, 196–197, 201, 233, 237 (*see also* CLASSIFICATION, Artifactual)
All the artifacts that share a diagnostic pattern of attributes, that is, a type.

ASPECT

Taxonomic *See* CULTURES, Series of

ASSEMBLAGE   46, 50, 105, 212 (*see also* ACTIVITY ASSEMBLAGE; CULTURAL ASSEMBLAGE; ETHNIC ASSEM-
BLAGE; HUMAN SKELETAL ASSEMBLAGE; MORPHOLOGICAL ASSEMBLAGE; RESIDENTIAL ASSEMBLAGE)
> Remains that are treated as a unit because they have been found together, not, as in the
> case of a class, because they are alike.

ASSEMBLAGES

Class of *See* ACTIVITY ASSEMBLAGES, Class of; CULTURAL ASSEMBLAGES, Class of; MORPHOLOGICAL ASSEM-
BLAGES, Class of

ASSOCIATION

Professional 161, 182, 188
> A group of individuals who specialize in the same activity. Synonym: profession.

ATTRIBUTE

Cultural 45–51, 53–54, 56, 125, 167–168, 237
> Any culturally distinctive quality of an artifact or of other kinds of remains.

Functional 48, 51, 173
> A quality of an artifact that enhances its utility and, as a result, indicates how it was used.

Morphological 99
> Any biologically distinctive quality of a human bone.

Stylistic 48, 51, 125, 131, 137
> A quality that expresses the nature of a people or a period.

Technological 48, 51, 173
> A quality that indicates the manner in which an artifact was made.

BASIC CULTURE *See* CULTURES, Series of

BEHAVIOR

Cultural 155, 157–158, 160, 164–165, 175, 183, 196–197, 199–200, 239
> The behavior of performing a cultural activity. It is directed toward the environment, real
> or imagined, rather than toward other members of one's group, as social behavior is.

Linguistic 156–158, 164, 199–200 (*see also* SPEECH)
> The behavior of speaking a language.

Morphological 155, 157–158, 164, 240 (*see also* REPRODUCTION)
> The behavior of reproduction, leading to, including, and following after sexual intercourse.

Pattern of *See* NORM

Social 156–158, 164–165, 183–184, 188–189, 199–200, 240 (*see also* INTERACTION)
> The behavior of interrelation among the members of a social group.

BIAS   71–73, 86, 111–113, 144–145, 175, 227–228, 242–243
>   Study of prehistory from a prejudiced, as opposed to an objective, point of view by fitting the archeological facts to one's theories instead of developing one's theories from the facts.

BONES

Class of   58
>   All individual bones, such as mandibles, that share the same diagnostic attributes. A "class of bones" should not be confused with a "class of morphological assemblages."

BRANCH   See SUBTRADITION

CENTER   217–220, 228–229, 241
>   A nuclear area or region containing superorganic systems that are more highly developed than those in the surrounding area or region.

CENTRISM   218 (see also ETHNOCENTRISM)
>   The tendency to pay more attention to central than to peripheral developments.

CHANGE   13–14, 17, 24, 143, 191–236
>   A difference that occurs along a continuity of cultural, morphological, social, or linguistic systems or traits.

Analogous   193–194 (see also ANALOGY)
>   An ethnographic or ethnohistorical parallel that a prehistorian uses in reconstructing patterns of change. Synonym: parallel.

Cultural   123, 129, 131, 143, 195, 206, 217, 226–228, 234, 241
>   The modification of a cultural system, or the development of a new system.

Developmental   127–128, 212
>   Change in form, as opposed to change in frequency or occurrence.

Ecological   128–129, 132–133
>   The modification of an ecosystem, or the development of a new system.

Ethnic   197, 206, 216, 218, 221, 229, 232–235, 238
>   Cultural, linguistic, morphological, and social change.

Frequency   127, 232
>   Change in popularity, as opposed to change in form or occurrence.

Linguistic   135–136, 195, 206, 228, 241
>   The modification of a language, or the development of a new one.

Model of   193–194, 197, 202–207, 211, 220, 222–225, 228, 241
>   A model used by prehistorians in reconstructing patterns of change.

Morphological   195, 205–206, 228, 241
>   The modification of a morphological system, or the development of a new one.

Occurrence   127
>   Change in occurrence, as opposed to change in form or frequency.

CHANGE (*continued*)

Organic   198–199, 204–205, 209, 216, 219–223, 228, 230, 235, 241
Change in a living organism.

Pattern of   See PATTERN OF CHANGE

Process of   See PROCESS OF CHANGE

Rate of   131, 136, 233–235
The speed of a series of changes.

Social   195, 206, 227–228, 241
The modification of a social system, or the development of a new one.

Superorganic   198–199, 205, 209, 216, 219–220, 223, 228, 230, 235–236, 241
Change in a cultural, linguistic, or social system.

Typological   127–129
Change in a type.

Units of   192–193, 215
The individual parts of a sequence of changes.

CHRONOLOGY   75–77, 102–139, 140, 144–145, 147, 187, 214, 239
A modification of a map in which latitude and longitude are combined in one dimension of space, so that the other dimension can be used to express time.

Absolute   106, 108, 111, 117, 129, 131–136
A chronology based upon absolute time.

Artifactual   119–120
A chronology of types or modes.

Cultural   108, 112–113, 115–121, 129–130, 136, 138–139, 141, 210
A chronology of cultural groups.

Ecological   See CHRONOLOGY, Geo-

Ethnic   114, 120–121, 138–139, 150
A chronology of more than one type of ethnic group.

Evolutionary   See SEQUENCE, Evolutionary

Geo-   113, 120, 122, 127–129, 131, 133 (*see also* VARVE ANALYSIS)
A chart that gives the temporal and spatial distribution of natural events. Synonym: ecological chronology.

Linguistic   120, 190, 234
A chronology of linguistic groups.

Morphological   120, 128, 234
A chronology of morphological groups.

CHRONOLOGY (*continued*)

Regional   *See* CHRONOLOGY, Sectional

Relational   208
> A chronology showing not only the distribution of peoples, etc., but also the principal traditions that connected them.

Relative   106, 108, 111, 113, 136
> A chronology based upon relative time.

Sectional   116–117
> A chronological chart delimited in space and time.

Social   120, 131, 234
> A chronology of social groups.

CIVILIZATION   94–97, 112, 116, 125, 137, 145, 149, 161, 170, 172, 211, 213–214, 217–218, 226–227, 234
> A culture that is divided into sustaining and professional co-cultures, each possessed by a separate co-people.

Phase of   97 (*see also* CO-CULTURE, Phase of)
> A division of a civilization composed of sustaining and professional co-phases, each possessed by a separate co-subpeople.

CIVILIZATIONS

Series of   97 (*see also* CO-CULTURES, Series of)
> Several civilizations linked by a diagnostic tradition.

CLASS   45–46 (*see also* ACTIVITY ASSEMBLAGES, Class of; ARTIFACTS, Class of; BONES, Class of; CULTURAL ASSEMBLAGES, Class of; FEATURES, Class of; MORPHOLOGICAL ASSEMBLAGES, Class of)
> A group of specimens that share a diagnostic pattern of attributes or a diagnostic complex of patterns.

CLASSIFICATION   32, 78 (*see also* IDENTIFICATION)
> The procedure of forming new classes, naming them, and defining them in terms of diagnostic patterns of attributes or complexes of patterns.

Activity   173
> The procedure of forming classes of activity assemblages and defining them in terms of functional and technological modes and types in order to reconstruct an activity.

Artifactual   45–48, 51–56, 78, 83, 96, 167, 173, 197, 237–238
> The procedure of forming classes of artifacts and defining them in terms of the patterns of attributes known as types.

Of bones   58
> The classification of individual bones, as opposed to morphological classification, which deals with skeletons.

Chorological   71, 72, 74–75
> The classification of assemblages, etc., in terms of their geographical distribution.

CLASSIFICATION (*continued*)

Chronological   51, 74–75, 77, 115
> The procedure of forming classes of artifacts by studying only their chronologically significant features (dimensions), in order to produce time-markers. Also, the procedure of classifying cultural assemblages in terms of these time-markers.

Cultural   66–67, 72–85, 89, 93–94, 96–97, 98–99, 125, 141, 147, 173
> Classification of cultural assemblages in terms of stylistically significant types and modes, and definition of the classes in terms of these kinds of diagnostics.

Ethnic   61–101, 116, 153, 226 (*see also* CLASSIFICATION, Cultural; CLASSIFICATION, Morphological)
> The procedure of forming classes of cultural or morphological assemblages.

Ethnoscientific   167
> The way in which a native people classifies the items of its environment.

Extrinsic   173
> The procedure of classifying remains, not in order to learn their nature, but in order to distinguish patterns of attributes or complexes of patterns that are indicative of the position of the remains in the dimension of form, space, or time.

Functional   173
> The procedure of forming classes of artifacts or features in terms of the attributes that rendered them useful in carrying out a people's activities.

Linguistic   80
> Classification of local populations in terms of their languages or linguistic remains.

Morphological   58, 65–67, 98–101
> The procedure of forming classes of morphological assemblages and defining them in terms of diagnostic complexes of morphological traits.

Natural-scientific   167, 221, 226, 237
> The procedure of forming classes in terms of the principles of natural science, so that the resultant units are cross-cultural, contrary to ethnoscientific units.

Partitive   55–56
> The procedure of forming classes of features of artifacts rather than whole artifacts and defining them in terms of modes rather than types.

Taxonomic   52–53, 75, 83, 93, 100 (*see also* TAXONOMY)
> The procedure of dividing and subdividing one's collection into progressively smaller classes in terms of a succession of arbitrarily selected attributes. The final classes are defined by the attributes used to form them.

Technological   173
> The procedure of forming classes of artifacts or features in terms of their technologically significant attributes.

Typological   51–55, 83, 93, 100, 173 (*see also* TYPOLOGY)
> The procedure of formulating a trial pattern of types, modes, or complexes; using it to

CLASSIFICATION (*continued*)
  Typological (*continued*)

      sort artifacts, features, or assemblages into classes; and repeating this process until satisfactory classes are achieved.

CLIMAX   219–220, 241
      The high point of a development, followed by a decline.

CO-CULTURE   94–97, 181 (*see also* CIVILIZATION)
      The subsystem of materiel, activities, and norms possessed by a co-people.

  Phase of   97
      A division of a co-culture.

  Professional   95, 181 (*see also* CO-PEOPLE, Professional)
      A co-culture consisting of nonessential activities, such as religion, burial, or trade.

  Sustaining   95, 181 (*see also* CO-PEOPLE, Sustaining)
      A co-culture consisting mainly of food production and other essential activities.

CO-CULTURES

  Series of   97 (*see also* CIVILIZATIONS, Series of)
      The co-cultures possessed by a series of co-peoples.

COMMUNITY   232, 234 (*see also* RESIDENTIAL COMMUNITY; SPEECH COMMUNITY)
      A group of people linked by common interests or practices.

COMPARATIVE DISCIPLINES   *See* DISCIPLINES, Comparative

COMPARATIVE STRATEGY *See* STRATEGY, Comparative

COMPLEX   *See* DIAGNOSTIC COMPLEX

COMPONENT   46
      An ethnically delimited part of a site. Synonyms: occupation, settlement.

  Cultural   42–44, 58, 75, 79, 169, 185
      The part or parts of a site that have yielded similar cultural remains. If the entire site has yielded similar remains, it is known as a "single-component site."

  Morphological   58, 99
      The part or parts of a site that have yielded similar morphological remains.

  Residential   153, 185–187
      The part or parts of a site that were occupied by a single residential community.

CONJUNCTIVE APPROACH   142, 143–149
      Inference of cultural, morphological, social, or linguistic traits from archeological remains, and articulation of those traits into an ethnic system. Synonyms: structural approach, synchronic approach.

CONTEXT   *See* SITE, Structure of

CONVERGENCE   194, 206–207, 211, 214, 231 (*see also* DEVELOPMENT, Parallel)
Innovation of similar ethnic traits in different parts of the world. Synonym: convergent development.

CO-PATTERN

Activity   See ACTIVITY CO-PATTERN

Professional   See ACTIVITY CO-PATTERN, Professional

Sustaining   See ACTIVITY CO-PATTERN, Sustaining

CO-PEOPLE   94–98, 103, 114, 151 (*see also* PEOPLE, Civilized)
A cultural subgroup that specializes in particular activities and performs them in terms of its own distinctive activity co-pattern.

Professional   95, 170, 172, 238 (*see also* CO-CULTURE, Professional)
A co-people that specializes in nonessential activities, such as religion, burial, or trade.

Sustaining   95, 170, 172, 238 (*see also* CO-CULTURE, Sustaining)
A co-people that specializes in food production and other essential activities.

CO-PEOPLES

Series of   97 (*see also* CO-CULTURES, Series of)
Several sustaining or professional co-peoples linked by a diagnostic tradition.

CO-SUBPEOPLE   97
A division of a co-people that corresponds to a subpeople.

CREATION   220–222
An explanation of change that attributes it to the purposeful actions of an individual.

CULTURAL ACTIVITY   *See* ACTIVITY

CULTURAL ASSEMBLAGE   42–44, 58, 71–89, 93, 96–98, 106, 112, 122–125, 129, 138–139, 141–142, 169, 173, 186, 237–238
The remains obtained from a cultural component.

Mixed   43, 80, 83, 89
A cultural assemblage consisting of the remains of two or more cultural groups.

Pure   80, 83, 89
A cultural assemblage consisting of the remains of a single people.

Transitional   81, 83, 99
A cultural assemblage from the border zone between two peoples, where the traits of the two are mixed.

Typical   81, 83
A cultural assemblage from the central part of the distribution of a people, where there is the least admixture with the traits of other peoples.

CULTURAL ASSEMBLAGES

Class of 75–81, 83, 86–89, 93, 96, 196, 233, 238
> All cultural assemblages that share a diagnostic complex of modes and types and hence are indicative of a people. Synonym: focus.

CULTURAL CLASSIFICATION *See* CLASSIFICATION, Cultural

CULTURAL COMPLEX *See* DIAGNOSTIC COMPLEX, Cultural

CULTURAL COMPONENT *See* COMPONENT, Cultural

CULTURAL DIAGNOSTIC *See* DIAGNOSTIC, Cultural

CULTURAL EQUIPMENT *See* EQUIPMENT, Cultural

CULTURAL GROUP 102–104, 138, 140–141, 144, 148, 151, 155, 185, 191, 199, 206, 211, 216–217, 240, 244 (*see also* CO-PEOPLE; PEOPLES, Series of; SUBPEOPLE)
> A group of individuals distinguished by a common set of cultural traits.

CULTURAL MATERIALS *See* MATERIALS, Cultural

CULTURAL NORM *See* NORM, Cultural

CULTURAL REMAINS *See* REMAINS, Cultural

CULTURAL SYSTEM *See* CULTURE

CULTURE 2, 5, 12–14, 18–20, 24, 27, 38, 40–41, 63, 69, 72–73, 77, 79–80, 85, 87–94, 96–97, 99, 111, 113, 115, 119, 123–124, 138, 141–144, 146–149, 151, 154–157, 159–162, 166, 170–171, 174–176, 189, 197–201, 205–207, 210–211, 213, 219, 224, 227–229, 232–234, 239, 246 (*see also* PEOPLE)
> The combination of materiel, activities, and norms that makes up a cultural system. Synonym: cultural period.

Co- *See* CO-CULTURE

Intrusive *See* INTRUSIVE CULTURE

Phase of 77, 91–93, 115
> The culture of a subpeople. Synonyms: facies, subculture.

CULTURE HISTORY *See* PREHISTORY; ETHNOHISTORY; ETHNOLOGY

CULTURES

Plural *See* PLURAL CULTURES

Series of 75–76, 91–94, 195
> The cultures possessed by a series of peoples. Synonyms: basic culture; taxonomic aspect, phase, or pattern.

DATING

Absolute 104–106, 111, 124, 131–136 (*see also* TIME, Absolute)
> Dating of an event with reference to a universal calendar, applicable throughout the world. Synonyms: calendrical dating, scientific dating.

DATING (*continued*)

   Artifactual 122, 125–128
        Forming a local sequence by the study of individual types or modes of artifacts.

   Calendrical *See* DATING, Absolute

   Chemical 128–129 (*see also* DATING, Hydration; DATING, Isotopic)
        Determining the relative ages of artifacts by comparing the amounts of a chemical, such
        as fluorine, that they have absorbed from the ground.

   Cultural 122–128
        Setting up a local sequence by stratigraphic or seriational study of diagnostic complexes
        rather than of types or modes per se.

   Geological 128–129
        Determining the relative ages of assemblages or artifacts by correlating the remains with
        geochronologies.

   Graphic 104–106
        Expressing time in terms of a chronological chart, which may be marked off in either
        absolute or relative time, rather than verbally.

   Hydration 129, 135
        Determining the relative ages of obsidian artifacts by comparing the amounts of water
        they have absorbed since deposition.

   Isotopic 133–135 (*see also* POTASSIUM-ARGON ANALYSIS; RADIOCARBON ANALYSIS)
        Calculating the absolute age of a specimen by measuring the proportion of a radioactive
        isotope that has decayed since the specimen was formed.

   Lexico-statistical *See* GLOTTOCHRONOLOGY

   Magnetic *See* ARCHEOMAGNETISM

   Potassium-argon *See* POTASSIUM-ARGON ANALYSIS

   Radiocarbon *See* RADIOCARBON ANALYSIS

   Relative 104–106, 111 (*see also* TIME, Relative)
        Dating an event with reference to another event that was limited in its distribution and
        variable in time from place to place.

   Scientific *See* DATING, Absolute

   Stratigraphic 122–129 (*see also* STRATIGRAPHY)
        Using superimpositions of assemblages or artifacts to set up local sequences.

   Tree-ring *See* DENDROCHRONOLOGY

   Varve *See* VARVE ANALYSIS

DEFINITION 48–50, 53–54, 56–57 (*see also* DIAGNOSTIC COMPLEX; DIAGNOSTIC TRADITION; MODE; TYPE)
        The procedure of selecting, recording, and illustrating the diagnostic attributes of classes,
        as opposed to description, which treats all of the attributes.

DENDROCHRONOLOGY   115, 132–135
>   Use of a local pattern of tree-ring growth to determine absolute time. Synonym: tree-ring dating.

DEPOSIT

Disturbed   33, 43, 80, 122, 133 (*see also* STRATIGRAPHY, Reverse)
>   A deposit that has been modified more than is usual by a human or natural agency.

Human   *See* REMAINS, Archeological

Natural   *See* REMAINS, Natural

DEPOSITION

Rate of   131
>   The speed of accumulation of a deposit.

DESCENT GROUP   161, 182
>   A group of individuals descended from a common ancestor.

DESCRIPTION   32, 49, 55, 58–59, 71, 222
>   The procedure of recording and illustrating the attributes of classes without, as in the case of definition, limiting oneself to the diagnostic attributes.

DETERMINANT   *See* DIAGNOSTIC, Cultural

DEVELOPMENT   202, 217–220, 223, 230, 241
>   Formation of a pattern of change.

Convergent   See CONVERGENCE

Cultural   111, 115–116, 137, 149, 175, 197, 211, 217, 224–225, 228–229
>   Development in cultural systems or traits.

Divergent   *See* DIVERGENCE

Ethnic   199, 211–214
>   Development in cultural, linguistic, morphological, and social systems or traits.

Linear   *See* EVOLUTION, Linear

Morphological   208, 212–213, 215, 230
>   Development in morphological systems or traits. Synonym: organic development.

Multilinear   *See* EVOLUTION, Multilinear

Organic   *See* DEVELOPMENT, Morphological

Parallel   115, 214–215, 228 (*see also* EVOLUTION, Multilinear; EVOLUTION, Unilinear)
>   Two or more similar developmetns taking place in different parts of the world.

Rate of   233
>   The speed of a series of changes.

DEVELOPMENT (*continued*)

Social   224–225
> Development in social systems or traits.

Superorganic   220, 230
> Development in cultural, linguistic, and social systems or traits.

Unilinear   See EVOLUTION, Unilinear

DIACHRONIC APPROACH   *See* ETHNOLOGY

DIAGNOSTIC

Cultural   75, 84–87, 90, 93–94, 97, 119, 207, 238
> An element of a diagnostic cultural complex. Synonym: determinant.

DIAGNOSTIC COMPLEX   238
> A pattern of traits that distinguishes a group of assemblages and defines it as a class.

Activity   173
> A pattern of types, modes, and other kinds of cultural norms that distinguishes a group of activity assemblages and defines it as a class.

Cognitive   86, 88
> The diagnostics that a people or race used to define itself, as opposed to those obtained by classifying its assemblages.

Cultural   75–76, 79, 84–92, 95, 97, 99, 141, 144–145
> A pattern of types, modes, and other kinds of cultural norms that distinguishes a group of cultural assemblages and defines it as a class. A diagnostic cultural complex also indicative of a people and a culture. Synonyms: determinants, cultural diagnostics, industry, style.

Extrinsic   86, 88, 173
> The diagnostic complex obtained by classifying cultural or morphological assemblages.

Morphological   84, 99
> A pattern of traits that distinguishes a group of morphological assemblages and defines it as a class.

DIAGNOSTIC SUBCOMPLEX   90–93, 97
> The pattern of modes, types, and other traits that characterizes a subpeople, its subclass, and its phase of culture.

DIAGNOSTIC TRADITION   91–94, 97, 210, 238
> A set of cultural or morphological traits that is diagnostic of a series of peoples or races.

DIFFUSION   112, 117, 121, 130, 137–138, 143, 145, 206–207, 209, 213–214, 220, 231, 234–235, 241 (*see also* GENE FLOW)
> The spread of superorganic traits from one ethnic system to another.

DIMENSION

Of form   2, 12–14, 18–19, 27, 62, 67, 74, 103, 141–145, 147, 149–151, 153, 171, 179, 203, 208, 210, 216, 219, 222–226, 237
> The total range of ecological and ethnic systems and traits reconstructed by the prehistorian.

Of space   2, 12–14, 27, 62, 74, 103–104, 114, 116, 138, 141, 150, 190, 203–210, 213–214, 216, 219–220, 223, 225, 237, 239
> The total range of points on the surface of the earth, arranged linearly rather than in two dimensions.

Of time   1–2, 18, 27, 62, 74, 103–104, 114, 116, 138, 141, 150, 190, 193, 203–210, 213–214, 216, 219–220, 222–225, 237, 239
> The total range of points in time since the formation of the earth.

DIRECT HISTORIC METHOD   76–77
> The procedure of working back from history to prehistory in order to establish a local sequence of periods or peoples.

DISCIPLINES

Analytic   7–11, 13–15, 17–18, 20–21, 25
> Disciplines that aim to determine the nature of the materials they study.

Comparative   16–21
> Disciplines that work topically from group to group instead of focusing upon particular groups of human beings.

Holistic   6–7, 13–15, 17–18, 24
> Disciplines that study the entire range of the dimension of form.

Synthetic   7–11, 13–15, 17–18, 20–21, 25
> Disciplines that synthesize a picture of life and times during a particular period.

Topical   6–7, 13–14, 17–18
> Disciplines that specialize in a part of the dimension of form.

DIVERGENCE   203, 206–207, 211–212, 214, 215 (*see also* MODEL, Phylogenetic)
> Furcate development, in which one system or trait gives rise to two or more new ones. Synonym: divergent development.

DWELLING SITE   *See* SITE, Residential

DYNAMICS   191, 194–198, 200, 230, 235–236 (*see also* PATTERN OF CHANGE)
> Study of the nature and patterning of changes. Synonym: historical reconstruction.

ECOSYSTEM   158
> The system of relationships among a community of organisms, including the community's adaptation to the inorganic environment.

ENTERPRISE   187
> An institution organized to carry out a cultural activity on a more or less permanent basis.

ENTERPRISE (*continued*)

Professional   161, 181–182
> An enterprise organized to carry out a professional activity.

Sustaining   161, 181
> An enterprise organized to carry out a sustaining activity.

ENVIRONMENT   2, 12, 19, 67, 142, 146–148, 151, 154–156, 158–159, 163–164, 179, 183, 194, 198, 200, 209, 212, 217, 228, 235
> The inorganic and organic conditions among which an ethnic group lived.

Micro-   *See* MICROENVIRONMENT

EPIGRAPHY   *See* PALEOGRAPHY

EQUIPMENT

Cultural   35–41, 44, 47, 58, 78, 119, 162, 167
> Equipment that is selected, if unworked, or made, if worked, by man in accordance with his cultural norms.

Natural   37–40, 162
> Equipment that is selected or made by wild animals rather than man.

Unworked   35, 38–39, 41, 167
> Structures, tools, etc., used by the inhabitants of a site without manufacture.

Worked   35–41, 48, 167
> Structures, tools, etc., modified by the occupants of a site in order to increase their utility. If worked by man rather than animals, they are called "artifacts."

ETHNIC ASSEMBLAGE   153 (*see also* CULTURAL ASSEMBLAGE; MORPHOLOGICAL ASSEMBLAGE)
> All the remains laid down at a site by a single ethnic group.

ETHNIC GROUP   5–6, 12–15, 16, 18, 61–101, 141, 154–155, 158–159, 179, 191, 198–201, 206–208, 210–211, 217, 219, 226, 232, 238, 243–245 (*see also* CULTURAL, LINGUISTIC, MORPHOLOGICAL, and SOCIAL GROUPS)
> A group of individuals distinguished by a common set of cultural, linguistic, morphological, or social traits. Synonym: superorganic group.

Literate   12, 14–15, 16
> An ethnic group that can be studied primarily in terms of its writing.

Nonliterate   12, 14–15
> An ethnic group with little or no writing, so that it must be studied primarily by the techniques of archeology or ethnography.

ETHNIC SUBGROUP   243, 245
> A subdivision of an ethnic group.

ETHNIC SYSTEM   *See* SYSTEM, Ethnic

ETHNOCENTRISM   218, 220, 243–244 (*see also* CENTRISM)
>The tendency to view other ethnic systems in terms of one's own and to assume that they are peripheral to it.

ETHNOGENESIS   232–233
>The development of a completely new ethnic system.

ETHNOGRAPHIC MODEL   *See* ANALOGY, Specific

ETHNOGRAPHIC RECONSTRUCTION   *See* CONJUNCTIVE APPROACH

ETHNOGRAPHIC TRAIT   *See* TRAIT, Ethnic

ETHNOGRAPHY   12–15, 16–18, 20–22, 24–25, 27, 31, 57, 67, 69, 142–150, 152, 154–155, 157, 167–169, 174–176, 191, 223, 227, 240
>Study of the nature of contemporary ethnic groups.

ETHNOHISTORY   9, 16, 17, 22, 57, 61–62, 168, 240 (*see also* HISTORY)
>Study of the nature of, and changes in, the ethnic groups who lived during historic time. Synonym: culture history.

ETHNOLOGY   13–15, 16–18, 20–25, 27, 59, 67, 69, 103–104, 108, 120, 148, 191–192, 211, 224, 226
>Study of the changes in contemporary ethnic groups and of the reasons therefor. Synonyms: culture history, diachronic approach.

ETHNOSCIENCE   167
>Study of scientific knowledge and its development among nonliterate peoples.

EVOLUTION   197, 202–207, 216, 223–229
>The overall development of the earth and of its inhabitants. Rather than a sequence of occurrences, such as an evolutionary sequence, evolution produces a pattern of changes.

Chemical   *See* EVOLUTION, Inorganic

Cultural   111, 113, 224, 228
>The overall development of cultural systems or traits.

Ethnic   144–145, 166, 175, 206, 211, 225–229, 233, 238, 241
>The overall development of cultural, linguistic, morphological, and social systems or traits. Synonym: human evolution.

General   *See* SEQUENCE, Evolutionary

Human   *See* EVOLUTION, Ethnic

Inorganic   197
>The earliest stage of evolution, marked by the development of matter.

Linear   211, 225–229, 233, 241 (*see also* EVOLUTION, Multilinear; EVOLUTION, Unilinear)
>The false assumption that ethnic systems and traits have developed along lines rather than intermittent traditions. Synonym: linear development.

Macro-   *See* MACROEVOLUTION

EVOLUTION (*continued*)

Micro- See MICROEVOLUTION

Morphological 120
>   The overall development of morphological systems or traits.

Multilinear 211, 219, 228–229 (*see also* DEVELOPMENT, Parallel)
>   The false assumption that ethnic systems or traits have evolved primarily in terms of centers, each composed of a long parallel line, instead of via short, intermittent traditions inside and outside centers. Synonym: multilinear development.

Organic 197, 201, 206, 212, 222–224, 241, 244
>   The second stage of evolution, in which the development of organisms was superimposed upon the development of matter.

Social 144–145
>   The overall development of social systems or traits.

Superorganic 197, 201, 223–226, 244
>   The third stage of evolution, in which the development of ethnic systems was superimposed upon the development of matter and of organisms.

Unilinear 111, 211, 225–229 (*see also* DEVELOPMENT, Parallel)
>   The false assumption that ethnic systems or traits have developed in the same way throughout the world, that is, in a single line. Synonym: unilinear development.

EXCAVATION UNITS 34–35, 42, 43
>   The units into which an archeologist divides a site in order to record its structure.

EXPLANATION 191–192, 194–195, 198–200, 225, 230, 235–236
>   Study of the factors causing changes, that is, of processes of change.

EXPLOITATION 158–159, 230, 239
>   Utilization of natural resources by an ethnic group.

FACIES *See* CULTURE, Phase of

FEATURE 50–51, 55–57, 238
>   Any part or aspect of an artifact, such as its material, an element of shape, or a design motif.

FEATURES

Class of 55–57, 59, 238 (*see also* CLASSIFICATION, Partitive)
>   All artifact features that share a diagnostic set of attributes, that is, a mode.

FOCUS *See* CULTURAL ASSEMBLAGES, Class of

FORM, DIMENSION OF *See Dimension*, Of form

FORMAL SEQUENCE *See* PATTERN OF CHANGE

FORMATION *See* PERIOD, Paleontological

FUSION   232–233 (*see also* ACCULTURATION)
> The formation of a new ethnic system by the merging of two previous systems.

GENE   176, 177, 198–199, 201–209, 211–214, 219–220, 230–233, 241
> The medium of change in organic evolution, corresponding to the norm in superorganic evolution.

GENE FLOW   280 (*see also* DIFFUSION)
> The spread of genes from one morphological group to another.

GENUS   54, 65–68, 98, 100, 103, 211, 221–222, 234, 241
> A group of related species.

GEOCHRONOLOGY   *See* CHRONOLOGY, Geo-

GEOLOGIC TIME   2–4, 8, 9, 26, 120
> The period of relative time before the first appearance of mankind. It is studied by means of paleontological analysis and natural-historical synthesis.

GLOTTOCHRONOLOGY   135–136, 140
> Use of changes in the basic vocabulary of a language to estimate absolute time. Synonym: lexico-statistical dating.

GRADE   204, 212–213, 215, 219, 226
> A division of a phylogeny consisting of several species etc. that have developed in a homologous manner.

HISTORIC TIME   2–4, 8, 9, 12, 14, 26–27, 67, 120, 127, 131, 141
> The period of relative time after the appearance of enough documentary evidence to work primarily by means of paleographic analysis and historical synthesis.

HISTORICAL GEOLOGY   4, 26–27, 122–123, 128, 242
> Synthetic study of the earth and its occupants, primarily before the appearance of man.

HISTORICAL RECONSTRUCTION   *See* DYNAMICS

HISTORY   3–4, 6–11, 14–15, 17, 25, 26–27, 29, 57, 59–60, 65, 67, 76, 103, 106–107, 112, 131, 150, 168, 181, 185–187, 189–190, 192, 217, 224, 243–245 (*see also* ETHNOHISTORY)
> The study of events and conditions during historic time from an ethnocentric point of view, using primarily paleographic, rather than archeological, evidence; also, the results of this study.

  Archeological   7–11, 29–30
> The use of archeological evidence to solve problems of the discipline of history. Synonym: historical archeology.

HORIZON STYLE   130
> A complex of modes or types that spread so rapidly over a region that it can be used to synchronize local sequences.

HUMAN-SKELETAL ASSEMBLAGE   58, 99
> The bones of a single skeleton, usually found buried in anatomical position. A "human-

HUMAN-SKELETAL ASSEMBLAGE (*continued*)

> skeletal assemblage" should not be confused with a "morphological assemblage," which consists of bones from a number of skeletons.

HYDRATION DATING   *See* DATING, Hydration

HYPOTHESES

Multiple working   20, 174–175, 189, 194, 199, 230

> All hypotheses that might possibly explain a set of archeological facts. After these hypotheses are formulated, the one that best fits the facts is selected.

HYPOTHESIS   175, 194, 230, 241

> A tentative assumption about prehistory that is tested against the archeological evidence.

Age-area   175–176

> The assumption that the more widespread a trait is, the older it is.

IDENTIFICATION   32, 45, 53–56 (*see also* CLASSIFICATION)

> The procedure of assigning specimens to established sets of classes in terms of the attributes or traits diagnostic of those classes.

Activity   173

> The procedure of assigning activity assemblages to already established classes in terms of the complexes diagnostic of those classes, in order to determine the distribution of activities.

Artifactual   53–56, 71, 96

> The procedure of assigning artifacts to already established classes in terms of the types diagnostic of those classes.

Of bones   58

> The procedure of assigning individual bones, rather than morphological assemblages, to established classes in terms of the diagnostics of those classes.

Cultural   67, 96–97, 99, 173

> The procedure of assigning cultural assemblages to already established classes in terms of the complexes diagnostic of those classes, in order to identify the peoples etc. that produced the classes.

Morphological   58, 65–67, 99

> The procedure of assigning morphological assemblages to established classes in terms of the complexes diagnostic of those classes, in order to identify the races etc. that produced the classes.

Partitive   55–56

> The procedure of assigning artifact features to already established classes of features in terms of the modes diagnostic of those classes.

INDUSTRY   *See* DIAGNOSTIC COMPLEX, Cultural

INFERENCE

Ethnographic   *See* RECONSTRUCTION, Ethnographic

Historical   *See* RECONSTRUCTION, Historical

INNOVATION   105–106, 114, 116–119, 121, 136–138, 199, 209, 214–215, 217–218, 220–221, 223, 231, 233–235, 239, 241 (*see also* MUTATION)
> The independent development of a norm or tradition within one or more ethnic systems. Synonym: invention.

INORGANIC EVOLUTION   *See* EVOLUTION, Inorganic

INSTITUTION   66–68, 151–152, 154–157, 173, 178–184, 188–189 (*see also* SOCIETY)
> A subgroup of individuals organized for a particular purpose or purposes by means of a network of interactions mediated by social norms.

Activity   161, 170, 180–182, 187, 240
> A subgroup of individuals organized primarily for the purpose of carrying out a specific activity, such as religion.

Relational   161, 182, 187, 240
> A subgroup of individuals organized primarily for the purpose of expressing relationships of descent, rank, etc.

Residential   152, 159, 161, 169–181, 184–187, 240
> A subgroup of people organized primarily for the purpose of living together as either a community, a household, or a territorial unit.

INTERACTION   154, 156–157, 179, 183–184, 188 (*see also* BEHAVIOR, Social)
> Behavior by means of which individuals influence one another.

INTERACTION GROUP   161, 182
> A group of individuals organized to influence the interaction of other individuals within a society.

INTERACTION SPHERE   *See* MACROSTRUCTURE

INTRUSIVE CULTURE   96
> A culture that has intruded into the area of another culture and has not been acculturated into the latter. Synonym: subculture.

INTRUSIVE PEOPLE   96
> A foreign people that has intruded into the area of another people and has not been assimilated to the latter.

INVENTION   *See* INNOVATION

KEY   53–54, 97
> The hierarchical list of diagnostic attributes that a taxonomic classifier prepares in order to facilitate the identification of members of his classes.

LANGUAGE   2, 6, 7, 12–14, 18–20, 24, 27, 38, 63, 67, 69, 135–136, 142–144, 151, 154–157, 165–166, 189–190, 197–201, 205–206 210–211, 213, 219, 226, 228–229, 232–234, 243 (*see also* SPEECH COMMUNITY)
> The combination of records, speech, and norms that makes up a linguistic system. Synonym: linguistic period.

LANGUAGE (*continued*)

Transitional 80
 The form of a language to be found on the boundary with another language, where there is so much mutual influence that the speakers of the two languages can understand one another.

LIFE   *See* WILDLIFE

LIMITED POSSIBILITIES

Principle of 214, 231 (*see also* CONVERGENCE; DEVELOPMENT, Parallel)
 The recognition that there are a limited number of ways of filling the needs of mankind, so that diverse peoples are likely to develop similar ways independently.

LINE   103, 202–205, 207–213, 215, 219, 225–226, 229
 A segment of a phylogeny marking the route whereby an initial genus etc. gave birth to subsequent species etc.

LINGUISTIC GROUP   119–120, 128, 139, 141, 147, 151, 156, 190, 191, 199, 206, 211, 216–217, 239, 244 (*see also* SPEECH COMMUNITY)
 A group of individuals distinguished by a common set of linguistic traits.

LOCAL AREA   *See* AREA, Local

LOCAL SEQUENCE   *See* SEQUENCE, Local

LOCUS

Activity   *See* ACTIVITY LOCUS

Residential   *See* RESIDENTIAL LOCUS

MACROEVOLUTION   54, 202–206, 211, 224, 229
 The overall development of organic groups on the level of species and above, that is, development in terms of closed systems that change phylogenetically.

MACROSTRUCTURE   149, 188
 The network of interactions among the members of different institutions. Synonym: interaction sphere.

MANKIND   159–168, 176–177, 178–184, 189–190 (*see also* MORPHOLOGY, Human)
 All individuals capable of producing cultural, linguistic, morphological, and social systems that include conceptual norms and hence are not based solely upon instinct and habit.

MAP   104, 106, 112, 117, 121–122, 134, 239
 A representation of an area in the two dimensions of space.

MATERIAL CULTURE   *See* MATERIEL

MATERIALS

Cultural   35, 37–40, 46–47, 58, 147–148, 155, 167–169, 176
 The remains of raw or processed materials brought to a site by its human occupants.

MATERIALS (*continued*)

Natural 38–39
>The remains of raw or processed materials brought to a site by its animal occupants.

MATERIEL 19, 154–155, 157, 160, 164–166, 168, 170, 174–176, 179, 183, 189, 239
>The materials, natural equipment, and artifacts of a cultural system. Synonym: material culture.

MATTER 2, 19, 197, 235, 244
>The materials of which the earth and its atmosphere are composed.

MICROENVIRONMENT 159, 230, 239, 241
>A division of a people's environment that is characterized by a homogeneous set of natural resources.

MICROEVOLUTION 202–206, 211, 224, 229, 241
>The overall development of ethnic groups within a species, that is, development in terms of open systems that change via the trellis model.

MICROSTRUCTURE 149, 188
>The network of interactions among the members of an institution.

MIGRATION 94, 158, 194–196, 209, 219, 229, 231, 235, 241
>Movement of individuals, with their ethnic systems, from one area to another.

MODE 56–57, 59, 66, 78, 83–84, 86–87, 97, 121–122, 125, 127, 130, 164, 167, 192–193, 238
>A pattern of attributes that distinguishes a group of artifact features, such as rim profiles, and defines it as a class.

Cognitive 57, 167–168, 238
>A pattern of attributes that a people uses to distinguish a class of features among its own artifacts.

Extrinsic 57, 167–168, 173, 238
>A pattern of attributes indicative of the behavior of manufacture or use, which the prehistorian obtains by classifying artifacts partitively.

Intrinsic 57, 167–168, 238
>A pattern of attributes expressive of the nature of a class of artifact features, which the archeologist obtains by partitively classifying artifacts.

MODEL 63–64, 146, 148, 153–154, 194, 197, 202–206, 219
>A theoretical diagram, as opposed to a substantive pattern, that is, an analogy, developed to assist in the reconstruction of prehistory. Synonym: theoretical pattern.

Anthropological 63
>A theoretical diagram worked out by anthropologists.

Of change *See* CHANGE, Model of

Ethnographic *See* ANALOGY, Specific

MODEL (*continued*)

Geographical 145, 148
> A theoretical diagram worked out by geographers.

Phylogenetic 103–104, 202–207, 212–213, 222–225, 228, 241
> The model of change in closed systems, along straight or branching lines. It is drawn in the dimensions of form and time, that is, on the side face of our cube of knowledge. Synonym: phylogeny.

Reticulate 203–204
> A model illustrating the manner of change in open systems that is plotted in the dimensions of form and time, that is, on the side face of our cube of knowledge. Synonym: reticulate pattern.

Substantive *See* ANALOGY

Trellis 203–208, 213, 223–224, 228–229, 241
> A model illustrating the manner of change in open systems that is plotted in the dimensions of space and time, that is, on the front face of our cube of knowledge. Synonym: trellis pattern.

MODES

Series of 127–128
> A number of modes that have developed one from another.

MORPHOLOGICAL ASSEMBLAGE 58, 81, 99, 138–139, 142, 177, 238
> The remains obtained from a single morphological component.

Mixed 99
> A morphological assemblage consisting of the remains of two or more morphological groups.

Pure 99
> A morphological assemblage consisting of the remains of a single race.

Transitional 99
> A morphological assemblage from the border zone between two races, where the traits of the two are mixed.

MORPHOLOGICAL ASSEMBLAGES

Class of 99
> All morphological assemblages that share a diagnostic complex of traits and are therefore indicative of a race, species, or genus.

MORPHOLOGICAL COMPONENT *See* COMPONENT, Morphological

MORPHOLOGICAL GROUP 102, 119–120, 138–139, 140–141, 151, 155, 176–177, 191, 206, 211, 239–240 (*see also* GENUS; RACE; RACES, Series of; SPECIES)
> A group of individuals distinguished by a common set of morphological traits.

MORPHOLOGICAL REMAINS *See* REMAINS, Morphological

MORPHOLOGY

Human   2, 5, 12–14, 18–20, 24, 63, 69, 99, 142–144, 151, 154–157, 176–178, 197–198, 203–204, 206, 210, 213, 226, 232–234, 241, 243 (*see also* MANKIND)
>The combination of individuals, reproductive behavior, and norms that makes up a morphological system.

MUTATION   198, 202, 209, 230 (*see also* INNOVATION)
>A change in a gene that takes place as it is passed to an offspring through sexual intercourse.

NATURAL EQUIPMENT   *See* EQUIPMENT, Natural

NATURAL HISTORY   6, 9–10, 31, 103, 221 (*see also* HISTORICAL GEOLOGY)
>Synthetic study of the lesser animals and plants, and their environments, both before and after the appearance of mankind.

NATURAL MATERIALS   *See* MATERIALS, Natural

NATURAL SELECTION   198, 201–202, 209, 225, 230
>The elimination of mutations that are not adapted to the environment in which an organism lives.

NORM   157–158, 207–210, 213–214, 219–220, 223–224, 231–236, 241–242
>A regularity of behavior that is based not only upon instinct and habit, but also upon conceptual thought, if only that of the investigator. It is the medium of change in superorganic evolution, corresponding to the gene in organic evolution. Synonym: pattern of behavior.

Conceptual   165
>A regularity in mental behavior, that is, in thought, that the members of an ethnic group express in their speech or record in their writing and in their artifacts, where it is observed or inferred by the investigator.

Cultural   38, 49–50, 54, 57, 66–69, 75–76, 83–87, 119, 121–122, 125, 130, 154–155, 157, 160, 162–168, 174–177, 184, 189, 196–202, 205–208, 224–225, 232, 238–239, 241
>A regularity in a people's activities, as observed or inferred by an investigator.

Ethnic   198–201, 221
>Any superorganic regularity in an ethnic system, whether cultural, linguistic, morphological, or social.

Linguistic   154, 156, 199–202, 205, 208, 224, 232, 241
>A regularity in a community's speech, as observed or inferred by an investigator.

Morphological   154–155, 176–178, 198, 202, 205, 208–209, 240, 241
>A regularity in the reproductive behavior of a race, as observed or inferred by an investigator.

Perceptual   165
>A regularity that the members of an ethnic group build into the products of their behavior, especially their artifacts, where it is observed by the investigator.

NORM (*continued*)

Procedural 165
   A regularity in physical (as opposed to mental) behavior exhibited by the members of an
   ethnic group or inferred from the products of their behavior.

Social 68–69, 154, 156–157, 178–179, 182, 184, 188–189, 199–202, 205, 208, 224–225, 240–241
   A regularity in a society's interactive behavior, as observed or inferred by an investigator.

Superorganic 98, 199–200
   A cultural, social, or linguistic norm, which does not belong to a morphological (organic)
   system.

OCCUPATION *See* COMPONENT

ORDERING

Chronological 102–139
   Arrangement of one's classes in terms of their positions in space and time. They can be
   arranged either verbally, in terms of areas and periods, or graphically, by plotting the
   classes on a chronology.

Phylogenetic 103–104
   Use of the phylogenetic model to order one's classes. This method is possible only when
   the classes were closed systems, which developed furcately.

Taxonomic 75–76, 115
   Use of taxonomic classification to order one's classes. The order of formation of the classes
   serves as the organizing principle.

ORGANIC EVOLUTION *See* EVOLUTION, Organic

ORGANIC GROUP 65–66, 98 (*see also* GENUS; RACE; SPECIES)
   A group of individuals defined in terms of their biological traits.

ORGANISM 158, 199, 201, 219, 235
   Any living object, or one that has died.

PALEOGRAPHY 6, 8–10, 27, 67, 131
   Study of the nature of written records, including inscriptions and documents, with the aim
   of determining their validity and meaning. Synonym: epigraphy.

PALEONTOLOGY 8–10, 27, 59, 126, 153, 222
   Study of the nature of extinct animals.

PARALLEL *See* ANALOGY; CHANGE, Analogous

PARALLELISM *See* DEVELOPMENT, Parallel

PATTERN 63–64
   Any configuration distinguished by anthropologists, as follows.

Activity *See* ACTIVITY PATTERN

PATTERN (*continued*)

Of attributes See MODE, TYPE

Of behavior See NORM

Of change See PATTERN OF CHANGE

Of development See PATTERN OF CHANGE

Residential See RESIDENTIAL PATTERN

Reticulate See MODEL, Reticulate

Settlement See SETTLEMENT PATTERN

Taxonomic See CULTURES, Series of

Theoretical See MODEL

Trellis See MODEL, Trellis

PATTERN OF CHANGE   123, 127–129, 132–133, 192–197, 199, 207–208, 212–213, 219–226, 230, 240–241

> A continuous sequence of changes; the product of development and other, more specific processes of change. Synonym: formal sequence.

Remnant   153, 192–194

> The traces of a pattern of change that have survived archeologically. The prehistorian uses them to reconstruct the original pattern of change.

PEOPLE   2, 5, 6, 12–14, 16–18, 24, 38, 41–44, 49–51, 58, 61, 64, 66–77, 79–80, 86–87, 94–100, 102–108, 111–130, 136–139, 141–152, 154–155, 159, 162–163, 165, 168–169, 171–172, 174–176, 178–180, 187, 190, 192, 196, 206–210, 215, 217–218, 220, 224, 233–234, 237–241, 243–244

> The individuals who deposited a class of cultural assemblages, who are characterized by the complex diagnostic of that class, and who therefore may be said to have had the same culture.

Civilized   94–97, 172, 181, 238

> A people divided into sustaining and professional co-peoples, each with its own co-culture.

Co- See CO-PEOPLE

Cognitive   88

> A cultural group defined by a cognitive complex, that is, by its own diagnostics.

Extrinsic   88

> A cultural group defined by an extrinsic complex, that is, by its archeological remains.

Intrusive See INTRUSIVE PEOPLE

Transitional   93

> A people that has adopted cultural traits from several neighboring subpeoples, becoming transitional between them.

PEOPLES

Plural   See PLURAL PEOPLES

Series of   91–94, 98, 100, 102–104, 114–115, 123–125, 128, 151, 207–210, 238–239
  Several peoples linked by a diagnostic tradition of cultural traits, which indicates that they
  have developed one from another, even though each possesses a distinctive culture.

PERIOD   120
  Any unit of time.

Cultural   76–77, 113, 136
  A local period that is culturally homogeneous. Synonym: culture.

General   108, 112
  An arbitrary unit of absolute time that is used in the absence of calendrical dates to mark
  off the vertical dimension of a chronology.

Linguistic   136
  A local period that is linguistically homogeneous. Synonym: language.

Local   51, 84, 108, 145
  A division of time within a local area. It may or may not be ethnically homogeneous.

Paleontological   129
  A local period that is homogeneous in its fossil remains. Synonym: formation.

PERIPHERIES   217–218, 220
  The areas that surround a center and contain less highly developed superorganic systems
  than those in the center.

PERSISTENCE   209
  Survival of an ethnic trait for an appreciable length of time.

PHASE

Of a civilization   See CIVILIZATION, Phase of

Of a co-culture   See CO-CULTURE, Phase of

Of a culture   See CULTURE, Phase of

Taxonomic   See CULTURES, Series of

PHYLOGENY   *See* MODEL, Phylogenetic

PLURAL CULTURES   96
  Cultures that are linked by a common social structure but not, as in the case of co-cultures,
  by a common cultural complex.

PLURAL PEOPLES   69, 96
  Peoples that share a common social structure.

PLURAL SOCIETIES   69
  Societies that share a common culture.

POLLEN ANALYSIS 129
>Reconstruction of a pattern of change in types of pollen. This reconstruction constitutes a geochronology, which the prehistorian can use to date his remains.

POPULATION

Local 154
>The population of a local area. A local population is normally composed of overlapping cultural, morphological, social, and linguistic groups.

POTASSIUM-ARGON ANALYSIS 134–135
>Calculation of the absolute age of volcanic rock by determining the amount of potassium 40 that has changed into argon 40 since the rock was formed.

PREHISTORIC ARCHEOLOGY *See* PREHISTORY; ARCHEOLOGY, Prehistoric

PREHISTORIC TIME 2–4, 8, 12, 14, 25, 26–27, 120, 131, 139, 141, 234
>The period of relative time between the first appearance of mankind and the development of written history. It is studied by means of archeological analysis and prehistoric synthesis.

PREHISTORY 1–25, 26, 31, 45, 49–52, 57, 59–62, 71–72, 76, 83, 96, 100, 103–104, 106, 108–109, 111–114, 116, 118–119, 122, 124, 131, 142–150, 153–154, 157–159, 162, 165, 168–169, 172–177, 180, 184–190, 192–196, 202, 211–213, 215, 217–220, 224–229, 233, 235–238, 242, 244
>Study of events and conditions during prehistoric time; also, the results of this study. Because of the absence or scarcity of writing, the reconstruction of prehistory has to be based primarily upon archeological evidence. Synonyms: culture history, prehistoric archeology, synthetic archeology.

PROCESS OF CHANGE 192, 194–196, 199–200, 230–233, 235, 241
>One of several contingent events postulated to explain a pattern of change. For example, changes in the nature of a system or trait may be said to be due to development, but one must also take into consideration other processes that have affected the development, such as mutation or ecological adaptation, in accordance with the principle of reductionism.

PROCESSUAL STRATEGY *See* STRATEGY, Comparative

PROFESSION *See* ASSOCIATION, Professional; INSTITUTION, Activity

PROTOHISTORY 73
>The transitional zone between prehistory and history.

PURE SCIENCE *See* SCIENCE, Pure

RACE 2, 5, 6, 12–14, 16–18, 24, 58, 61, 65–69, 90, 98–101, 103, 114, 128, 141, 144, 150–151, 154–155, 177, 184, 197–199, 203–206, 209, 223, 238, 240
>The individuals who deposited a class of morphological assemblages, who are characterized by the complex diagnostic of that class, and who therefore may be said to have had the same morphology.

Cognitive 100
>A morphological group defined by a cognitive complex, that is, by its own diagnostics.

Sub- *See* SUBRACE

RACES

Series of 100
Several races linked by a diagnostic tradition but differing in the rest of their morphologies. Synonym: stock.

RADIOCARBON ANALYSIS   133–135, 239
Estimation of the absolute time of events by calculating the amount of decay in the radioactive isotopes of carbon. Synonym: radiocarbon dating.

RANK GROUP   161, 182, 188
A group of individuals organized on the basis of prestige or wealth.

RECONSTRUCTION

Ethnographic   140–149, 168–176, 177–178, 184–189, 190, 192–196, 212, 220, 229, 230, 239–241
The re-creation of an ethnic trait, pattern, or system by recovering the pertinent archeological evidence and interpreting it in terms of ethnohistorical or ethnographic analogies. Synonym: ethnographic inference.

Historical   192–194
The re-creation of a pattern of change by recovering the pertinent archeological evidence and interpreting it in terms of models of change and analogous changes. Synonym: historical inference.

RECORDS

Historical   3, 6, 8, 27, 59–60, 67, 106, 131, 154, 156–157, 164, 189–190, 192, 220
A speech community's writings about itself.

REDUCTIONISM

Principle of   235–236
The recognition that changes must be explained not only on the superorganic level, in terms of processes such as development and diffusion, but also on the organic and inorganic levels, in terms of processes such as adaptation and exploitation.

REGION   103–104, 120–121, 136–137, 215
The series of local areas included in a cultural chronology. Synonym: cultural area.

REMAINS

Archeological   35–41, 61, 128, 135, 143, 145–149, 151–153, 162, 192, 196, 237–238
Remains deposited through human, as opposed to natural, agency. Synonym: human deposit.

Context of   See SITE, Structure of

Cultural   18, 35–40, 41–58, 61–62, 66, 80, 99, 141, 151, 168–169, 174
The remains of human activities at a site.

Morphological   18, 35, 38–40, 41, 57–58, 61–62, 65–66, 99, 177
The remains of the human beings who occupied a site and of their domesticates.

REMAINS (*continued*)

Natural 35, 37–41, 128
Remains deposited through natural, as opposed to human, agency.

Residential 180, 185
The remains deposited by a residential community.

REPRODUCTION 154–156, 176–178, 240 (*see also* BEHAVIOR, Morphological)
The behavior of reproducing a morphological group, leading to, including, and following sexual intercourse.

RESIDENTIAL ASSEMBLAGE 80, 83, 153, 185–187, 240
An assemblage consisting of all the remains deposited at a site by a single community.

RESIDENTIAL COMMUNITY 14, 147, 149, 152, 161, 169–171, 180–182, 184–189, 240
A group of people who live together in a band, village, town, or city. Synonym: settlement.

Nomadic 185–186
A band or village that moved frequently from place to place.

Sedentary 185
A band, village, or larger community that remained in one place.

RESIDENTIAL COMPONENT *See* COMPONENT, Residential

RESIDENTIAL LOCUS 152, 186
A part of a residential component occupied by a household or other division of a community.

RESIDENTIAL PATTERN 151–152, 187–189
The manner in which a society's residential institutions are distributed over the landscape.

Original 152–153, 159, 181, 184–189, 240
The full residential pattern, as observed by an ethnographer or recorded in a society's writing.

Remnant 153, 180, 184–188
The archeological traces of a residential pattern.

RETICULATE MODEL *See* MODEL, Reticulate

REVOLUTION 209–210, 233
A radical change in people's lives that extends across several different kinds of systems.

ROLE 183
The part played by a member of an institution.

SCIENCE

Applied 10–12, 15, 16, 242–244
Practical use of the results of academic research.

SCIENCE (*continued*)

Pure   15, 242–245
>An academic discipline the aim of which is to discover the truth about the world and its occupants, not to improve them.

SEQUENCE   203, 206, 216, 225
>A pattern of occurrences, as opposed to a pattern of changes.

Artifactual   122, 124–129, 220
>A local sequence of types or modes, as opposed to peoples. Synonym: typological sequence.

Cultural   122, 126–128, 220
>A local sequence of peoples, as opposed to types or modes.

Evolutionary   202, 204, 206, 222–225, 228
>The overall sequence of ever more advanced forms of matter, life, and ethnic systems. It is a record of occurrences rather than changes, contrary to evolution itself. Synonyms: evolutionary chronology, general evolution.

Formal   *See* PATTERN OF CHANGE

General   *See* SEQUENCE, Evolutionary

Geological   124
>A local sequence of geological units, such as formations.

Linguistic   128
>A local sequence of languages.

Local   117–120, 122–129, 153, 239
>A temporal sequence of ethnic units that is set up within a local area.

Racial   124, 128
>A local sequence of races.

Social   124, 128
>A local sequence of institutions or societies.

Typological   *See* SEQUENCE, Artifactual

SEQUENCE DATING   *See* SERIATION

SERIATION   192, 212
>Use of patterns of change in cultures, types, or modes to set up a local sequence. Synonym: sequence dating.

Artifactual   125, 127, 232
>Seriation of types or modes.

Cultural   123–125
>Seriation of cultures.

SERIATION (*continued*)

Developmental 127–128
> Seriation based upon the development of cultures, types, or modes one from another.

Frequency 127
> Seriation based upon changes in the frequency of cultures, types, or modes.

Occurrence 127
> Seriation based solely upon the distribution of cultures, types, or modes.

SERIES

Of civilizations *See* CIVILIZATIONS, Series of

Of co-cultures *See* CO-CULTURES, Series of

Of co-peoples *See* CO-PEOPLES, Series of

Of cultures *See* CULTURES, Series of

Local 130, 209
> A series that is limited to a local area.

Of modes *See* MODES, Series of

Of peoples *See* PEOPLES, Series of

Of races *See* RACES, Series of

Of societies *See* SOCIETIES, Series of

Of speech communities *See* SPEECH COMMUNITIES, Series of

Of types *See* TYPES, Series of

SETTLEMENT *See* COMPONENT, RESIDENTIAL COMMUNITY

SETTLEMENT PATTERN 148, 151, 189
> The overall name for both activity and residential patterns.

Remnant 153, 184
> The traces of a settlement pattern that have survived archeologically.

SITE 33–37, 39–45, 48, 58, 71, 74–75, 84, 98, 115, 118, 120–121, 133, 142–143, 147–148, 150, 152–153, 169–170, 175, 193, 237
> Any place in which an appreciable number of archeological remains have accumulated.

Contents of 33–40, 43, 45, 169
> The natural and human remains in a site.

Dwelling *See* SITE, Residential

Primary 33
> A site with its remains still in approximately the same positions in which they were deposited, so that it may be said to retain its original structure.

SITE (*continued*)

Residential 80, 142–143, 153, 171–172, 185–187
> A site containing the remains of habitation. Synonym: dwelling site.

Secondary 33
> A site resulting from the transportation of remains from their original place of deposition by either a natural or a human agency. Such a site retains the content of the original site (at least in part) but lacks that site's structure.

Structure of 32, 33–34, 43, 45, 169
> The position of archeological remains relative to one another and to the natural features of a site. Synonym: context of the remains.

Typical 84, 238
> A site that has yielded an assemblage typical of a people and culture.

SITE ASSEMBLAGE *See* SITE, Contents of

SITE UNIT *See* SYSTEM, Ethnic

SOCIAL GROUP 119–120, 139, 141, 147–148, 151, 156, 185, 187, 189, 191, 199, 206, 211, 216–217, 239, 244 (*see also* INSTITUTION; SOCIETY)
> A group of individuals distinguished by a common set of social traits.

SOCIAL STRUCTURE 2, 5, 7, 12, 14, 18–20, 24, 27, 63, 69, 96, 142–143, 146, 151, 154–157, 161, 173, 178–189, 192, 197–199, 201, 205–206, 210–211, 213, 219, 226, 228–229, 232–234, 240, 243–244 (*see also* SOCIETY)
> The combination of institutions, interactive behavior, and norms that makes up a social system.

SOCIETIES

Plural *See* PLURAL SOCIETIES

Series of 209
> Societies that have developed one from another and are characterized by a diagnostic tradition of social traits.

SOCIETY 2, 5, 6, 12–14, 16–19, 24, 61, 66–69, 114, 128, 151–152, 154–156, 159, 178–179, 182, 184–185, 188, 206, 209, 234, 240–241, 244 (*see also* SOCIAL STRUCTURE)
> All individuals organized into similar institutions on the basis of similar social norms.

SPACE

Dimension of *See* DIMENSION, Of space

SPECIES 54, 65–67, 98, 100, 103, 155, 177, 197, 202–207, 210–213, 216, 219, 221–224, 234, 238, 240–241, 244
> A group of organisms that can interbreed but, theoretically at least, cannot breed with the members of other species. Each species is composed of several races.

SPEECH   154, 156–157, 164–165 (*see also* BEHAVIOR, Linguistic)
> The behavior of speaking a language.

SPEECH COMMUNITIES

Series of   209
> Speech communities that have developed one from another and are characterized by a diagnostic tradition of linguistic traits.

SPEECH COMMUNITY   2, 6, 12–14, 16–18, 24, 61, 65, 67–69, 114, 151, 154–156, 206, 209, 234 (*see also* LANGUAGE)
> A group of individuals distinguished by a common language, which enables them to understand one another's speech. Synonym: linguistic group.

STAGE   111, 113, 116, 123, 145, 172, 204, 206, 212–216, 220–221, 225–229, 241
> The level of development achieved by ethnic groups in one or more traditions.

Cultural   215
> A level of development within cultural traditions. Like cultural traditions themselves, it is usually limited to a single kind of activity.

Generalized   216, 220
> Segments of different traditions that are all on the same level of development.

Morphological   215
> A level of development within a morphological tradition or traditions.

Specific   115, 215–216, 220
> A segment of a tradition, as opposed to an age, which is a section of a chronology.

STATUS   183
> The rank of an individual within an institution.

STOCK   *See* RACES, Series of

STRATEGY   77 (*see also* TACTICS)
> The logical order of procedure, or research design, that is followed under ideal conditions.

Analytic   7–9, 12–15, 17–18, 20–21, 25, 27–29, 31–33, 45, 52, 62, 83, 96, 153
> The research design that aims to determine the nature of archeological remains. It provides evidence for use in the synthetic and comparative strategies.

Comparative   16–21, 27–28, 62, 174
> The research design in which the results of archeological analyses and prehistorical syntheses are used to learn about the nature of, and changes in, mankind as a whole. It proceeds by formulating hypotheses and testing them against the evidence. Synonyms: experimental strategy, processual strategy, scientific strategy.

Experimental   *See* STRATEGY, Comparative

Processual   *See* STRATEGY, Comparative

Scientific   *See* STRATEGY, Comparative

STRATEGY (*continued*)

Synthetic 7–9, 12–15, 17–18, 20–21, 25, 27–28, 31, 44–45, 52, 62–65, 77, 81–82, 89, 94, 96, 100, 107, 119, 124, 127, 131, 139, 142–143, 153, 193
> The strategy that aims to reconstruct the prehistory of ethnic groups and their environments. It works primarily with archeological evidence obtained through analysis.

STRATIGRAPHY 122, 129, 153, 239 (*see also* DATING, Stratigraphic)
> Superimposition of deposits in two or more layers.

Artifactual 125–127, 129
> Superimposition of artifacts.

Cultural 122–125, 129
> Superimposition of cultural assemblages.

Geologic 128–129
> Superimposition of geologic deposits.

Reverse 122
> Reversal of a sequence of strata due to disturbance.

STRUCTURAL APPROACH *See* CONJUNCTIVE APPROACH

STRUCTURE

Social *See* SOCIAL STRUCTURE

STYLE *See* DIAGNOSTIC COMPLEX, Cultural

SUBCLASS 53–54
> A division of a class of artifacts or assemblages.

SUBCOMPLEX *See* DIAGNOSTIC SUBCOMPLEX

SUBCULTURE *See* CULTURE, Phase of; INTRUSIVE CULTURE

SUBPEOPLE 90–93, 97–98, 100, 102–104, 114–115, 151
> A part of a people characterized by a diagnostic subcomplex and possessing a separate phase of the culture.

Transitional 93
> A subpeople that has adopted cultural traits from several neighboring subpeoples, becoming transitional between them.

SUBRACE 100
> A part of a race characterized by a diagnostic subcomplex and possessing a separate submorphology.

SUBSTANTIVE RESEARCH 64–65, 139, 140, 215, 238
> Study of the substance of a discipline, as opposed to study of its systematics.

SUBSYSTEM

Cultural *See* CULTURE, Phase of; CO-CULTURE; INTRUSIVE CULTURE

SUBTRADITION 115
> Two or more furcate parts into which a tradition has split. Synonym: branch.

SUBTYPE 53, 55
> A pattern of attributes that distinguishes a division of an artifact class and defines it as a subclass. Synonym: variety.

SUPERCLASS 55
> A grouping of classes of artifacts.

SUPERORGANIC EVOLUTION *See* EVOLUTION, Superorganic

SUPERORGANIC GROUP 65–66, 98 (*see also* PEOPLE; SOCIETY; SPEECH COMMUNITY)
> A group of individuals defined in terms of their cultural, social, or linguistic traits.

SUPERORGANIC NORM *See* NORM, Superorganic

SUPERORGANIC SYSTEM *See* SYSTEM, Superorganic

SUPERTYPE 55 (*see also* TYPES, Series of)
> A pattern of attributes that distinguishes a group of classes of artifacts and defines it as a superclass.

SYNCHRONIC APPROACH *See* CONJUNCTIVE APPROACH

SYNCHRONIZATION 118–120, 129–131, 239
> Synthesizing local sequences into a regional chronology.

SYNTHESIS

> *Ethnic* 217, 232–233, 241
> > The process of formation of a new ethnic system from norms drawn from a number of previous systems.

SYNTHETIC ARCHEOLOGY *See* PREHISTORY

SYNTHETIC DISCIPLINES *See* DISCIPLINES, Synthetic

SYNTHETIC STRATEGY *See* STRATEGY, Synthetic

SYSTEM

> *Closed* 203, 206–208, 211–212, 219, 233–234, 241
> > A system that is unable to exchange elements with any other system.

> *Cultural* 141–142, 148, 154, 157, 160–161, 167–168, 176, 180, 184, 191–192, 194, 197, 202, 205, 208, 211, 231–232, 235, 238–241, 244
> > A culture or subculture.

> *Ethnic* 140–190, 191–236, 241, 244–245 (*see also* CULTURE; MORPHOLOGY; SOCIAL STRUCTURE; LANGUAGE)
> > The set of cultural, morphological, social, or linguistic traits that is possessed by an ethnic group. Synonym: site unit.

> *Inorganic* 199
> > A system that is composed of matter, as opposed to life or superorganic traits.

SYSTEM (*continued*)

Linguistic   141–142, 154, 157, 191–192, 202, 205, 208, 211, 231–232, 235, 238–241, 244
A language or dialect.

Morphological   141–142, 154, 157, 176, 191–192, 202, 208–209, 232, 235, 238–241, 244
The morphology of a race, species, or larger unit in the Linnaean system.

Open   203, 205–208, 211, 213, 220, 233–234, 241
A system that is able to exchange elements with other systems.

Organic   199, 208, 231
A system that is composed of living organisms or of the remains of organisms.

Social   141–142, 148, 154, 157, 180, 184, 191–192, 202, 205, 208, 211, 231–232, 235, 238–241, 244
A social structure.

Sociocultural   149
A combination of a culture and a social structure.

Sub-   *See* SUBSYSTEM

Superorganic   199, 208, 231
A cultural, social, or linguistic system, as opposed to a morphological system.

SYSTEMATIC   64–68, 139, 140, 148, 150, 151, 171, 207, 210, 215, 238
The formation of a discipline's basic units of study and the ordering of those units in a systematic manner.

TACTICS   27, 63–64, 77, 89, 94, 100, 124, 127, 131, 139, 193 (*see also* STRATEGY)
The order of procedure, or research design, that is followed when conditions are less than ideal and it is necessary to adapt one's procedure to the nature of the evidence encountered.

TAXONOMY   53–55, 65, 67, 74–75, 89, 91, 93, 98, 147, 207, 221–222, 225 (*see also* CLASSIFICATION, Taxonomic)
A hierarchy of classes formed by means of taxonomic classification, so that all the classes in the lower levels of the hierarchy are exact divisions of the classes in the higher levels.

TIME

Absolute   112–119, 126, 129, 239 (*see also* DATING, Absolute)
A measurement of time that is applicable throughout the world and does not vary from place to place. Synonyms: calendrical time, elapsed time, scientific time.

Calendrical   *See* TIME, Absolute

Dimension of   *See* DIMENSION, Of time

Elapsed   *See* TIME, Absolute

Geologic   *See* GEOLOGIC TIME

Historic   *See* HISTORIC TIME

Prehistoric   *See* PREHISTORIC TIME

TIME (*continued*)

Relative   112–114, 118–119, 126, 136–138, 214, 225, 239 (*see also* DATING, Relative)
> A measurement of time that is based upon events that are restricted in distribution and vary in time from place to place.

Scientific   *See* TIME, Absolute

TIME-MARKER   51, 125, 129, 141, 214
> An artifact type that is diagnostic of a local period or of a series of contemporaneous periods. Synonym: type fossil.

TOPICAL DISCIPLINES   *See* DISCIPLINES, Topical

TRADITION   204, 207–221, 226–229, 231, 233, 241
> A segment of the trellis model that marks a route whereby an appreciable number of genes or norms have passed from one ethnic group to another. The term is also applied to the genes and norms that have passed via the segment.

Cultural   115, 124, 206, 208–209, 215, 228, 238
> A complex of cultural norms that can be traced from one people to another. Cultural traditions are often limited to a single activity.

Diagnostic   *See* DIAGNOSTIC TRADITION

Linguistic   208–209, 228
> A complex of linguistic norms that can be traced from one speech community to another.

Local   130, 215, 218, 229
> A complex of types or modes that remains constant throughout a local sequence.

Morphological   208–209, 215
> A complex of morphological traits that can be traced from one race to another.

Social   208–209, 228
> A complex of social norms that can be traced from one society to another.

Systematic   *See* DIAGNOSTIC TRADITION

TRAIT

Cultural   60–68, 72, 94, 96, 141–142, 146, 148–149, 151, 153, 175–176, 195, 197, 223, 238
> An element of a cultural system.

Ecological   153, 187
> An element of an ecosystem.

Ethnic   13, 145, 147–149, 155, 196, 211, 214, 220, 225–226, 231, 245
> An element of an ethnic system. Synonyms: ethnographic trait, trait unit.

Linguistic   66–68, 141–142, 146, 228
> An element of a language.

Morphological   66–69, 142, 146, 155, 198, 223, 235
> An element of a morphological system.

TRAIT (*continued*)

Organic 66, 220
>   Any trait of the human body, whether morphological or physiological.

Social 66–68, 141–142, 148–149, 153, 223
>   An element of a social system.

Superorganic 66–67, 199–200, 220
>   Any cultural, social, or linguistic trait.

TRAITS

Complex of 195–196
>   A set of linked traits.

TRAIT UNIT *See* TRAIT, Ethnic

TRANSFORMATION 232–233
>   The formation of a new ethnic system by more or less gradual development from a previous system, so that the two form a series and are linked by a diagnostic tradition.

TRELLIS MODEL *See* MODEL, Trellis

TYPE 45, 48–53, 56–57, 59, 66, 78–79, 83–84, 86–87, 97–98, 119, 121–122, 125–127, 130, 143, 167, 192, 237–238
>   A pattern of attributes that distinguishes a group of artifacts and defines it as a class.

Cognitive 52, 86, 167–168, 238
>   A pattern of attributes that a people uses to categorize some of its own artifacts and to assign them to a class. Synonym: emic type.

Descriptive *See* TYPE, Intrinsic

Emic *See* TYPE, Cognitive; TYPE, Extrinsic

Etic *See* TYPE, Intrinsic

Extrinsic 51–52, 86, 125, 167–168, 173, 197, 238
>   A pattern of diagnostic attributes obtained by classifying artifacts in terms of features of selected kinds, such as tempering materials, rim profiles, and design motifs, in order to bring out the stylistic, chronological, functional, or developmental significance of the artifacts. Synonyms: emic type, functional type, historical-index type.

Functional *See* TYPE, Extrinsic

Historical-index *See* TYPE, Extrinsic

Intrinsic 50–52, 86, 125, 167–168, 197, 238
>   A pattern of diagnostic attributes obtained by classifying artifacts in terms of all kinds of features, in order to obtain an expression of the inherent nature of the artifacts. Synonyms: descriptive type, etic type, morphological type, natural type, phenetic type.

Morphological *See* TYPE, Intrinsic

TYPE (*continued*)

Natural   See TYPE, Intrinsic

Phenetic   See TYPE, Intrinsic

TYPE ARTIFACT   45, 50
> Any artifact selected to serve as a standard for a class in identifying new artifacts.

TYPE FOSSIL   *See* TIME-MARKER

TYPES

Series of   127–128 (*see also* SUPERTYPES)
> A number of types that have developed one from another.

TYPOLOGY   54–55, 93
> A set of classes formed by means of typological classification. If the classes are hierarchical, they need not be exact subdivisions of one another, as in the case of a taxonomy.

VARIETY   *See* SUBTYPE

VARVE ANALYSIS   133
> Use of a pattern of varves to estimate absolute time. Synonyms: geochronology, varve dating.

VENTIFACT   40
> An object fashioned by the wind.

WILDLIFE   2, 19, 197–198, 235, 244
> The morphologies and capabilities of wild animals and plants.

WORKED EQUIPMENT   *See* EQUIPMENT, Worked

WORK GROUP   156, 161, 181, 183, 187, 240
> A group of individuals organized temporarily in order to carry out a particular activity.